TOPICAL BUDGET

The Great British News Film

Poster design by Augustus John for the *War Office Official Topical Budget*.

THE GREAT BRITISH NEWS FILM

TOPICAL BUDGET

LUKE McKERNAN

BFI Publishing

Published in 1992 by the
British Film Institute
21 Stephen Street
London W1P 1PL

British Library Cataloguing in Publication Data

  McKernan, Luke
    Topical budget.
    I. Title
    070.43

ISBN 0 85170 305 4

Cover design by Geoff Wiggins

Front cover stills: background image – Harold Jeapes
filming in Egypt or Palestine 1917–1918; small
pictures from top to bottom – Lloyd George and
daughter at Chequers (*Downing Street in
Buckinghamshire*); the wedding of the Duke of York
and Lady Elizabeth Bowes-Lyon (*The Royal
Wedding*); land girls in Essex (*Women Hay Makers*);
public protest at war-time food prices (*Hands Off
Baby's Milk*); a Conservative cabinet meeting at 10
Downing Street (*The New Government*).

Typeset in Monotype Plantin by Discript, London
and printed in Great Britain by
Page Bros. Norwich

For my parents

CONTENTS

ACKNOWLEDGMENTS

Much of the research for this history was made possible by an eight month sabbatical offered as part of the BFI's internal research programme. I am grateful to Colin MacCabe for this opportunity, and for overseeing it, and to David Francis for encouraging it in this form.

Three people in particular have been of great help to me. Roger Whitney, former Non-Fiction Films Acquisition Officer at the National Film Archive, acquired the *Topical Budget* collection and the accompanying records and paperwork, and without his foresight and efforts there would be no history such as this. He has given me much help and advice throughout. Secondly Dr Nicholas Hiley has generously allowed me to make much use of his researches into the news media of this period, and I have incorporated a great deal of this into my text. I am also grateful for our many discussions about newsreels, and to have encountered someone as pleased to have uncovered the smallest fact relating to a cameraman as I have been. Lastly, my thanks to Jim Ballantyne of the British Universities Film and Video Council for all his help and enthusiasm.

I work in the Cataloguing Department of the National Film Archive, and my thanks are due to past and present members involved in the research: Simon Baker, Anne Burton, Anna Calvert, Roger Holman, Fiona O'Brien, Caroline Sage and Don Swift; and to those at the NFA generally who have helped and supported me: Elaine Burrows, Phil Crossley, June Elvy, Anne Fleming, Jane Hockings, Clyde Jeavons, Joan Kempster, David Meeker, Jackie Morris, James Patterson, Colin Rattee, Markku Salmi and former Deputy Curator Michelle Aubert. My thanks also to the staff of the Imperial War Museum Department of Film, particularly Jane Fish, Sid Mills, Neil Pilfold and Paul Sargent.

Sadly, no one who ever worked for the Topical Film Company now survives, but I have received kind welcome and much help from their families. I must thank especially Clifford Jeapes for talking to me about this period, and for letting me see his papers and other records relating to his father and uncle, William and Harold Jeapes. Next my thanks go to the descendants of F. A. Enders: Peter Enders, David Enders and Mrs Patricia Payton, and especially John Enders for letting me see the papers he holds relating to FBO and the Topical Film Company. I am also grateful to Mrs Rosemary Cooper, daughter of Fred Wilson, and her husband William, and to David Hutchins and his sister Irene, son and daughter of 'Bunny' Hutchins, for all their help and hospitality.

Many other people have provided me with information: Bob Allen, Colin Bakke, Robin Bishop, Kevin Brownlow, John Edwards, Roy Flower of the ACTT History Project, Ken Goodman, Alec Jeakins, John O'Kelly, Lisa Pontecorvo, Norman Roper, Bill Whittemore and Jim Wilde. My thanks to all of them.

My thanks go to all who read the text at various stages of its existence, and for all their encouragement and advice. Christine Gledhill has been a patient and sympathetic editor, and I am indebted to Ed Buscombe and Roma Gibson for all their help.

Copyright material from the Beaverbrook papers is reproduced with permission from the House of Lords Record Office. I am grateful to the Canadian War Museum for permission to use the Augustus John poster design. I am most indebted to the McKernan Partnership.

Picture Credits

The photograph of F. A. Enders is the property of Mrs Patricia Payton. Photographs of William and Harold Jeapes are the property of Mr Clifford Jeapes, with the exception of the photograph of Harold Jeapes filming in Jerusalem, which is reproduced by permission of the Trustees of the Imperial War Museum, as is the photograph of Frank Bassill and the frame still from THE DELIVERANCE OF LILLE BY HAIG'S MEN. All other frame stills from *Topical Budget* copies are National Film Archive copyright. The frame still from *Pathé Gazette* is British Pathé News copyright. The photograph of Fred Wilson is the property of Mrs Rosemary Cooper. The photograph of J. B. McDowell comes from the McDowell Collection in BFI Stills, Posters and Designs. The cartoons of cameramen are reproduced from the *Kinematograph and Lantern Weekly*. The Augustus John poster design is the property of the Canadian War Museum. All pictures and photographs are reproduced with permission.

Note

Lengths of films referred to in the text are given in 35mm footage. Run at silent speed (16 to 18 frames per second), this roughly equals one foot per second. Where the footage is given with a plus sign (for example, 58+ feet), this means that only the length of the picture is known, and not of the accompanying opening titles. All lengths otherwise include titles. Where only the titles and intertitles have been given, these are in quotation marks, and the presence of three dots between titles indicates the pictures, which I have not always described. Where there are descriptions they are my own, unless otherwise noted, and are taken from the catalogue to the *Topical Budget* newsreel which accompanies this history. Such descriptions derive from the films themselves, wherever possible. When other sources have been used these are noted.

INTRODUCTION
Topical Budget and the Silent Newsreel in Britain

The history of the newsreels is the history of popular cinema. They were founded when films moved from the fairgrounds and variety halls to theatres of their own, and they gradually died out as the mass audience drifted away from the screen and into the living room. But for fifty years or more they were an essential part of the entertainment package that the cinema offered. They were popular, employed skilled staff who ensured that a high technical and professional standard was maintained, and were a major factor in broadening the outlook and experience of millions. They have bequeathed a visual record of those fifty years that is of rich and permanent value. And for their first twenty years they were silent.

There was never any silence, of course, in the silent cinema, and one must think of the newsreels of that time as being accompanied by music. But the coming of sound brought about the one major shift in their evolution. The soundtrack, and most importantly the commentary, brought the newsreels authority and journalistic credibility – so much so that the popular memory of them is of rousing music and a dominant commentator, and not the images on the screen. The existence of a commentary led to an increased sophistication in pictorial style as pictures were shot and edited with the spoken word in mind. The silent newsreel, apart from the use of short titles to introduce the subject, had to rely on an entirely visual means of communication. Pictorially they were simpler and more direct than sound newsreels. Today the worst of them appear clumsy and amateur, but the best are skilful compressions of visual information.

During the twenty years that the newsreels were silent, three companies held sway over the newsfilm industry in Britain. *Pathé Gazette* and *Gaumont Graphic* were produced by the British arms of the international Pathé and Gaumont companies, French-based organisations with a worldwide network of production and distribution ideal for supporting a newsreel. Third came *Topical Budget*, an entirely British operation, produced by the Topical Film Company. That this newsreel, only one of a number of native newsfilm outfits in existence around the time of its founding in 1911, should survive and indeed thrive for so long is down to professionalism, luck and a world war.

1

When production ceased in 1931 it was not through lack of success or inability to adapt to sound, but because those that then remained in control had insufficient interest in newsfilm. This history tells how this one newsreel made its contribution to our visual record of the past.

The roots of *Topical Budget* can be traced back to 1816. In that year the firm of J. Wrench & Son, opticians, was set up at 50 Gray's Inn Road, London.[1] By the late 1890s the firm was run by Alfred Wrench and had moved into the area first of magic lanterns and then of cinematography itself. The shop had a darkroom in the basement and supplied its own projector which became the chief rival to Paul's Animatograph. Cecil Hepworth brought his first film to be developed to Wrench's shop and James Williamson bought his first projector there. Alfred Wrench himself was a film pioneer and in 1897 filmed Queen Victoria's Diamond Jubilee procession and the naval review at Spithead.

Around this time Will Barker and William Jeapes entered film production, both with a special aptitude for actuality film. These two, together with the American Charles Urban, who founded the Warwick Trading Company in 1898, were to establish the foundations of the newsfilm industry in Britain, although only Jeapes would go on to found a British newsreel.

Barker, a former commercial traveller who began his career in films as a showman exhibiting in halls up and down the country, founded his Autoscope Company at the Wrench premises in 1900. Subsequently he was to merge with the Warwick Trading Company in 1906, guiding them through their great period of actuality film-making, before leaving to form his own company, Barker Motion Photography, in 1909. His great passion was for newsfilm and he dominated this branch of the film industry in its earliest years. Later he was to boast that seven out of ten news cameramen working in the 1910s had begun with him,[2] and certainly a great many *Topical Budget* cameramen began their careers with Barker. Meanwhile Jeapes, who likewise had begun as a showman in 1897, exhibiting films with a Paul projector, founded the Graphic Cinematograph Company in 1902 and produced what he later claimed was the first attempt at a newsreel in Britain, *Jeapes's Animated Graphic*. The *Animated Graphic* was in actual fact a film show, was irregularly presented in music halls and variety theatres, and in any case was predated by the Biograph shows at the Palace Theatre in London which regularly presented footage of the Boer War and could therefore be said to have provided the first ever newsfilm service.

Nevertheless, what mattered about Barker and Jeapes' efforts was their commitment to the topical actuality film, a branch of film-making that came to be known and sold as 'topicals'. Moreover, the *Animated Graphic* indicated for the first time a wish to imitate newspapers (the *Daily Graphic* was a contemporary illustrated paper). Film is an imita-

2

tive art, and film producers sought both inspiration and public approval by reproducing established forms on the screen. Producers of fiction films naturally turned to novels and plays; once it was clear that film of an event could be processed and screened while that event was still fresh in the public memory, producers of actuality films began to think in terms of newspapers. In May 1906 there was a freakishly early attempt at a newsreel cinema, 'The Daily Bioscope', which showed Gaumont news and fiction items in a converted shop opposite Liverpool Street station.[3] Unable to supply enough fresh newsfilm, it failed to find an audience and soon reverted to normal film fare. Barker followed Jeapes' efforts with his *London Day By Day* in July 1906, the first attempt at a daily newsreel (it took its name from a column in the *Daily Telegraph*), in which a story was removed and a new story added each day. The attempt was defeated by the weather.[4] A friendly rivalry built up between the two, both Barker and Jeapes taking pride in screening an event such as the Grand National that same evening, and fighting to acquire and then to defend the exclusive rights to such events. Both developed expertise in the hurried, irregular production methods which topicals demanded and which many companies (at a time when most produced all types of films) were unwilling to adopt. They worked together for a period under the Warwick banner, producing topicals and sound films using the Warwick Cinephone system, an

William Jeapes (left) and Will Barker in 1908, during their time together at Warwick. The cameraman with them is J. B. McDowell.

3

invention of Jeapes'. Some (if not all) of these sound films were directed by Frank Danvers Yates, formerly an actor, later to be a *Topical Budget* cameraman.

No film company at this time could survive on the production of topicals alone. Although cameramen and equipment and know-how were available, there was no network of cinemas to provide the regular audience on which the newsreel was to depend. A newsfilm can be defined as an actuality item of current interest for a specific audience.[5] Such a film has built-in obsolescence – it must be replaced by fresh material once it has lost its topicality. To be able to produce a regular supply of such material there must be a regular audience. Thus in the era before cinemas (largely before 1910), when topicals were only one kind of film and all kinds were sold at the same price, they had to be kept on the market for the same length of time as a travel or fiction film. Therefore topicals had to feature events of lasting interest. Major ceremonies of state, celebrated annual events and big sporting occasions were the favoured subjects since these kept their sale value. Otherwise stories of an on-going nature, such as a war or the suffragette issue, could be filmed and the same film exploited over a period of time. The Graphic company supplemented their income by producing a number of fiction films between 1905 and 1908, directed by Harold Jeapes (William's brother) or Arthur Melbourne-Cooper, and they also supplied equipment and a film titling service.

This all changed in June 1910 with the introduction of *Pathé's Animated Gazette*, the first British newsreel in the accepted sense. In France the newsreel *Pathé Journal* (originally *Pathé Fait-Divers*) had been founded in 1908, and the British version followed its example. It featured a collection of actuality items, each around a minute in length and related only by a shared topicality. It was issued weekly to begin with, and comprised items taken by two British-based cameramen, supplemented by further material from Pathé's international organisation. Staff were a mixture of French and British under the editorship of Valentia Steer, and initially all developing and printing took place in Paris, a delay which could scarcely have helped topicality.[6] Nevertheless it was clearly a successful and popular innovation, and Pathé soon had a number of competitors. The following month Jeapes, still with Warwick, formed the *Warwick Bioscope Chronicle*. In October 1910 Gaumont produced the *Gaumont Graphic*; as with Pathé, to begin with their films were sent to Paris to be developed and printed. Production methods improved, and by August 1911 the three newsreels were all being issued bi-weekly. That same month, Jeapes (having left Warwick) formed the Topical Film Company with Herbert Wrench of the Wrench family firm, with offices at 50 Gray's Inn Road, and on 1 September 1911[7] the first issue of Topical Budget was released.

No. 1 of The Topical Budget. News by animation is the coming fashion and therefore the multiplication of the number of moving picture newspapers will be hailed with delight both by exhibitors and public alike. Competition stimulates business, and therefore, with the advent of each new comer in the field there is bound to be a levelling up all round. This week the Topical Films Co., of 50 Grays Inn Road, W.C., have published the first number of the Topical Budget and we are bound to admit that they have scored a decided triumph. The photographic quality was A1, whilst the editing had been so capably managed that the edition included the Royal Naval and Marine Tournament, the Fleet Street £20,000 Fire, The Ebor Handicap, the King of Italy at the Military Hospital, Roman Dread-nought's last Voyage, Amateur Punting Competition at Shepperton and the Latest Fashion in Gowns. Issued with a punctuality that did the proprietors infinite credit The Budget was shown at the Alham-bra, by Jury's Pictures, The Pyke Circuit, Ruffell's Bioscope and Walturdaw's. The Budget appears to have leapt at a single bound into popularity, and that in a week when opportunities for illustrated news were remarkably scarce. Next week's number is promised to be a bumper and as Topical Films Co., are laying themselves open to this class of work exhibitors would be wise to keep their eye on them.[8]

Topical Budget was released weekly at first, but by November 1911 had turned to bi-weekly production and was issued every Wednesday and Saturday, matching *Pathe's Animated Gazette*, but not *Gaumont Graphic* which was issued on Mondays and Thursdays. The stories were standard newsreel fare, and they had secured nationwide distribu-tion. Everything in this press notice indicates a well-planned product, put together by professionals who knew the topical business and their market. What was remarkable about the Topical Film Company, how-ever, was that for the first time theirs was a company without anything else to offer except a newsreel: no fiction films, no sidelines in equip-ment or exhibition, no parent company to support the venture or aid distribution. Such a move on the part of Jeapes and Wrench is a measure of how firmly established the newsreel had become in the cinema programme and how ideal a proposition it was to the right kind of producer.

The newsreels in Britain soon settled into a generally accepted format: around five items per issue, each item around a minute long, two issues per week to match the practice of programme changes in the cinemas.[9] At this time the newsreels were usually regarded as a form of 'topical' and continued to be referred to as such up to the 1920s. For they were the same length, around 300 feet, were sold initially at the same price, and were produced by people who had made their reputations with topicals. However there were major producers of topicals who never produced a newsreel, such as Jury, Urban and, most notably, Barker.[10]

The term 'newsreel' was unknown at this time. F. A. Talbot, in his book *Moving Pictures. How They Are Made And Worked* (London, 1912), gives a detailed picture of the new phenomenon in film production. The relevant chapter is entitled 'The Animated Newspapers' and in the space of a few pages Talbot manages to refer to newsreels as animated newspapers, weekly topical features, moving picture newspapers, moving newspapers, animated newssheets, film newspapers and cinematographic newspapers.[11] The term 'newsreel' seems to have been used first in America for *International Newsreel* in 1917, although the term had occurred in publicity there as early as 1914.[12] In Britain it did not become current until the 1920s, and the Topical Film Company generally referred to their own and rivals' product as 'budgets', a term also occasionally used by others. All the newsreels took their names from newspapers – thus *Pathé's Animated Gazette*, *Warwick Bioscope Chronicle*, *Gaumont Graphic*, *Topical Budget*, *Eclair Journal* (founded in March 1913) and *Williamson's Animated News* (founded in May 1913), the six British newsreels in existence by the start of the First World War (three of them French in origin). The word 'budget' was a common term for a newspaper or journal at the time (for example, *Pall Mall Budget*) although this sense of the word is now obsolete. The term 'newsreel' will be used throughout this history.

Newsreels rapidly became an important part of the cinema programme. Talbot observed: 'Although the animated newspaper has been amongst us for only a few months, yet it has already developed into an institution.'[13] At this date there were still no feature films and a variety of films of roughly equal length went to make up the desired programme. Although newsreels might be pushed to the back of the show and did not have the drawing power of fiction films, it became essential to exhibit them and to keep showing the same company's newsreel each week. They were also shown as part of music hall and variety shows, generally at the end of the performance. This latter practice faded out with the rise of cinemas, but the night Marie Lloyd died in 1922 after a show at the Empire, Edmonton there was a *Topical Budget* on the bill.

Barker still dominated the topical business, which was not exclusively newsreel at this time, with excellent staff and facilities; but he was defeated by cost-cutting practices by the others and a stubborn refusal on his part to offer competitive wages. The newsreels cut their prices from the accepted 4d per foot for topicals to 2¼d or 2½d per foot for single items, and a round five or six pounds for the week's two issues at 600 feet. That they were able to do this indicates how cheaply they were prepared to operate, and how much more reliable the market was for them. For there were fundamental differences between the topical and the newsreel, as F. A. Talbot noticed:

There are many incidents of daily occurrence which are of absorbing passing interest, such as the launch of a battleship, a railway collision, a big fire, or a public demonstration. Such subjects are not adapted to presentation as individual films, being insufficiently momentous to grip the public for several minutes in the same way as the International Yacht Race, or some other dramatic item in our complex social and industrial life.[14]

This simple statement of affairs neatly describes the newsreels, their appeal to certain producers, and their limitations. The interest they aroused was indeed both absorbing and passing, demanding fresh material of the same kind over and over again, so that the newsreels were sustained by their own logic. Talbot's list of subjects reads like the typical newsreel issue; this reliable formula needed little change, and saw little thereafter. For the length of the single-story topical the newsreels offered several short items in a single issue, raiding the newspapers, the social and sporting calendars, and the whim of the moment to make up a varied, undemanding, entertaining mixture; topical, absorbing, passing.

Little is known now about *Topical Budget*'s early years. William Jeapes and Herbert Wrench were the managing directors and Jeapes was designated Editor. However, staying true to the imitation of the newspaper world, Jeapes' was a managerial role and it was a news editor who directed the cameramen, chose assignments, organised the filming, and selected the film shot for inclusion in the newsreel. The exact role of editor and news editor is unclear and seems to have differed from company to company. Jeapes would certainly have had an influence over his news editors, although equally influential were the output of their rivals (strong competition led to a strong need to imitate) and the standard round of stories that were universally held to be suitable newsreel material.

Harold Jeapes was the main cameraman, as he was for all of his brother's various film ventures, and William Jeapes himself filmed a number of items for Topical in these early years. The other cameramen known to have worked for Topical before 1914 are F. W. Engholm, Harrison Ward (who had been with William Jeapes at Graphic) and Walter Evan Davies. Their first news editor was George Woods-Taylor. As was to prove the norm he had Fleet Street experience, having spent a number of years as a press photographer. Newsreels came to prefer their news editors to have a background of journalism. Woods-Taylor doubled as a cameraman, which became occasional practice for other news editors, particularly on stories requiring a large team. Topical would have had no more than four cameramen at this stage, and (except for exceptional circumstances during the war) this remained the standard number until the 1920s. The number of cameramen for a

William Jeapes, with aviator Pierre Verrier, filming at the Hendon air races, March 1913. His camera is a Debrie.

newsreel then gradually rose to five or six in the mid-1920s, and eight by the end of the decade, although in Topical's case this had probably dropped back to four. There were any number of freelance cameramen available to swell the numbers when the occasion demanded.

On 25 September 1913 the company, as evidence of its success and growing confidence, was registered as the Topical Film Company Limited, its offices still at 50 Gray's Inn Road. The directors of the new company were Major T. McDonnell Madden, Donald Wilson Player, George Jeffrey, Herbert Holmes Wrench and William Cecil Jeapes. The share capital was £20,000, divided into 20,000 shares of £1 each. The company had been purchased from Jeapes and Wrench, who each took 5,500 shares. In April 1914 they followed the general trend within the film industry and moved to 76–78 Wardour Street. By the end of their first year as a limited company they were able to announce a net profit of £1,693 3s 5d.[15]

What information survives about *Topical Budget* at this time indicates steady, unambitious progress and a routine product: launches, processions, horse-races, the occasional international item. Newsreel filming at this period was basic – single-shot items were not uncommon, and all the opportunities for a creative film treatment that the longer topicals might have promised seemed lost. In terms of actuality film technique, the newsreel in its earliest years was a retrograde step, though an advance in presentation. The big newsreel stories were in fact of topical length, for a whole issue would be devoted to the FA Cup Final or the Lord Mayor's Show. Topical showed some interest in other film activities, producing the occasional 'interest' film, 'locals' for individual cinemas, and in May 1914 were even contemplating producing comic films. In 1912 they sent Eugene Lauste, cameraman and celebrated inventor of the first sound-on-film process, to film material for them in Africa.[16]

As for the newsreel, the major event of the period was the Balkan War,[17] which broke out between September 1912 and May 1913, and again between June and July of 1913. Topical sent out cameramen immediately, but in common with the other companies spent a great deal of money with very little in return save the glory of having tried:

> The expenses of the Balkan War ran the leading cinema firms into thousands of pounds each, for which they practically received no return whatever, owing to the strictures of the censorship and the difficulties of the campaign – quite the worst which has ever been faced by the war correspondents and photographers in the world. The photographers evaded the censors and took risks innumerable to secure some really good pictures of the campaign, but all in vain. Horses, tents, equipments, and even thousand-pound motor-cars were lost, stolen, or abandoned on every side, and after the battle of Tulu Burgas many of the correspondents were left out in the wind and cold with nothing in the world except their cameras and the clothes they stood up in. Many of them lived for nearly a week on nothing but a handful of mouldy biscuits.[18]

Nevertheless, Topical's cameramen managed to secure some pictures, as they advertised in the following bold manner:

> Beware of Balkan Burlesques!! It is only permitted <u>Conjurors</u> to deceive! The Special War Edition of the Topical Budget Contains a remarkable series of Absolute Actualities Secured by one of the

Budget's intrepid correspondents in the pestilential and Cholera stricken regions Around Constantinople. Train-loads of victims arriving from the front – Awe-inspiring scenes at the San Stefano Cholera Camp – the dead and the dying – Doctors helpless – Constantinople Harbour alive with Battleships – Turks defending the Railway at Hademkeui – Bluejackets from H.M.S. Weymouth guarding the American Embassy, etc., etc., etc. This complete war series ready for delivery Friday, Nov. 29th. Length (approximately) 360ft.[19]

The reference to 'burlesques' is a jibe at the faking of news scenes, which had been common at the turn of the century, and still arose on occasion from less scrupulous companies. What *Topical Budget* actually showed is a matter of conjecture, but it is unlikely to have inspired much awe. In August 1914 a greater war broke out.

The First World War brought the newsreels and *Topical Budget* in particular into prominence. On the declaration of war most companies producing newsfilm sent out cameramen to film on the continent despite talk of a ban on war films and a subsequent official ban on any cameraman filming British troops at the Front. Topical sent three cameramen into Belgium, including Engholm, who brought them much prestige when he filmed the German entry into Brussels. However the cameramen in general found themselves away from the action and often in danger from the locals who held them to be spies. The footage sent back by Topical's cameramen was of variable quality, the best of it going into a series of longer-length topicals, and the more trite material finding its way into the newsreel, to judge from the surviving films. Despite the brave efforts of the cameramen and some individual films of interest, it was a very limited picture of the war that made its way onto British screens, and no picture at all from the Western Front, due to the enforcement of the ban on cameramen. The government (and Lord Kitchener in particular) saw filming the war as a security hazard, at best an unnecessary nuisance, and as yet gave little thought to film propaganda.

Despite the lack of war coverage by the start of 1915, there was a healthiness about Topical's product at this time that shows the resilience of the newsreel format. *Warwick Bioscope Chronicle* and *Williamson's Animated News* did not last long into the war, but the four newsreels that survived did so by mixing local product with purchases from and deals with companies in Europe, together with material from roving cameramen still attempting to capture war footage and exchanges between companies.[20] *Pathé Gazette*, *Gaumont Graphic* and *Eclair Journal* all retained some links with France but what is remarkable is that Topical were able to operate equally well without any such international links, depending instead on thorough coverage of the home front and exchanges on the open market. That they thrived in this manner is largely due to the self-sustaining nature of the newsreels. The topical-length story could not work under such circumstances; it showed up all too clearly the poverty of its material. The newsreel, however, with its short items coming one after the other, turned this to its advantage. One minute Tommies would be seen marching away to war, the next there was a football match in England, then Belgian refugees, then royalty or a society wedding, then the launching of a ship, then a munitions factory. If newsreels could not portray the actuality of war, they could construct the illusion of continuity. The war was progressing, life went on as before at home, they could show aspects of life as it was going on in various locations at that very time, they could appear in control of events if only they mixed variety with contemporaneity. It was an admirable way in which to exploit limited resources and it suited the newsreels' passive nature. It also provided a reassuring vision of things – all of which the film propagandists were to discover rather later in the war.

The first moves towards government-sanctioned filming of the war followed an agreement made between the War Office and the Cinematograph Trade Topical Committee in October 1915. The Committee, which had its basis in pre-war trade negotiations, was formed with the idea of co-ordinating efforts to organise the filming, distribution and censorship of war footage from British cameramen. From the very outset of the war the film trade had been keen both to prove itself loyal and to exploit the situation financially, but felt frustrated by the government's indifference to its wishes. All the major topical companies, including the Topical Film Company, were involved in the Committee, although Jury and Gaumont dominated.[21] In view of this united front, and following the special efforts of J. Brooke Wilkinson of the British Board of Film Censors, permission was eventually granted for filming of British troops at the Front to begin under the direction of the Committee, which was renamed the British Topical Committee for War Films. In November 1915 the first two cameramen, Geoffrey Malins and Edward Tong, set out for the Western Front. None of the material taken at this stage was to be made available to the newsreels.

The first films produced by the British Topical Committee for War Films were a failure, both financially and as war reportage. Produced as six series of short films between January and June 1916, they gave little impression of what was happening, and the government finally came in, taking over the Trade Committee and forming the War Office Cinematograph Committee (WOCC). This was run by William Jury, Sir Reginald Brade from the War Office, and Max Aitken (soon to become Lord Beaverbrook). This action followed the release of the first major film made from material taken at the Western Front, *The Battle of the Somme*, which was a great success and a revelation as a film. The WOCC produced other feature and medium-length films before going a stage further and deciding to use a newsreel as a regular outlet for its films. After considering the four possible newsreel companies then in operation (the ailing *Eclair Journal* was not to last much longer), they took over the Topical Film Company in May 1917, and the name of the newsreel became the *War Office Official Topical Budget*. The company was used to produce newsreel and individual items of longer length. However problems arose with content and sales, and in November 1917 the WOCC bought up Topical for the duration of the war and three months thereafter. Captain W. Holt-White (formerly editor of Beaverbrook's *Canadian Daily Record*), was brought in as head of the editorial department to improve production methods. William Jeapes was put in charge of the technical department, Patrick McCabe came over from Pathé as news editor, and Harry Rowson was put in charge of sales.

As the Official newsreel, the *War Office Official Topical Budget* had exclusive access to material shot by the Official cameramen on the various fronts, and eventually became the chief means by which war footage was screened in Britain. There had been some shying away from the alarming images in longer films such as *The Battle of the Somme*, with the newsreel showing troops marching, captured prisoners, battle sites and the situation in Britain, but very little of the actual conflict. In the cameramen's defence it should be noted that the work was naturally hazardous, their equipment awkward, army officialdom interfering, and much of the fighting unfilmable since it took place at night. Moreover the longer films had been more matter of fact than overtly propagandist, whereas the newsreel clearly aimed at restoring national morale and presenting a positive image abroad. Although the newsreel was distributed in many countries it was not possible to put the fullest effort into propaganda overseas and most attention was devoted to content and sales for the home market. Lord Beaverbrook later spoke a little inaccurately but nevertheless proudly of their achievement:

> The Topical Budget shown in every picture palace was the decisive factor in maintaining the morale of the people during the black days of the early summer of 1918.[22]

In February 1918 the newsreel was given a second name, *Pictorial News (Official)*, and released its most celebrated film, that of General Allenby's entry into Jerusalem, filmed by Harold Jeapes and Frank Hurley, which took up the whole of one issue.[23] In June the WOCC's role was taken over by the newly formed Ministry of Information, but little changed in the manner of production, especially as the new Minister of Information was Lord Beaverbrook, who remained in control of the company. Mixing home footage with film from the various war fronts, and making fuller use of the potential of the newsreel form, the *Pictorial News* proved increasingly successful in terms of both technique and sales right up to the end of the war.

In February 1919 the WOCC relinquished its interest in the Topical Film Company, which was then bought up by the newspaper proprietor Edward Hulton, probably as a result of his friendship with Lord Beaverbrook. Former owner William Jeapes returned as managing director, while Lord Beaverbrook went on to control *Pathé Gazette*. Hulton was the first person from big business really to take an interest in the British film industry, and the first newspaper man to do so, since Beaverbrook's involvement with Topical was not related to what were at that time his minor newspaper interests. Hulton decided to put Topical on a stronger footing and took control of a distribution company, Film Booking Offices (FBO), the two operations being run in tandem throughout the 1920s. Hulton owned the *Daily Sketch*, among other titles, and Topical's offices were moved to the newspaper's premises in Shoe Lane, though the labs and editorial department remained at Wardour Street. They kept the name *Pictorial News* until May 1919, when they became *Topical Budget* once more. For a short period between 1922 and 1923 they called themselves the *Daily Sketch Topical Budget*.

A number of the WOCC staff stayed on with the company. Holt-White remained in charge of the editorial department, and the cameramen included Walter Evan Davies, Harold Jeapes and Fred Wilson (joining them after a spell with Charles Urban's American newsreel *Kinograms*), all of whom had been Official cameramen, as well as John 'Bunny' Hutchins who during the latter half of the war had worked in the darkroom and as an occasional cameraman. Patrick McCabe remained as news editor for a short while, before being replaced by Charles Heath in 1920. Over sixty cameramen are known to have worked for Topical at one time or other between 1919 and 1923. There were always the core number of five to six cameramen, but any number of freelancers and those out of work were employed to help cover large events such as the Cup Final or Grand National, when fifteen or more cameramen could be used by each newsreel company. There were now just the three main newsreels, *Pathé Gazette*, *Gaumont Graphic* and *Topical Budget*, with occasional competition from smaller outfits such as *Scottish Moving Picture News* or the short-lived attempt at a daily newsreel, *Daily Cinema News*. The first American company to set up a British branch was Fox, whose *Fox News* was a small operation first started in April 1920.

The early 20s was a period of stabilisation and popularity for the newsreels, Topical included, although Hulton instigated costly improvements and refurbishments resulting in a couple of years when they made no profit. Newsreels thrived on a stable environment. Just as they first emerged when a large network of cinemas was first established, so they fitted into the settled pattern of cinema programming that had become established by the 1920s, with a programme of short items (newsreel, cartoon, travel film and so on) supporting a main feature film. It meant an assured market and an easily planned product. This inevitably led to predictable news coverage, but was made compelling by increasing versatility on the part of both cameramen and editorial staff. Although sales fluctuated unevenly throughout Topical's existence, in terms of technique and quality they showed steady progress from 1915 to a peak around 1922–3, their finest years. The chief aims of the silent newsreel were to reflect current topics and to entertain, and there was as much emphasis on pictorial quality and entertainment value as newsworthiness. The years under Sir Edward Hulton's control generally were a period of great vitality for *Topical Budget*, with impressive sporting coverage, a 'find a British film star' competition organised in conjunction with the *Daily Sketch*, much material from Ireland, and some notable coups: a cameraman inside the Hall of Mirrors for the signing of the Versailles peace treaty (Harold Jeapes), a cameraman (Ken Gordon) with the British Expeditionary Force in North Russia in 1919, and the filming of Bonar Law's cabinet in session at 10 Downing Street. Analysing one cameraman's activities for a year (Hutchins from November 1922 to November 1923), it is seen that he covered 176 assignments, half of them teamed with other cameramen, that 38 of these were never used, and that of all assignments 37 featured royalty, 24 horse-racing, 13 football, 11 weddings and 11 politicians. He filmed abroad three times. On three assignments he obtained no picture. These years saw the huge rise in popularity of the young Prince of Wales, who found his every move dogged by cameramen, and a boom period in sport, particularly football. Such stories were deemed news by public and newsreel producers alike.

The Topical Film Company did not make newsfilm exclusively. There were two prestigious feature-length films in the early 1920s, *50,000 Miles With The Prince of Wales* (1920), filmed by Will Barker, and *Across India With The Duke of Connaught* (1921), the material from both of which was originally shown as part of the newsreel, as well as the many locals and specials (short films commissioned by individual cinemas) which were a reliable source of revenue. Also at this time Topical introduced regular regional stories for their editions in Manchester, Liverpool, Glasgow, Leeds and elsewhere, generally using freelance cameramen and the FBO offices in those towns. They also developed a cheerful style of titling and intertitling (frequently based on weak puns) and decorative title 'pages'. In 1924 they moved their offices to 22 Soho Square (sharing with FBO), retaining the labs and editorial department at Wardour Street. Hulton was still chairman and the main managerial figures were William Jeapes and F. A. Enders of FBO.

On 23 October 1924 there was a fire at the company's Wardour Street premises. Much of the building was burnt out, and one member

F. A. Enders, managing director of FBO from 1923, and of the Topical Film Company from 1925.

15

of staff subsequently died from her injuries. Production, however, was unaffected and the next issue came out on time. While rebuilding took place, Topical had to send their printing out to other firms, which led to problems with staff and photographic quality. This, coupled with an internal newsreel war when Pathé introduced cost-cutting and their additional longer newsreel, *Pathé Super Gazette*, led to a fall in sales. After rebuilding, printing resumed at Wardour Street.

Shortly afterwards William Jeapes left. In part dissatisfied after losing control of his company during the war, and then seeing it bought up by Hulton, he departed in May 1925 to form another newsreel, *Empire News Bulletin*, with his brother Harold as main cameraman. Later that same month Sir Edward Hulton died and the company was bought up by Enders, who became the dominant figure behind Topical and FBO. Enders was not a newsreel man like Jeapes, but he was an astute businessman under whose regime the newsreel was more successful than it had ever been before. However this was counterbalanced by an increasingly routine product, attractively packaged but lacking the vitality of a few years earlier. In 1927 Topical did an exchange deal with the William Randolph Hearst company, producer of *MGM International News*, which brought *Topical Budget* a ready source of international stories, with the emphasis on 'entertainment' rather than 'news' since the latter tended to lose its news-value in the time it took to cross the Atlantic. Nevertheless the deal did provide Topical with interesting stories on American figures, aviation, China and the like which they could not hope to cover on their own, helping them all the more to match the efforts of the richer newsreels. However this increased dependence on outside material only emphasised the weakness of Topical's own product.

In June 1929 *British Movietone News* was launched, the first British sound newsreel.[24] Gaumont attempted to bring out a matching sound newsreel on the same day, but their equipment failed. Not to be outdone, it would appear that Topical had disc sound effects (the stories were the Trooping of the Colour and the Derby) to accompany their newsreel at some theatres, but this was to be their only foray into sound.[25] Topical had always struggled against the competition from Pathé and Gaumont, who enjoyed greater resources and assured exhibition outlets, and a decision was made to develop the laboratory work, culminating in the building of Brent Laboratories at Cricklewood in 1930. Both newsreel and distribution company were to be allowed to wind down, but many cinemas took a long time to adjust to sound and Topical were still supplying material in 1931. The number of cameramen was reduced, and they resorted more and more to library material. The last issue, number 1022–1, was released on 26 March 1931:

The news that the Topical Budget is to fade out from among

16

news-reels is a break with a past, when 'topical' was a better-known word than 'news-reel'. The claim for recognition by newer ventures into the field with sound and talkie resources has given the Topical Budget a difficult time. There seems a possibility that it will continue in another form – there are hints of amalgamations of the kind which Fleet Street knows. At the moment the Kine understands that nothing definite has been arranged.[26]

The very words 'Topical Budget' now sounded antiquated. The Chronicles, Graphics and Journals belonged to the past, when imitating the newspapers seemed a necessary pretence, whereas the five main newsreels of the sound era proclaimed by their very names that the newsreel had found its identity and, of course, its voice: *British Movietone News*, *British Paramount News*, *Gaumont-British News*, *Universal Talking News*, and (ever the exception) *Pathé Gazette*, who did not become *Pathé News* until 1946.

The *Topical Budget* library of negatives remained at Brent Labs, and the Topical Film Company continued (as did FBO), concentrating solely on laboratory work. In 1937 the name was changed to Brent Laboratories Limited and a new Topical Film Company was formed which produced instructional films for builders and craftsmen. Jeapes' *Empire News Bulletin* evolved into *Universal Talking News* and most of the former *Topical Budget* cameramen still active went on to work for him or for *British Movietone News*. Universal were the outsiders of the main sound newsreels, run cheaply, using solely silent cameras and adding commentary and sound effects in the studio. In many ways they were the continuation of what Topical had been in the silent era.

'*The past is a foreign country; they do things differently there.*' Histories of film may have found little place for the newsreels, but newsreel libraries continue to be exploited by television. Old newsfilm remains familiar, and yet unfamiliar. It is difficult to associate these grey scenes from the past with the slick televisual presentation that encompasses them. Frequently they have been handled in a cavalier manner with disparate images taken from a variety of sources, edited together to form a kind of filmic wallpaper behind a dominant commentary. Such suppression of the image indeed began when the newsreels themselves discovered sound: what we see is conditioned by what is said.

To enter that other country it is necessary to learn its language. Those grey scenes were created: an editor chose them, a cameraman filmed them, they were presented in the form of a newsreel. To see them as a product of human endeavour – human ingenuity, pragmatism, idleness, blindness – is to re-witness their creation, to recognise the past. And credit must be given for what we have inherited. The newsreel editors may have been complacent and conservative, but they could also be creative, and the cameramen deserve our admiration.

Theirs was a privileged position: they were journalists, their own directors and cinematographers, and the innovators of many newsfilm techniques. There is freer, more imaginative camerawork in the best of the newsreels than in most silent fiction films made in Britain.

Topical Budget did not think in terms of a record of the past; they thought about what was happening next week. Therein lies the life and fun of the newsreels: the hectic race to find good pictures, to dodge the bad weather, best your rivals, and get the results into the cinemas on time. The skill and enthusiasm of the early newsfilm producers and cameramen, their experiments and decisions, have given us our moving picture of their times, and shaped the pattern of visual news-telling that is with us today.

THE WORLD WAR
A View from the Home Front

War Office Official Topical Budget

We are informed by Mr. Jeapes, the managing director of the Topical Film Co., that the entire concern has been placed at the disposal of the War Office Cinematograph Committee for the period of the war, in order to issue a bi-weekly Topical Film Budget showing all the principal events of interest in connection with the war.

This will include pictures from the British Fronts, French, Italian, Portugese, and other films, and also those of American troops in the field.

This will in no way interfere with the official war films, which will be put out as usual, but the Topical Budget will be released on the same terms, and the service of the official operators will be available.

The Budget, being released twice a week, on Tuesdays [sic] and Saturdays, will always be up to date, each issue consisting approximately of 350 feet. The great success attained by the Topical Budget under Mr. Jeapes proves that this is an item which is indispensable to every programme, and though the War Office Cinematograph Committee is not in a position to handle it in foreign countries, there is little doubt that arrangements will be made to ensure it a world-wide circulation.

All the proceeds are devoted to military charities. Mr. Ernest Waters, late of Cricks and Martin, the American Co., David Horsley etc., has been appointed outside representative of the War Office Official Topical Budget, the offices of which are at 76 Wardour Street.[1]

On 28 May 1917 *Topical Budget*, a minor British newsreel with an audience of little more than half a million, found itself taken over by the British government, renamed *War Office Official Topical Budget*, and over the next year and a half widening that audience to over three million at home and abroad. It became the chief channel for British film propaganda, but the new controllers were to find that it was hard enough just to operate a newsreel, never mind make it a tool of official information.

1914–1917

The declaration of war took the film trade, like the country, by surprise. Initial reactions centred around fears of a loss in business. They worried not only about the country's future but also about unemployment, falling audiences, loss of foreign contacts and staff joining up. This was just as soon counteracted by a sense of opportunity, of being able to exploit the situation and show that the trade could rise to the occasion.

August 1914 saw a remarkable amount of activity on the film front as every company sought to bring out something to capitalise on the crisis. Old travel films were advertised as showing the sites where battles were being fought, dramatised reconstructions of current political events were hastily put together, and an exhibitor wrote to the *Bioscope* to say, 'the serious crisis in Europe has afforded opportunity for enterprise, which should bring its own reward.'[2] Patriotic sentiments or the promise of military scenes just in the titles of films were enough to draw enthusiastic audiences.

All the newsreel and topical companies responded by sending out cameramen in the hope of filming something at the Front. The experience of the Balkan wars had taught them the value of the publicity, even when the chances of securing material were slim, the right preparations to make, and the few chances of filming anything worthwhile. But enthusiasm must have been high: Pathé, Gaumont and Eclair were confident in the advantages offered by their French contacts; Jury's announced that they were sending six cameramen to the Front; Cherry Kearton, new owner of the Warwick Trading Company, announced that he had sent out three men, and before the end of August he had created a new bi-weekly war magazine, *The Whirlpool Of War*. William Jeapes announced through the trade press that Topical had sent out three cameramen,[3] and later reports reveal that two of these were F. W. Engholm and George Woods-Taylor. Things were just as active on the home front, with films of troop movements and men joining up to fight said to be in great demand.

The realities of the situation soon darkened the mood. The public quickly tired of reconstructions, library material and marches – they wanted actuality film of the fighting. Not three weeks into the war it was being reported that the current situation in Belgium made such filming impossible:

You may like to hear what are the chances for photography or cinematography during this war. I would answer, having been in the mill, none at all, at any rate, not at present. For days it was death to venture in the streets of Brussels with a camera. It is better now, but still, the man alone must be wary. The authorities put the bann [sic] on photography, the mob made it impossible. To try and take a picture was to risk death. The camera was the badge of a spy, and the mob would tear a suspect limb from limb if the guards did not

20

arrest him first . . . The spy fever has simmered down somewhat now that about a hundred spies have been shot in Brussels . . . There is no chance of going to the front, but perhaps, later, when the Germans are driven back and the mists roll away from the general disposition of the troops they will get an opportunity to move. That is the hope, but the cinematographer hardly shares it. He is told that the British military authorities are against cinematographers going to the front, and I know it is not only the Belgians who are raising obstacles, the French also have put up the bar . . . The difficulties of the cinematographer, naturally, are infinitely worse than those of the ordinary still-picture man. He has, for such times, a cumbersome apparatus to trail about with, and this impedes his action, for he cannot set it up, take his picture and hustle it away before the crowd become aware of his intentions. What his difficulties will be when he gets up country if he gets away from Brussels at all, are impossible to guess.[4]

To the distraught Belgians, anyone not speaking French must be speaking German and was liable to be attacked. With native hostility, no co-ordination of activities and little access to military areas, the cameramen were obliged to film much the same sort of light stories they would have filmed back at home, only behind Belgian lines. Despite some extravagant claims from some sources, very little material of any interest was getting through and none of it from the war front. The cameramen themselves, resourceful and stubborn as a breed, travelled remarkably widely and had adventures enough; Frank Danvers Yates (a future *Topical Budget* employee), filming for Cherry Kearton, reported on his return to London that he had had:

. . . quite an exciting time, having penetrated into the firing line on the strength of a provisional pass which was lightly regarded even by the Allied Forces, backed up by his own tactical resource. He was in Ostend when a company of Uhlans was dispersed by a handful of gendarmes, and has visited Louvain, Malines and Naumur, his camera has been confiscated on several occasions, and he himself has been arrested in Amiens, but he is returning full of enthusiasm and with the determination to secure pictures of still greater interest.[5]

Clearly Yates was having an enjoyable time, but equally clearly he had not filmed much of interest, nor been in a position to do so.

All things conspired against the topical companies. It was hard enough obtaining permits to film with the Belgian army behind lines. The British military authorities were said to be forbidding filming of any kind, and at home there were threats of the complete censorship of any films of the war, as the following letter shows:

F. E. SMITH, Esq.,
   Press Bureau, War Office,
      Whitehall.

DEAR SIR, – As proprietors of a British newsfilm, would you inform us if the statement as per enclosed Press cutting, is intended to apply to general pictures of the troops mobilising, and on the march?

   Of course, we do not intend to take, and have not attempted to film, any pictures of forts or defences that would be of the slightest use to an enemy, and, furthermore, we should like to state that the whole of our staff are British subjects.

We are, yours faithfully,
THE TOPICAL BUDGET,
EDITOR,
August 10, 1914.[6]

Despite rumours, no such overall ban was introduced beyond the refusal to grant permits to cameramen wishing to accompany the British forces, which was effective enough in itself. The threats were also partly alleviated by the film trade imposing self-censorship in the guise of the British Board of Film Censors (BBFC), whose statement of approval appeared at the front of all war films shown on British screens:

   The sections of this film dealing with the National Crisis have been passed by the British Board of Film Censors.

Some material was being sent back by the cameramen, enough for it to be exploited in a variety of forms, and there were shocking scenes of urban destruction, and uplifting scenes of soldiers on the march. But the topical companies were unable to progress beyond such coverage and by the end of 1914, with Belgian permits now removed and the British authorities denying any access to military locations, they had to admit defeat and retreated to largely home coverage.

The Topical Film Company was comparatively fortunate during this period. Of the three cameramen the company sent out, it is known that George Woods-Taylor filmed in France, taking what was later claimed to be the first film of the British Expeditionary Force in France, while F. W. Engholm was extremely active in Belgium, apparently filming in Antwerp, Brussels, Ghent, Liège, Louvain, Ostend, Termonde and Ypres. Certainly Engholm was able to send back a large amount of material, some of it of high quality. While still including such material in the newsreel, Topical decided to release a series of war topicals, each around 400 feet in length:[7]

TABLE I

Series of war topicals released by the Topical Film Company

	Title	Length (ft)	Release date
1.	*England Declares War*	340	
2.	*War Scenes in Belgium*	645	
3.	*Our Cavalry's Magnificent Horsemanship by the 18th Hussars (Queen Mary's Own)*	520	
4.	*The Battle of Louvain*		
5.	*Defence of Belgium*		
6.	*The German Army Entering Brussels*	400	14.9.1914
7.			
8.	*The German Occupation of Historic Louvain*	700	24.9.1914
9.	*The Battle of Lebbeke*	561	5.10.1914
10.	*Great Battle before Antwerp*	650	8.10.1914
11.	*The First Film of British Troops in France*	300	12.10.1914
12.	*The Evacuation of Ghent and Ostend*	450	
13.			
14.	*Scenes in and around the Belgian Capital*	550	2.11.1914
15.	*The Battle around Dixmunde, Nieuport and the Yser Canal*	455	16.11.1914
16.	*With the English Troops around Arras*	560	20.11.1914
17.	*King George on the Battle-Field at Ypres*	400	14.12.1914
18.	*With the British Forces in France*	650	4.1.1915
19.	*India's Reply*	350	18.1.1915
20.	*With a Skirmishing Party in Flanders*	450	8.2.1915
21.	*In the Argonne a Fight for the Wood*	435	1.3.1915
22.	*Russia's Great Haul*	350	8.3.1915
23.	*Scenes on the Austro-Servian Frontier*	365	29.3.1915

While such material was coming in, it seemed wisest to exploit it in the longer topical form, and *Topical Budget* suffered somewhat as a result. Certainly the surviving newsreel items for this period are insignificant snapshots of Belgian life, done in the run-of-the-mill manner of home news stories, whereas the surviving topicals are often impressive. *The German Occupation of Historic Louvain* is an astonishing film. Beginning with various shots of houses and churches shattered by shellfire, it then features a series of remarkably close shots of the German army both relaxing and marching in the town. The structure of the film itself, progressing as it does from scenes of destruction to the casual army of occupation to final shots of goose-stepping soldiers, conveys (without the need for censorious titles) the impression and shock of the invasion. One eloquent panning shot follows German troops as they leave by train, the camera continuing to pan as the train passes by, revealing the ruined buildings left behind. Topical claimed that the film was taken 'by our own correspondent', and Engholm was certainly in the area at the time, but the closeness of the cameraman to the Germans suggests that he is more likely to have been an American independent who subsequently sold his footage to Topical.[8]

Engholm was responsible for other fine films in the series, however. His *With a Skirmishing Party in Flanders* is a lively, dramatic account of a party of British troops passing through ruined towns, fighting on their way. The battle scenes cannot be genuine, though they are possibly training exercises, but with the camera positioned low down and the skirmishing party cautiously advancing through scrubland and firing at the enemy such scenes still have the look and feel of the real thing. *With the British Forces in France*, probably taken by George Woods-Taylor (to whom can be attributed numbers 11, 16, 18 and 19 in the series), is less impressive, showing the movement of stores and ammunition well behind the lines, but on the evidence of these films both cameramen were able to film British troops with some freedom, at least for a while. The newsreel companies always tended to imitate one another, and both Pathé and Gaumont issued a series of war topicals alongside the regular newsreel. Most imaginative among these efforts was Cherry Kearton's *The Whirlpool of War* series, a hybrid of the topical and newsreel forms, which Kearton operated in parallel with *Warwick Bioscope Chronicle*.

The last of the series of war topicals came out at the end of March 1915 and thereafter the newsreel ran on its own. The cameramen all returned to Britain, and such material from the continent as appeared in *Topical Budget* came from outside sources. However, advertising for the twenty-second topical in the war series, *Russia's Great Haul*, refers to 'our correspondent with the Russian Forces'. Certainly there is a surprisingly large amount of Russian material in *Topical Budget*, particularly in 1916, which would seem to indicate a regular source, and it is known that Frank Danvers Yates filmed for Cherry Kearton in Russia at this time. Too little information survives from this period to make any more than guesses about roaming Topical cameramen, as war footage in the newsreel could just as easily, and indeed was more likely to, have come from foreign companies and cameramen. After the initial burst of activity and enthusiasm, Topical settled down to reporting the war from home.

By the start of 1915, there had been a complete change in the British newsfilm industry, and already it bore a closer resemblance to the arrangement of the 1920s than it did to the state of things just six months before. *Williamson's Animated News*, *The Whirlpool Of War* and *Warwick Bioscope Chronicle* all folded. Producers of the single-story topical found the market for these had dropped, and so concentrated on renting (as in the case of Jury's), or turned to fiction film production, Barker's being the most spectacular amongst these efforts.

24

Two thirds of all cinemas now took a newsreel, four of which remained. Of these, *Pathé's Animated Gazette* and *Gaumont Graphic* were dominant. From an estimated total cinema audience of 10,000,000, Pathé had 30 per cent of the market, or a 1,600,000 audience per issue; Gaumont had 22 per cent of the market, or a 1,100,000 audience per issue. Topical lagged behind with 11 per cent of the market, or 600,000 per issue. The audience figures for *Eclair Journal* were still lower.[9] How this last newsreel survived until possibly 1917 is unclear, but certainly for a period between June and October 1916 they were being supported by Topical, possibly to the extent of merely being *Topical Budget* under another name. Surviving items for both newsreels for this period are identical save for the change in company logo, but the style of titling is Topical's.[10] The reasons for this extraordinary state of affairs seem lost, but after October 1916 *Eclair Journal* either regained their independence or disappeared altogether.

Although Topical had only a small share of the newsreel market, they prospered. In September 1915, at the end of their second year as a limited company, they could boast a profit for the year of £9,205 13s 3d.[11] 1915 is the first year for which a sizeable proportion of Topical's output survives; with additional information from coverage in the trade press, this makes it possible to see how this native newsreel was taking shape and dealing with news in wartime. Furthermore an account in a contemporary journal gives some idea of the newsreel's work and thinking:

In a good many respects the news film – which has nowadays become such a regular feature of all picture-palace shows – is like a pictorial newspaper shorn of the greater part of its letterpress. Only, of course, the illustrations are put into motion, and consequently become far more realistic than those that appear in print.

It would, therefore, be accurate to say that the news film is the picture paper of the moving picture world; an animated record of passing events. And immediately it becomes natural that, like an ordinary picture paper, it should be edited, controlled from an office, and fed by representatives in all parts of the world.

As a matter of fact, the editing of a news film, bears many points of resemblance to the editing of a daily picture paper. If you were to visit the editorial offices of *The Animated Gazette* at Messrs' Pathé, or of the *Topical Budget* at the Topical Film Company (both in Wardour Street) you would find quite a number of people busily engaged in reading the day's papers with scissors in their hands. For this is one of the means by which subjects suitable for filming are found, and it results in quite a sheaf of cuttings being placed upon the editor's table for his consideration. At the same time, moreover, letters, telegram messages are constantly arriving from agents and employees in all parts of the world, describing events which have happened or which are about to happen.

Under the Editor's Eagle Eye
The editor of a news-film has to be a man with a 'nose for news' and a comprehensive mind. He has to decide, often in a few seconds, not merely whether a thing is worth doing, but whether it can or cannot be done in cinematographic form. And all day long he is considering and rejecting or accepting subjects suggested to him, and is sending expert operators off to diverse scenes of action in all corners of the kingdom.

In his room a tape machine ticks away the news of the moment, and every now and then this machine is consulted lest anything of value should have escaped attention.

Many events that have already happened are 'covered' without delay. The dropping of bombs on Southend, for example, was an outrage which naturally could not be recorded in the happening, but within a very few hours a whole tribe of cinema men were on the spot, photographing the visible signs of havoc caused by the bombardment. But the events which appeal most strongly to the editors of these news films are those which are advertised beforehand, for the simple reason that they can be photographed in the happening . . .

The Press and the Cinema
. . . The great aim of the editor is to have film reproductions of subjects which are illustrated in the daily papers; but many of these are not suitable from the film point of view. In some cases there is nothing to lead up to the event; in others the comparative darkness of the interior of a building defies the cinema camera, because it calls out for flashlight exposures, which are utterly out of the question. The Press photographer, moreover, has a tremendous advantage over the cinema operator, because he can use photographic plates that are considerably faster than the fastest film. And just now there are other difficulties.

The Secret Movements of the Military
'The present time', declares the Editor of *The Topical Budget*, 'is an extremely bad one for security subjects, as to be topical they must be of a military nature, and nearly all the big military reviews are held almost in secret. Permits can, as a rule, be obtained, but the difficulty is to find out in time when and where they are being held.

'Even when you have secured the negative the trouble does not end there. The film has to be passed by the Censor. To give you an instance, we filmed H. M. the King and Lord Kitchener reviewing the Canadians on Salisbury Plain, but it was *over seven weeks* before this film was released for exhibition by the Censor. Of course, we quite appreciate that it is necessary to censor topical films, but that

26

does not make the task of obtaining subjects any easier. Just lately, however, the recruiting offices have realised the value of the topical film from a recruiting point of view, and therefore greater facilities have been granted.'[12]

The 'editor' speaking may be either William Jeapes or news editor George Woods-Taylor, a former press photographer. The account of news-gathering in the office presumably combines what the reporter found at Pathé and Topical. Other evidence, in particular the complaints raised when the WOCC took over *Topical Budget*, indicate a humbler, more haphazard system. Certainly only Pathé would be receiving much information from international services, and it is unlikely that Topical made much use of a news agency's ticker-tape service until after the war. What is interesting is the open admission that they took their lead from illustrations in the newspapers.

Censorship had been introduced at the start of the war, but it was only in wartime that the newsreels were subjected to outside censorship, 'topicals' and 'locals' being officially excluded from the attentions of the BBFC when it began operations in January 1913. There is, of course, no mention in the above excerpt of attempting to film military scenes on the continent, which had been completely banned, and if it took seven weeks for a harmless military review to pass the censors it is no surprise that Topical's output at this time gives little idea of the war. The last comment, however, is of the greatest interest, since it certainly ties in with the kind of stories which were beginning to appear in the *Topical Budget*. 1915 saw a number of items that can be readily interpreted as designs to aid recruiting:

VC APPEALS FOR RECRUITS
'Corp. Holmes, VC attends a recruiting march meeting on Clapham Common and appeals for recruits to help the men at the front.'[13]

MORE MEN WANTED
'E. G. Hemmerde Esq. KC, MP appeals for recruits for Lord Kitchener's new army of 300,000 men.'[14]

WOMEN'S MARCH THROUGH LONDON
'A vast procession of women headed by Mrs Pankhurst, march through London to show the Minister of Munitions their willingness to help in any war service.'[15]

AN INCENTIVE TO RECRUITING
'Recruiting Sergeants avail themselves of the interest shown in the war trophies and secure many recruits in answer to the King's call for men.'[16]

Here then is one of the first instances of the authorities accepting the popularity of the cinema and making it work for them. Topical approved of their being used in this way since they approved of the cause, but it should be observed that they could also report on protests about recruiting methods, as in these two items (actually from 1916):

MARRIED MENS' [sic] PROTEST MEETING
'London attested married men hold a Single Men First protest meeting at Tower Hill. Mr W. Dyson speaking to the meeting, calling on the Government to fulfil the pledge.'[17]

LONDON HUSBANDS' PROTEST
'Passing the resolution at the protest meeting of attested married men in Hyde Park.'[18]

Topical's output in 1915 was a mixture of processions, protests, personalities and occasional glimpses of the war in Belgium, Serbia or Russia, depending on availability of material for purchase. They could best record how the war had come to Britain; SOUTHEND AIR RAID[19] shows Zeppelin bomb damage in English towns, with the charred body of a dog being held up to the camera; ANTI-GERMAN RIOTS[20] shows German-owned shops being wrecked as a reaction to the sinking of the *Lusitania*. They kept up the diet of standard newsreel stories, but hardly anything was shown that was not coloured in some way by the war. Thus a fête was news if convalescent soldiers attended it; captured German guns were a highlight of the 1915 Lord Mayor's Show; football players in a match were shortly to join up; a dog show was in aid of a war charity; the bride at a society wedding had a brother at the Front.

This was a home front picture of the war, produced by people with little access to military footage and no personal experience of the all-pervasive news story of the day. But, compelled to portray fragmentary information of a necessarily limited nature, *Topical Budget* found that they actually profited by the situation. As noted above, the material necessary to make topical-length films of the war saleable or interesting was unavailable, and with the growing length of fiction films, and their dominant position in the cinema programme, there was less and less audience interest in lengthy actuality films. But a varied package of short items, showing aspects of topical stories of common interest, left little time for boredom and promised a wide coverage of events. There were some complaints in the trade papers about the slight nature of the short newsreel item, but perhaps the newsreel producers knew rather more about their audience's attention span. By design or by choice, the newsreels had secured a formula that was to see them through the war, and indeed through to the age of television.

Thus from 1915, and particularly through 1916 until the company was taken over by the War Office in May 1917, Topical began to operate with some degree of inventiveness and imagination. It was a view from the home front, but it was for a home front audience. Editorially they were still rather inflexible, and the inventiveness lay in individual news items rather than the newsreel as a whole. The length, 300 feet, and the number of items, five, were rigidly adhered to. If a story ran over regulation length it was divided into two items. However, some issues do show an interesting variety of items. Issue 262–1 (release date 30 August 1916) features a football match, a protest march over food hoarding, news that Rumania had joined the war on the side of the Allies, military sports and a religious ceremony in Serbia. It opens with the start of the football season, and closes with an official ceremony. It covers a serious issue affecting life on the home front, includes a light-hearted item, and finds use for some stock footage of the Rumanian army. Or an issue might be largely devoted to a single theme. Issue 245–2 (release date 6 May 1916) is unusual in having a 284-feet item on the Dublin rebellion, but a follow-up issue, 247–1 (release date 17 May 1916), has four items on the aftermath: crowds outside Bow Street police station awaiting news of the trial of Roger Casement; Sir John Maxwell inspecting the OTC at Trinity College Dublin; a march past of the Irish Association Voluntary Training Corps; and an item entitled GERMAN RIFLES showing the rifles and pikes collected by troops following the rebellion. But such was the frequent struggle to find fresh news material that it was usually enough just to have found five topical stories, without worrying about the balance or overall content of an issue.

In a number of the individual news items for this mid-war period one can find clear creativity and imaginative camerawork. The task faced by the cameraman was to convey what was, literally, a moment of actuality. Some did this simply by filming single-shot items: CANADIANS AT THE ABBEY[21] features troops and band marching past the camera. Once the procession is past the item is over; there are no shots from other angles and no other scenes. Such literal descriptions on film were already known to be primitive, but examples of single-shot items still occur as late as 1918.[22] The march past of troops naturally lends itself to such simple coverage, although the visual monotony might be alleviated somewhat by the cameraman placing himself at a point where the marchers turned a corner – this catches the eye more and gives the appearance of troops approaching and moving away simultaneously. One march past, although again employing just one shot, ingeniously uses variety of speeds to create visual interest.[23] The cameraman placed himself on the back of a vehicle which then drove from the rear to the front of a marching column. One gets the march, the fresh camera angle looking down on the men, and the two differing speeds of the marchers and the travelling camera. With the customary cheery looks towards the camera that characterise so many of the newsreel items of the period, it is a striking and memorable single shot.

However, most items comprised up to half a dozen shots, necessarily describing the action from a number of angles. The growing sophistication in newsreel filming at this time can be illustrated through the problem of how to film a bridge being built. Army training activities were an obvious choice for the newsreels since they were safe, manageable and available. One such regular activity was the building of small pontoon bridges and here the nature of the story can be seen to have formed the news item that seeks to describe it. It takes a long time to build a bridge; seen as a whole activity it makes tedious viewing. But it is also a co-operative effort: wood has to be brought up, knots tied, planks laid, pontoons floated, people have to cross over, an official supervises the action. Over this length of time the cameraman has plenty of opportunities to capture each of the parts which go to make up the whole action and complete the bridge. The finished film begins with a river; it ends with a river spanned by a bridge.[24] In between come various shots indicating this process. This may seem too obvious, but it is an important step in newsreel construction: a created moment of actuality rather than a literal recording. Just as Topical learned to turn fragments of information into a record of life in wartime, so they learned to represent a story through selection and montage. Circumstances created both newsreel and newsreel style.

WOMEN HAY MAKERS[25] is a fine example of just such a created moment. The story features women employed on an Essex farm. The phenomenon of women workers, in factories and on the land, intrigued, even enthralled the nation, and they were featured regularly in *Topical Budget*. This item comprises seven shots, the cameraman's task being to illustrate the work being done on the land; this was not an event, past or present, but a part of life in wartime Britain that could be recorded.

WOMEN HAY MAKERS
'Mrs Wood daughter-in-law of Field Marshal Sir Evelyn Wood is organising farm workers at Warden's Hall, Willingale. Haymaking in full swing at the Essex Farm.'

The film opens with a medium shot, the camera panning left to right, of a group of women turning over hay in a field. The second shot shows a woman driving a horse-drawn rotary machine moving at an angle towards the camera, and third is a deftly executed reverse angle shot of the machine passing away from the camera. There follows a medium shot of one woman raking hay, then a carefully composed similar shot with two women raking, one in the foreground, the other further back down a curving line of mown hay. The sixth shot shows them loading hay onto a horse-drawn cart, and the final medium shot shows similar action, with the camera panning slowly from right to left. With the rural setting, women farm workers and careful composition, the end result is

30

a memorable portrait of its subject; indeed one with painterly qualities and emblematic of its times. By exercising his imagination, and clearly taking a great deal of effort over camera positions and arrangement of his subjects, the cameraman has created a small, but beautiful film.

The pastoral images of this news item come from due attention to the potential of the subject-matter. A different subject produces a different result. The story for BOWLS AT BLACKPOOL,[26] a bowling tournament, is hardly promising, and might have been idly filmed in three or four static shots. However full use has been made of the visual opportunities on offer:

BOWLS AT BLACKPOOL
'Scenes at the final of the bowling tournament, which is one of the big events held at Blackpool towards the end of the season.'

As with WOMEN HAY MAKERS, a single cameraman has taken the film (as was common for this period), but, with the exception of the final shot, he has restricted himself to one position in the stand, looking down on the green. First is a slow panning shot from left to right as the bowlers bowl towards the camera's corner of the green, followed by a close shot of people watching from windows to the cameraman's left. Third is a medium close shot looking directly down at the bowls in one corner, the camera moving slightly as men come to gather them. A similar shot follows, taken a little to the right. For the fifth shot the

Land girls in Essex in 1916. From *Women Hay Makers*.

camera begins by looking down as before, then tilts up as it follows a bowl sent away from the camera to the other corner of the green, the bowler running after it, then stopping. The final shot has the camera body positioned on the ground with a bowl being sent towards it. Once again the nature of the subject has been allowed to create the style of the film; rather than just show the game as a whole, the cameraman has been directed by particular aspects of the action.

Imaginative films such as these can be seen in the wider context of British film-making of the period. Although the newsreel companies operated quite separately from the producers of fiction film, both were exhibited at the same cinemas, and the difference can be quite marked. At a time when one might find the camera in a British studio actually bolted to the floor to prevent anyone from moving it,[27] the newsreels did, on some occasions, demonstrate a far greater awareness of the possibilities of communicating through film – an awareness derived from a greater trust in the medium. Producers of fiction film persisted in seeing the theatre as their ideal, whereas the makers of actuality film, forced for the most part to work in the open air and to describe the various aspects of their subject within the constraints of the newsreel format, often produced the more vital work.

Nevertheless it must be admitted that the number of poorly or indifferently filmed news items far outweighs the attractive ones. It is not wholly fair, of course, to judge ephemeral news stories in such a manner, for they were intended to be seen and then almost instantly forgotten, but the triviality of so much of the output of the newsreels (all of whose output was largely similar) must have exasperated those living through the most terrible of wars then known. Much of it appears to be just one long parade, and, more than the tedium, some of the films are lazily, even clumsily constructed. Filming was largely done with hand-cranked cameras. The cameraman would set his camera up in what he hoped would be a good position, and the moment something interesting occurred he would start turning the handle. If it turned out to be not quite so interesting, or was taking its time (for example, a person approaching the camera), he would stop. If the action picked up, he would start up again. The result is a large number of awkward jump-cuts in newsreels of this period. Today these blemishes jar on the eye, but it is possible that the contemporary audience came not to notice them. (Present day television interviews often feature a jump between one interesting comment and the next, and not all viewers are aware that a cut has been made.)

But thanks to considered filming by the few there are pleasing records of the time in *Topical Budget*. KHAKI BANK HOLIDAY[28] is an attractive, informal picture of a fair on Hampstead Heath, mixing swings and roundabouts with background recruiting meetings. DEVON-SHIRE HOSPITAL BUXTON and THERMAL MINERAL WATER BATHS,[29] unusually filmed indoors, are two consecutive items showing various

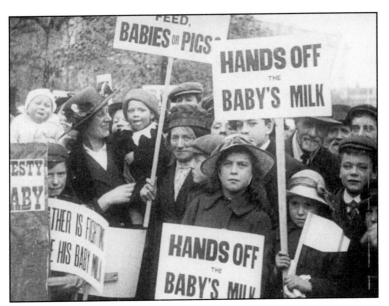

Public protest at the price of milk in war-time. From *Hands off Baby's Milk*.

treatment methods for soldiers with 'Rheumatism, Sciatica, and allied diseases'. Wounded and convalescent troops resting in Britain were an obvious choice of subject for the newsreels, and the greatest fascination was with the blinded. WORKING UNDER DIFFICULTIES,[30] showing blind soldiers learning carpentry at St Dunstan's Hospital, is one example of many such items, in which blind soldiers show new skills, race one another in rowing-boats, or play pushball, a voguish sport of the time. As has been noted above, women working on the land offered attractive, pastoral images, but scenes of women workers in munition factories were also common. Another regular subject was scenes of protest, and marches were a staple newsreel feature because they could be planned for in advance and were simple to film. If people were waving banners it was almost as good as hearing them speak. LUSITANIA DAY[31] gives prominence to a banner that reads, 'Hang All Pro-German Peacemongers'. HANDS OFF BABY'S MILK,[32] featuring a protest meeting in Hyde Park about the high price of milk, includes placards that read, 'Down With Food Trusts', 'Hands Off The Baby's Milk', 'Father Is Fighting Give His Baby Milk' and 'Which Shall You Feed, Babies Or Pigs?' The item ends with a close-up of a baby crying.

Military exercises were also a popular subject because they could at least give the appearance of proximity to the fighting. LAND MINE EXPLOSIONS and OCCUPYING THE CRATER,[33] two consecutive items from the same issue, show men of the Royal Engineers in a realistic training exercise, running down trenches, setting off an explosion and donning gas masks. Another way to suggest the war without actually being able to show it is demonstrated by an item such as LONDON TERRITORIALS.[34] The film merely shows troops marching down an English country road, but the intertitles point out that one such battalion was involved in a recent battle in France. The short item allowed the newsreels to get away with such tricks – film commemorating an event without showing actual footage of it. This was to be developed later in the war, when scenes of British troops on the Western Front were given to represent action the audience knew had taken place that week, whereas actual film of the action would be a few weeks in arriving. TORPEDOING A LINER[35] reveals another kind of lie. The film shows an aeroplane flying over a warship, which then explodes spectacularly. The titles are ambiguous:

TORPEDOING A LINER
'A faint idea of the "pirate huns" latest crime against civilisation, is portrayed in the torpedoing of a ship where the terrific explosion destroys everything.'

These lines have to be read twice before it is clear that the film is only giving an impression of the German sinking of two ships earlier in the week – and audiences of the time only had the chance to read them once. Actually, there is a jump-cut between the aeroplane passing over and the explosion, which clearly has been staged for the camera. But it was enough to have roused emotions. Such deceptions were the nearest Topical ever came to fakery in their newsreel.

Material bought from foreign companies gave *Topical Budget*'s audience a patchwork view of the war on the continent. Often such films came in batches, and the newsreel would make a special feature of one war location over a number of successive issues. So in March 1916 they featured a number of items showing Russian troop movements, from a source based in Petrograd. The military authorities on the Eastern Front were more amenable towards cameramen than those on the Western, and Topical were able to give regular coverage to the Serbian army and people, and British and other Allied troops in Macedonia and Salonika.[36] Apart from the occasional big gun firing, none of these items showed any fighting, but they did give a clear impression of the range of the war, and the varieties of landscapes and peoples involved. THE ARMIES OF THE ALLIES[37] features a group of soldiers, each one representative of the various races then fighting for the Allied cause in the Balkans. Towards the end of 1916, a number of items headed 'Official Belgian Film' appeared in *Topical Budget*. Taken by Belgian Official cameramen, they are for the most part no less trite than the poorest items taken in 1914; BELGIAN SOLDIERS' PILLOW FIGHT[38] is typical.

Topical also got hold of film taken by German cameramen. In November 1915, in a personal deal between William Jeapes and Frederick Wile, Berlin correspondent of the *Daily Mail*, the Topical Film Company acquired the prints of a large number of German propaganda films. Wile had secured the prints and turned to Jeapes for help in printing and distribution. Suitably edited, selected German films were the main feature of a programme of films running at the Scala cinema in London between January and June 1916, and elsewhere in the country. The programme caused a considerable stir, but only one issue of *Topical Budget* apparently made use of the material:

GERMAN BLUFF
'Part of the film issued by the German Government to Neutral Nations illustrates the "kindness" of the Hun soldier to the Belgian women and children. Of course this scene is carefully acted for the camera.' Acted sequence in which a Belgian family is met on the road by two German soldiers. One inspects the father's papers while the other chats to the children. The family then passes on its way.

THE HUN'S CONSCIENCE
'The murderers of Nurse Cavell deem it necessary to show how they are regarded by the inhabitants of the countries they have invaded. "A guilty conscience needs no accusing".' Acted sequence in which a Belgian couple and their daughter come out of their house with a German soldier, who gives them assurances and chalks a message in German, stating that the people living there are 'good people', on the outside of the door, with the admiring approval of the family.[39]

Any film picture of a war is going to be random and inadequate. War is vast movements or individual dramas. A film record falls somewhere in the middle ground, showing people in the grip of these forces, but unable to offer any understanding of their predicament. Topical's coverage of the first half of the war is sometimes foolish, sometimes memorable, mostly all that could be expected given the circumstances. But as a witness of the home front experience of the war, showing the military intrusion into normal life, the continuity of human activity, and short glimpses of the war's varied locations, somehow familiar from public discussion, *Topical Budget* fulfilled its function. In these first years of the war the silent newsreel found its form.

The Official Period
When the War Office decided to employ a newsreel as an outlet for Official film, it was the culmination of various efforts towards a campaign of filmed propaganda. A newsreel seemed to be a sensible and manageable means of packaging and exhibiting limited material from widespread sources. The creation of the *War Office Official Topical Budget* coincided with a coalescing of those various efforts, and led eventually to the creation of the Ministry of Information and a unified

policy for film propaganda.

It was the forcefulness of Britain's first Minister of Information, Lord Beaverbrook, that largely shaped these events. In 1915 he was Sir Max Aitken, Member of Parliament for Ashton-under-Lyne; seeking to represent his native Canada, he created and made himself head of the Canadian War Records Office (CWRO) in London in January 1916.[40] The CWRO's purpose was the promotion and recording of the Canadian war effort, and this involved securing the services of a Canadian Official cameraman. Thus it was that in July 1916 a Briton, Oscar Bovill, was sent out to the Western Front as Canadian Official cinematographer, the fourth person to be appointed as an Official cameraman with the forces of the British Empire.

The first three had been Geoffrey Malins, Teddy Tong and J. B. McDowell. Following some persistent lobbying by the cinema trade, led by J. Brooke Wilkinson of the BBFC, initial government reluctance towards any kind of war filming had been broken down. Fears of security risks and condescension towards the lowly cinema and its audience were gradually overcome as tight censorship regulations were devised and an agreement drawn up by which the cinema trade would collaborate over the production and distribution of British war films. The trade had put up its unusually united front via the Trade Topical Committee, which had arbitrated the allocation of exclusive rights to major events before the war, and which put itself forward as the organisation to control war filming to government satisfaction. The Committee comprised the major producers of actuality film: Barker Motion Photography, British and Colonial, Eclair, Gaumont Film Company, Jury's and the Topical Film Company, the Kineto company (representing Charles Urban) joining shortly afterwards. Pathé was strikingly absent, and it is likely that, had negotiations broken down with the Committee, the War Office might have turned to a single company, probably Pathé.[41] As events later turned out, the War Office were indeed to turn to just one firm: the Topical Film Company. Between March and October 1915, the Committee agreed terms with the War Office concerning costs, cameramen and the allocation of profits. The Committee was renamed the British Topical Committee for War Films, and on 2 November 1915 Geoffrey Malins of Gaumont and Teddy Tong of Jury's (representing the two dominant firms within the Committee) were sent out to the Western Front.[42]

All film shot was War Office copyright and was to be shown exclusively in Officially produced films. The films were sold at 4½d per foot, and the bulk of the proceeds were to be shared equally between the seven participating members of the Committee, with 1d per foot royalty going to the War Office for military charities. No firm could make individual use of the material, and none of it was available to the newsreels.[43] The action was a boost for the cinema trade, but the first films sent back by Malins and Tong were a disappointment. Mostly depicting scenes of drilling and training, all well behind lines, the six series of short films, around 500ft each and released between January and June 1916, were the product of official interference and organisational naiveté. The cameramen were given little opportunity to film as they had anticipated, nor does it seem that anyone really knew what was being asked of them. How were they to film the war? Not surprisingly, they returned scenes not unlike the newsreel footage they understood.

But government-sanctioned film from another source was having a greater effect. Wellington House, the British propaganda outfit run by Charles Masterman, had shown an imaginatively early interest in the cinema, and commissioned Charles Urban to produce *Britain Prepared*, a feature-length film released in December 1915. This showed the Fleet at sea, army training at Aldershot and munitions manufacture. There were no scenes of conflict, but with its plain, matter-of-fact approach the film gave an impressive sense of the scale of Britain's military undertaking. Sequences were filmed in the Kinemacolor process, a complicated and costly experiment not subsequently repeated during the war. *Britain Prepared* was more prestigious than successful, but the experiment, and the reaction from audiences at home and abroad, largely overcame whatever official suspicions may have remained about the value of the cinema as a propaganda weapon.

Thus there were three organisations with a stake in the official filming of the war: Wellington House, the British Topical Committee for War Films, and shortly afterwards the CWRO. The next stage came when Teddy Tong retired ill, and J. B. McDowell of British and Colonial joined Malins at the Front in June 1916. In August the first film compiled from their efforts, the feature-length *The Battle of the Somme*, was released to amazement, acclaim, horror and considerable box office success. The story of the production and the effect of what is the most famous and familiar film of the war has been told in detail elsewhere.[44] The film is simple in structure – preparations for the attack, briefly the attack itself, and the aftermath. It is not a record of the appalling slaughter, but its directness, the strikingly composed shots, the mud and the tedium, all haunt the spectator. For us today it shows the pity of war; in 1916 it was a magnificent spectacle, the first film of the war genuinely alien and awe-inspiring.

The Battle of the Somme did not greatly influence subsequent war filming in terms of subject-matter, for which it was almost the only statement necessary, but it gave confidence and enthusiasm to those who had taken up the cause of filming the war. Here Max Aitken returns to the picture. The alliance between the cinema trade and the War Office had always been an uneasy one, and in October 1916 the Committee was dissolved as the government took its first direct move into film production with the creation of the War Office Cinematograph Committee (WOCC). This new committee was headed by three representatives of the previously conflicting groups: Sir Reginald Brade, Secretary of the War Office, the film renter William Jury (who had worked with both the British Topical Committee for War Films and Wellington House) and Max Aitken, whose CWRO became virtually synonymous with the WOCC from here on. The War Office now hoped to have greater control over the production of its films, and to keep hold of the profits which it perceived to be going largely to the film trade.[45]

Official film up to this point had been exhibited in a variety of forms, from 400-foot shorts to full-length features. But right from the start the propagandists had been faced with the problem of selling film in the market-place. The label 'official' was not enough; indeed to some it was a disincentive, and too many poor films claiming to depict the fighting had been released for the war itself to be a guaranteed draw. Moreover the war was dragging on and on and the public was naturally dispirited. Thus there was an even greater need for an effective film propaganda campaign, coupled with the increased difficulty of making such a campaign acceptable and profitable – British exhibitors saw no sense in putting country before profit.

The propagandists therefore required a reliable means of exhibiting their product in an unreliable market. Two people were credited with suggesting a newsreel,[46] but it must have seemed an obvious solution. A major film such as *The Battle of the Somme* was marvellous to produce, but the often routine film material available would not stretch to many such features; moreover, the subsequent features were less successful.[47] Another influence was the recently founded French official newsreel, *Annales de la Guerre*, clearly an idea to imitate.[48] The WOCC were chiefly concerned about the public's weariness with the war and war films as presently constituted, and they approached each of the four newsreels then in operation in the hope of organising a fresher, more marketable product. *Pathé's Animated Gazette* and *Gaumont Graphic* were unlikely choices, too independent and complex for easy takeover, and *Eclair Journal* was heading for extinction. Furthermore, the WOCC were acquainted with Topical because they had been using them as agents for Official films coming in from Salonika. Topical's chances were therefore already high, but clever negotiating by William Jeapes ensured success.

Topical had been faltering for some while. What had previously been a sometimes creative mixture of purchased and home front footage had dulled into routine. There were more processions than protests and revitalisation was badly needed. It is likely that the WOCC sounded out William Jeapes in March 1917 on the possibility of the Topical Film Company co-operating with them in the production of an official newsreel. Jeapes, sensing the opportunity, responded both as an individual and as company managing director. Thus, while negotiating terms for the newsreel, he was promoting himself and his brother Harold, a cameraman. The WOCC were looking for someone to cover events in Egypt and Palestine, and Harold Jeapes was suggested for the posting; at the same time, the American Ariel Varges, then filming in Salonika, was suggested for Mesopotamia.[49] Meanwhile William Jeapes was given an honorary lieutenancy and made assistant to J. C. Faunthorpe, operations manager for the WOCC in France.[50] Quite what was the thinking behind this posting is unclear. Jeapes had no experience of the Front (he had applied for and gained exemption from military service in May 1916), and concern was raised over his lack of military know-how. Having announced that he would leave on 2 May for a two or three-week trial at least, the WOCC changed their minds, replacing him with the son of the Canadian banker Sir Herbert Holt, Andrew Holt, who had been pronounced unfit for ordinary military duties following an operation. Holt left on 10 May, but William Jeapes' services were to be retained for the projected Official newsreel. It appears that Jeapes had been quite successful in promoting himself to the WOCC:

> The truth of the matter is that the present style of Film is played out. The public is jaded and we have to tickle its palate with something a little more dramatic in the future, if we are to maintain our sales. From this point of view one is naturally compelled to look at the matter from an entirely commercial standpoint.
>
> The material, of course, will be the same, but the treatment which Jeapes would give it would be entirely different. A masterly piece of music has to be played by a master musician to get the best effects, and Jeapes has a reputation for being one of the finest Producers of Films in the world.[51]

Obviously the WOCC were still undecided about the idea of a newsreel if they were planning to send the managing director of Topical out to France only a week before deciding to employ him at home. This is further illustrated by the loose agreement drawn up by the WOCC and Topical. Plant, staff and all facilities were to be put at the disposal of the WOCC, who would offer the newsreel exclusive access to film shot by the Official cameramen on the various war fronts, but Topical would remain in control of the newsreel operation. The WOCC saw the newsreel as a means to distribute and exhibit the material coming in, and not yet as something on which they wished to impose any vision or directive for a propagandist message. They also wished to have all their operations channelled through the existing operation of a single company. It was agreed that all profits would go to war charities.

> Jeapes has very generously given us complete use and control of his business premises, rent free, on the basis of continuity of operations . . . The Budget service of course is undertaken on account of the declining interest in the long story films.[52]

Jeapes was able to exploit the trust held in him by the WOCC in order to dictate terms, using his new-found influence to secure the staff and facilities he required. For instance, he said that he required John Hutchins, then a driver with the Reserve Horse Transport Depot, to run the darkroom, and on 30 May Hutchins was duly released from military duties.[53] The name *Topical Budget* was to be retained, and Topical's own home-based cameramen would continue to supply material. The number sequence and release pattern were to be unbroken, and staff and directorate remained in place. The only differences were the 'Official' tag, the exclusive access to war footage, and the fact that a newsreel that might possibly have been heading for extinction was now controlled by people in whose interest it would be to ensure its survival.

On Saturday 26 May 1917 issue 300–2 of *Topical Budget* was released; on Monday 28 May the WOCC officially took over the Topical Film Company; and on Wednesday 30 May issue 301–1 of the *War Office Official Topical Budget*[54] came out, featuring a number of short items taken by the Official cameramen in France:

CAMERONS CLEARING ROADS (37ft)
TAKING UP BOMBS (20ft)
18 POUNDER BATTERY (12ft)
SHELLS BURSTING ON GERMAN LINES (9ft)
GERMAN PRISONERS ON RAILHEAD (36ft)
DRESSING STATION FOR WOUNDED PRISONERS (28ft)
BANTAMS AFTER BATTLE (42ft)
MAKING DUGOUTS ON GROUND CAPTURED FROM GERMANS (20ft)

ALLIED LABOUR DEMONSTRATION
'A great demonstration of Allied workers march past the Allied Ambassadors at the French Embassy.' (26ft)[55]

During this period there were seven Official cameramen working on the various fronts whose film was to be used in the newsreel. Harold Jeapes had left for Egypt on 16 May, Ariel Varges was heading for Mesopotamia, J. B. McDowell, Harry Raymond, Oscar Bovill and Bertram Brooks-Carrington were on the Western Front, and F. W. Engholm was with the Navy. There were other Official cameramen whose work generally did not make its way into the newsreel. Two cameramen were probably retained for coverage of the home front, but they were not given Official status. Some of the cameramen in Europe were granted honorary Canadian commissions by Beaverbrook, and William Jeapes retained his honorary lieutenancy.

The WOCC had entered into their agreement with the Topical Film Company with insufficient consideration of the likely results. Presumably they were aware that *Topical Budget* was only a moderately successful newsreel, but it was assumed that the attractions of the Official war films would sell themselves. Beyond this vague expectation of success, little thought had been given to how a propaganda newsreel might be run, and it was only when the sales returns came in that they realised their naiveté and began to reflect on what they wanted from their acquisition. The fact was that the *War Office Official Topical Budget* was hardly being noticed at all. Sales for issue 301–1 were 78. Sales for issue 325–2, six months later, were only 82.[56]

Soon after the WOCC had taken over the newsreel it became clear that the situation was unsatisfactory, and Beaverbrook responded quickly by calling in someone from the Canadian War Records Office to take over the newsreel's Editorial Department. This was Captain W. Holt-White, who was to become a figure of the greatest importance to the newsreel for the next eight years.

Holt-White had been invited to join the CWRO in December 1915, acting as Max Aitken's assistant on the CWRO's formation in January 1916. Exempted from military service through ill health, he was granted an honorary lieutenancy, then a captaincy, and in January 1917 became editor of Beaverbrook's daily paper for the Canadian troops, the *Canadian Daily Record*.[57] Before the war, Holt-White had been a journalist, including a period spent in Germany, had written two low-brow biographies of King Edward VII and Theodore Roosevelt, and a number of six-shilling Wellsian novels, virtually all of which are in the invasion-fantasy mould then common: Britain is threatened by anarchists or Germans or both, usually in airships, and is saved by dashing earls, beautiful heiresses or enterprising journalists. His last, *The Super-Spy*, was written in 1916 and is in part a reflection of his experience of the cinema at the CWRO. A German plot to infiltrate British finance prior to a war involves a beautiful actress acting as a spy while appearing in British films. A German film producer in Britain persuades the War Office to make a fictionalised feature film, to be called *Mobilization*, showing how British troops would prepare for war. Witnessing these scenes and the subsequent film, the Germans would know how best to invade! The fears expressed are part of the same ignorance and suspicion of the cinema that existed among the military establishment in 1914 and so hampered the initial recording of the war on film. But naive as his fiction may have been, Beaverbrook had selected an able journalist, and Holt-White was to be the key creative figure behind the *War Office Official Topical Budget*, and the engineer of its growing success throughout 1918.

Holt-White had joined Topical by July 1917, while remaining in charge of CWRO publicity, and on 8 August he wrote a detailed report for Lord Beaverbrook on the current state of the newsreel. The main problem was a clash between the demands of the WOCC and those of an ordinary newsreel. According to Holt-White, William Jeapes insisted that:

. . . he had run the business for years and had made a success of it, and that it was contrary to the contract to interfere with it. His impression appears to be that the Topical Film Company's business remains intact, and is really not subject to my control.[58]

There were three departments, Editorial, Sales and Publicity. Regarding the first, Holt-White felt that the newsreel was not doing enough to justify its exclusive status, and that it needed more from the war than just France. There was a need for exchanges with companies in Europe, for better footage from the Western Front ('any "Tank" stuff goes down in the Cinema Theatres'), and snippets from the lives of personalities such as Sir Douglas Haig or the Prince of Wales. His report gives a damning picture of the normal state of Topical's news-gathering:

To all intents an Editorial Department does not exist, but I have begun to create one. At present there is no organisation which can prevent such setbacks, as being beaten by Pathé on 'The American Troops in Training', which they are featuring this week. This was the first subject I ordered on Friday last, but of course Pathé had got ahead of me.[59]

The newsreel had to make the fullest use of its Official status and acquire the permits necessary to secure the most desirable pictures. Holt-White had opened negotiations with Buckingham Palace, the Admiralty, the War Office, the Foreign Office, the Ministry of Food and the US Embassy, and had received promises of advance warning of stories from the news editors of the *Daily Express* and *Daily Mirror*. 'I am relying very largely on special stunts to pull the Budget up' he wrote, suggesting such ideas as 'The Prime Minister's busy weekend', 'The new First Lord at work', 'Practical illustrations on "How to do it"', 'Lord Rhondda studying the fundamentals of Food Economy at his week-end farm', and a projected series on 'Cabinet Ministers' Wives in War Time'. Such ideas suggest that Holt-White was either frustrated at the constraints of the newsreel form, or as yet unaware of the differences between a newsreel item and a newspaper article. William Jeapes was quite correct to protest that he knew his job best, and Holt-White said that he had no intention of criticising Jeapes, though he was still dissatisfied. There was no adequate statement of sales, or any idea of sales within a region, so he had drawn up just such a statement: 'We can now see where we are – but this is not very much to boast of.' He advised against too strong a publicity campaign until they could be confident in what they had to show. A statement of accounts also needed to be drawn up; he had no idea of the margin of profit or of their expenses.

Holt-White's report is severe, and perhaps not wholly just. The issues of the newsreel between May and August 1917 indicate the competent output of an average newsreel, and the crisis that existed resulted from the WOCC requiring something more than the average. After experimenting a little with the format for the first few issues, showing several short interconnected items on aspects of military life in France alongside standard items, by June the newsreel had settled back into a surprisingly familiar routine, usually with just one war-front item per issue and this frequently just troop inspections. It is hardly the coverage to be expected of a newsreel with, in effect, exclusive access to the war. The organisation for Official filming that had existed up to that point had been geared to the more leisurely requirements of longer films, which would be put together once sufficient material was available. A newsreel required a continual supply of film and needed the cameramen to adjust their work pattern accordingly. Issue 308–2 (21 July 1917) included a 197-feet special item on King George V's visit to the Western Front, and by August the newsreel was beginning to take on the appearance of having authoritative coverage. Issue 310–1 (1 August 1917) features two items on German prisoners employed in reconstruction work in France; French armoured vehicles riding through a bomb-damaged town; and a striking picture of French troops moving through a familiar war landscape, with bomb craters, debris, a few branchless trees, and mud, as shells are seen exploding in the distance. Returning to Britain, the final item shows members of a crowd breaking into a pacifist meeting in a church. Issue 312–2 (18 August 1917) is given over entirely to the arrival in London of the first contingent of the American army. Holt-White was pleased with the whole operation on this occasion:

> We had four Operators on the American march this morning and I think we have some very good exclusive pictures. Each operator had a special permit signed by Sir Reginald Brade, which worked wonders.[60]

Film of such an event could hardly have failed to be impressive, but Topical's account includes a close shot of Admiral Sims and the American Ambassador Walter Page, looking out from a balcony at the American Embassy, taken from the adjacent balcony, and further close shots from within the forecourt of Buckingham Palace of the King, Queen and Prime Minister Lloyd George watching the march past. It was necessary not only to have exclusive access, but to be seen to have exclusive access.

From September to November the newsreel continued to build on this strengthening position, although there was still no improvement on sales. The first Admiralty Official films appeared in October, and the first films taken by Ariel Varges and Harold Jeapes in Mesopotamia and Egypt in November. There was an equal balance between entertaining home footage and informative snippets from the various war fronts.

Occasionally an item such as PUSHING ON IN FLANDERS[61] shows scenes from the Western Front that we now equate with the war: a flat, devastated landscape, with some crosses in the foreground and explosions in the distance. But they had not lost a newsreel's knack for the ludicrous:

HANDICAPPED WAR HEROES
'Australian legless soldiers participate in sports. Much amusement is caused by the hairdressing contest.'[62]

A few items are brilliantly done. THE PIGEON AS POSTMAN,[63] filmed in England, illustrates how messages are sent by homing pigeon. A soldier is seen putting a pigeon into a basket. Two motorcyclists with baskets drive away down a country road. A soldier comes up with a basket to two officers in a trench. There is a close-up of one of the officers writing a note. Another close-up shows the soldier attaching the note to the pigeon's foot. He releases the pigeon. The pigeon is seen landing on the roof of a large coop. A soldier hands the message to a telegraphist, who taps it out. The final shot shows the message, printed out on an official form, which reads: 'Notice – Please do not shoot homing pigeons. They are performing valuable national work.' A clever finish to an excellently dramatised and constructed newsreel item.

It was acknowledged that the newsreel was improving steadily, but it had so far failed to capitalise on the Official tag, and sales had remained static. The newsreel was attracting too little attention, and so fresh press notices were issued in September which made the WOCC's acquisition of the newsreel sound as if it were a new event.[64] Holt-White was still bemoaning the situation in a memo to Beaverbrook in October:

I should greatly appreciate an early opportunity of talking to you about the Budget, especially in regard to sales. The position is absolutely hopeless, and under the present system I do not think we can look for any extra copies to be sold at all.[65]

Beaverbrook decided to drop the gentlemen's agreement between the WOCC and Topical, and took steps to purchase the company outright. The newsreel contents were now more than satisfactory, but this made its fuller exploitation only the more imperative. The purchase was completed by November.[66] All of Topical's directors, including Jeapes and Wrench, resigned and the new directors appointed were Lord Beaverbrook, William Jury, Major Andrew Holt and Lieutenant R. D. Scott, the latter two both from the CWRO. Jeapes was reported to be antagonistic towards the whole affair, however he retained some token control, as the signatory authority for the company was agreed as being any one director and Jeapes jointly. He was also allowed to keep his room.

Some problems persisted. In October a sales manager had been brought in, W. Orton Tewson, a former journalist who had been handling WOCC films in the USA and Canada, but a personality clash between him and William Jeapes only made matters more difficult. Scott reported in December:

> I do not think Jeaps [sic] and Tewson will ever pull along together, because each hides from the other what he is doing. . . . It is quite clear that the business cannot be run on the present unfriendly basis. I saw Mr Jury this afternoon and he says that he is quite willing to do what he can to make matters smooth, but I doubt his success.[67]

They even hid the mail from one another. But shortly into the new year Jeapes found himself officially under Holt-White's direction in the newly devised company structure. Operations were divided into three new sections, under the control of Holt-White as Head of the Editorial Department. William Jeapes was now to run the technical side, overseeing the printing of the newsreel; Harry Rowson was put in charge of sales and distribution; and Patrick McCabe, recently fired by *Pathé Gazette*, possibly to some extent as a response to the improving status of the *War Office Official Topical Budget*, was brought in as news editor, 'watching events' and directing the cameramen.

This structure was in place and operating efficiently by April 1918, by which time the newsreel had also had its name changed. In December 1917 the newsreel became *War Office Official Topical Budget And Pictorial News*.[68] In November the idea had been mooted that the name be changed to 'War Office Pictorial News (Official)',[69] and the various titles of the newsreel during its Official period bear witness to the battle between Jeapes and the propagandists. This history has referred to the newsreel as *War Office Official Topical Budget* for simplicity's sake, and because this name remained constant throughout. On all paperwork, and in most advertisements, the name was simplified to *War Office Topical Budget*. But from issue 301-1 to 317-1 (30 May 1917 to 19 September 1917) the opening title of the newsreel proclaimed it to be *Topical Budget. Official War Office News-Film*, with the words 'War Office Official Topical Budget' appearing on each intertitle next to the issue number, and on the end title around a picture of Britannia. This end title was to remain unchanged throughout the Official period. Issue 317-2 (22 September 1917) saw the opening title change to *War Office Official Topical Budget*, issue 318-1 saw it revert to the former style, then for issue 318-2 *War Office Official Topical Budget* became the accepted name at the beginning and end of the newsreel. But the WOCC had decided to adopt a simpler name, preferring to drop the word 'war', and to use instead 'pictorial', it being noted that the most popular newsreel in the United States was called the 'News Pictorial' (meaning *Hearst-Selig News Pictorial*). There was a growing realisation that for the newsreel to work, they had to let it run as (and appear to be) a normal newsreel; they had to blend their exclusive war footage with standard newsreel fare, balancing commerce with propaganda. It had been part of the WOCC's agreement with the Topical Film Company that the name *Topical Budget* be used throughout,[70] and it was some while before they were at least able to push the name to the back of the newsreel. Issue 319–2 (6 October 1917) peculiarly reverted back to *Topical Budget. Official War Office News-Film*, but it then remained as *War Office Official Topical Budget* until December. The clumsy *War Office Offical Topical Budget And Pictorial News* then appears to have been retained until issue 339–2 (23 February 1918), at which time the newsreel finally became *Pictorial News (Official)*, the word 'official' appearing discreetly beneath the first two words:

> I hear that the *War Office Official Topical Budget and Pictorial News* will in future be known as the *Pictorial News (Official)*. The title is an appropriate one, and in its shortened form should add to the popularity and kudos the *Topical Budget* has attained. That it supplies a long-felt want and is appreciated by picture-goers is proved by the fact that the number of copies now issued twice weekly is twice as great as formerly.[71]

From here onwards the newsreel was known as *Pictorial News (Official)* at its beginning, and as a sop to Jeapes, who had now lost all control over his newsreel, as *War Office Official Topical Budget* at its end.

By February 1918 sales had indeed doubled and under Holt-White's editorship the newsreel was becoming an imaginatively packaged product, authoritative and watchable. Beaverbrook admitted the need for the newsreel to appear, in name and form, as a recognisably commercial prospect:

> It is sometimes found desirable to produce and distribute films which have no apparent propaganda value. This applies more particularly to The Pictorial News, which as a bi-weekly news service must necessarily include many pictures having no direct bearing on propaganda aims. As a whole, however, The Pictorial News is an instrument of undoubted propaganda value.[72]

Sales of the newsreel began to increase. From the lame 81 reported at the start of November 1917, 85 were reported by the end of the month, 100 the next month, 115 at the start of January 1918, 124 by the end of that month, and 150 in March.[73] With the increase in cinema attendances to nearly twenty million a week, the system of hiring 'runs' which ensured that a single copy would be shown in a number of cinemas, and the growing number of cinemas accepting a newsreel (virtually all of them by this time), the audience for the newsreel by mid-1918 was around three million.[74] The distribution of Official films in Britain was undertaken by Jury's Imperial Pictures, but the newsreel was both sold direct to some exhibitors and made available for hire via a number of renting firms.

Although they were now satisfied that they had a popular product that was worth promoting, the WOCC had to fight to persuade the film trade of their good intentions. The trade had seen its early initiative become independent and powerful, capable of producing exclusive films that the public wanted to see. To counter fears of 'government trading', the WOCC also launched a propaganda campaign aimed at exhibitors. It was argued that the WOCC and its newsreel were self-supporting, that it was the peculiar nature of film propaganda that it had to be run on business lines, and that experience had shown that a wider circulation could only be gained by stressing the merits of the films rather than the propaganda message. Although it could not be denied that competition was being offered to the other newsreels, it was emphasised that all profits went to war charities. The film trade still hovered between commerce and patriotism. A lunch was held for members of the cinema trade in December 1917, at which exhibitors were invited to include the *War Office Official Topical Budget* in their programmes and to support the government in its propaganda aims, and this was a marked success, indicative of the good relations that now started to exist between the WOCC and the trade. Advertising became more confident. In January 1918 Beaverbrook tried to get Augustus John, then an Official war artist to the Canadian Corps, to design a poster for the newsreel. John expressed enthusiasm for the project, but for reasons unexplained, the large 'cartoon' he produced, featuring a soldier on the march looking upwards beyond three branchless trees, with a blank section left for the name of the newsreel, was never used. Perhaps the downbeat image, with its possible suggestion of the crucifixion, was considered inappropriate – or perhaps it was rejected simply because it had too little to do with film. Then again, maybe it was just an idea that was abandoned.[75]

The newsreel started to sell well because exhibitors were happy to show it, and they were happy to do so because it was popular. By the time the newsreel changed its name to *Pictorial News (Official)* in February 1918, it had achieved a form that pleased exhibitors, propagandists and audiences alike. Its success as entertainment is clear from the evidence of the surviving issues; its success as propaganda is more questionable, though Beaverbrook clearly believed that it helped buoy up the nation during the difficult last year of the war. Primarily the newsreel was a vehicle for the film taken by the Official cameramen, who were in place long before an Official newsreel was even contemplated. The intention behind such filming was not just to provide positive images of the war, but also simply to record and exhibit the war on film. This duty was felt by all who were involved, and indeed the images, it was believed, would speak for themselves. It was not a problem of how to show the war, but rather of showing what they had to the best advantage. Once the WOCC had learned the newsreel business (and despite their problems between May and November 1917, the experience they gained at that time laid the foundations for the subsequent success), it was only doing their job to produce an attractive newsreel with the material available. Their confidence was their best weapon, and the newsreel reinforced their faith in the validity of their work. Audience faith in the British war effort was similarly relied upon.

The first issue under the name *Pictorial News (Official)* coincided with the release of the most famous film in the newsreel's history, and one of the most celebrated of the war. On 9 December 1917 General Allenby and the Egyptian Expeditionary Force captured Jerusalem from the Turks. It was a military triumph and a great boost to the Allied war effort, with the date's proximity to Christmas further increasing the significance of the action. On 11 December Allenby and his men made a symbolic entry on foot into Jerusalem. The newsreel could, of course, only show stock footage of Allenby for the issue following these events (329–1, 12 December 1918), but two cameramen were in place to cover the official entry. Harold Jeapes was the Official cameraman covering Egypt and Palestine, and on this occasion he was accompanied by the Australian Official cameraman, Frank Hurley. GENERAL ALLENBY'S ENTRY INTO JERUSALEM was released on 23 February 1918:

GENERAL ALLENBY'S ENTRY INTO JERUSALEM
'Before the ceremony. The Commander-in-chief conversing with commanders of Allied detachments and attaches.' General Allenby talking to various officers. 'General Sir Edmund Allenby, Commander-in-chief E. E. F., entering the Holy City, accompanied by Allied Commanders and military attaches.' General Allenby marches at the head of a long column of officers and men. 'Reading Sir Edmund Allenby's proclamation.' High angle view looking down at crowds in square and man reading proclamation from raised platform, with Allenby and other officers standing by. 'Reception of religious and civic dignitaries.' Various people being presented to Allenby. 'After leaving the Holy City the Commander-in-chief mounted his horse outside Jaffa Gate and rode away through the streets of the suburbs.' Allenby and party riding away through the Jaffa Gate. 'In the streets after the ceremony.' Panning shot showing crowds in the streets.[76]

The fame of GENERAL ALLENBY'S ENTRY INTO JERUSALEM derived from the significance of the event. The film itself now seems visually uninteresting, an adequate report of the main events – the entry itself and the reading of the proclamation – but suggesting little in itself of what was, for one participant, 'the supreme moment of the war'. That participant was T. E. Lawrence ('Lawrence of Arabia'), who was lent a uniform for the occasion, and whose fortuitous appearance among those officers walking behind Allenby has made the film of still greater value.[77] It was subsequently released as an individual film and shown with great success the world over in a variety of forms and lengths and under a variety of titles. Its popularity stemmed from its simplicity and its symbolism. Longer in its separate release version than a newsreel, yet much shorter than some of the more wearisome films of the war, the entrance on foot and the proclamation promising religious freedom could be translated favourably worldwide. Impressive to the contemporary audience, it successfully conveyed to them the sense of triumph occasioned by the event.

The following issue, 340–1 (release date 27 February 1918), was the first to refer to the new Ministry of Information. The opening titles now read:

PICTORIAL NEWS (Official)
Under the direction of the Ministry of Information. All profits are devoted to purposes connected with the War.

The Ministry had been created in February 1918, with Lord Beaverbrook at its head, out of the ashes of the Department of Information,

Harold Jeapes (top right) in Jerusalem, 11 December 1917, filming the reading of Allenby's proclamation.

49

which had also had its stake in Official film production and distribution. With the creation of the MOI, all the various conflicting strands of the British propaganda effort, and with them the film campaign, were brought under one roof and one person's control. The struggle to make the newsreel work was only part of a larger struggle to control all aspects of the British propaganda campaign, and the newsreel's success came hand in hand with the resolution of that struggle.

In June 1918 the MOI took over the WOCC's role, becoming owners and controllers of the Topical Film Company, although the shares in the company remained with the WOCC members. Since Beaverbrook controlled both, little upset was caused by the change-over. Beaverbrook and Jury resigned as directors of Topical, their places being taken by T. M. Till and G. W. Dawkins. The arrangement, just as it had been with the WOCC, was to run for the duration of the war and three months thereafter. The MOI were to pay all costs and to receive all income.[78] Beaverbrook also resigned from the WOCC, as did William Jury on his appointment as Director of Cinematography at the Ministry, and A. E. Cutforth and Colonel C. W. Sofer Whitburn took their places. Sir Reginald Brade resigned from the WOCC in July 1918 and was replaced by Sir Edward Goulding MP. Beaverbrook still personally held the majority of the shares in the Topical Film Company. The profit made by the *War Office Official Topical Budget* between May 1917 and June 1918 was £6,280,[79] all of which went to war charities.

Such was the view from the home front. The other side of the newsreel was represented by the cameramen. On the Western Front, where the movements of the cameramen were co-ordinated by J. C. Faunthorpe, there were a number filming material for the newsreel, but no more than five at any one time, and then only towards the end of the war. In May 1917, when the newsreel was first taken over by the WOCC, there were four, although given the time delay (on account of the elaborate censorship system), it is likely that some of Geoffrey Malins' last work for the WOCC made it into the newsreel.[80] The main four were J. B. McDowell, Harry Raymond, Bertram Brooks-Carrington and Oscar Bovill of the CWRO. Of these, Brooks-Carrington was shortly to retire, probably on account of nervous strain. It was one of the peculiarities of the agreements allowing Official filming of the war that no one could become a cameraman if he was A1 medically.[81] A forlorn note in July 1917 states the need for top quality operators to match those of the Americans, but complains that the man the MOI wanted (probably Walter Evan Davies), was A1 and therefore refused to them. As the note observes, 'B grade men break under the strain.'[82] The first Official cameraman with Malins, Teddy Tong, had retired sick, and the long periods of duty put a great strain on all the cameramen, which naturally affected their work.

The person with the longest such period of duty was J. B. McDo-

J. B. McDowell (right) carrying his Moy Bastie camera, his batman carrying the tripod, Western Front 1917–18. 'The camera weighs about 40 lbs to begin with, but after carrying it along roads and over broken country . . . it seems to weigh about four hundredweight . . .' (McDowell in *Daily News*, 4 October 1916, p. 5).

well, who remarkably worked virtually without a break from June 1916 until the end of the war. In August 1917 he briefly returned to England to help with the editing of material he had shot, and was on leave in London in late January 1918, returning to France in March. What is still more remarkable is the high quality of work which he continued to produce throughout this period. Faunthorpe described McDowell's work as unbeatable, and the French admitted that they had no one as good.[83] Admired equally by his fellow cameramen and his superiors, McDowell was also given the direction of all Official cameramen on the Western Front from April 1918, overseeing the production, developing and printing of all film taken, while continuing as a cameraman himself.[84] Reliable and trustworthy at a time when other Official cameramen were causing trouble, his films for the newsreel include some convincing scenes of military action, the funeral of Baron von Richthofen and the recording of a direct hit by a shell on a passing cavalry line.[85]

Among those causing trouble was Harry Raymond, who was transferred from the Western Front to Italy in November 1917. The only Official cameraman to be based in Italy, he remained there until February, returning once more in April, and spent much of his time complaining about the bad weather, the lack of transport, and the

51

difficulty of finding any good subjects. Major Andrew Holt (Faunthorpe's assistant) wrote a number of patient, helpless letters noting that his stuff was fine but that they really needed more film of 'our men'. Oscar Bovill, the CWRO cameraman on the Western Front whose work appeared in the newsreel, caused greater problems. Although praised for his earlier work with the CWRO, he began to be troublesome after returning to the Western Front in March 1917. He made demands for an assistant (beyond the batman attached to each cameraman), ran up too many travel expenses and was suspected of being too enamoured of French night-life.[86] By the time the *War Office Official Topical Budget* was launched, they were considering getting rid of him. His films at Vimy were criticised in particular, since his descriptions did not match what he had shot (titles describing military action were dependent in the first instance on the notes supplied by the cameraman). There may also have been a lack of dedication towards the Canadian cause which especially irritated his superiors at the CWRO. He offered his resignation in June 1917, but was taken on again in August 1917 as one of the home front cameramen. Despite praise for his work on the American march through London, he was subsequently criticised by Jeapes for a lack of care and judgment in his work and for considerable waste of negative. He resigned once again in November 1917 and became an observer with the Royal Air Force.

Raymond's replacement on the Western Front in December 1918

Frank Bassill filming a Chinese labour battalion celebrating the Chinese new year on the Western Front, for issue number 342–2 (*The Chinaman's New Year*, 16 March 1918).

was Frank Bassill, but he too gave cause for concern. Apart from worries about his health, it was felt that he filmed too far behind the lines, and both chose and photographed his subjects poorly. He remained on the Western Front until the end of the war, but clearly the London staff felt frustrated by some shoddy work by men out of their reach. For both Bovill and Bassill it was stated that they were capable of excellent work, but that they required supervision. In part it must have been fatigue, since the men who came fresh to filming the war in 1918, Walter Buckstone and particularly Fred Wilson, filmed some noticeably bright and inventive items.

Such reports of difficulties with cameramen have to be set against the evidence of the films themselves. All of the Official cameramen were experienced and competent workers, well able to spot a newsfilm story and to encapsulate it within a minute of film. What they probably most lacked was a true news editor, Faunthorpe and Holt being able administrators but ignorant of the cinema world and the demands of newsfilm. Perhaps it would have been a good idea to have had William Jeapes working in France after all (it is unclear how far McDowell's duties extended after April 1918). Whatever the true state of things, many of the individual items for this period are very fine indeed. HAIG'S MEN HIT OUT,[87] which is divided into two sections, one depicting a 'battle scarred-village whence the Huns were driven in fierce hand-to-hand fight' and the other showing French gun batteries in action, reveals particular skill on the part of the cameraman in the first section. The sequence shows British troops in the ruins of a shelled village, with various shots of the destruction and one of a dead horse in the street. But each shot is a panning shot from right to left across a street, leading to a point of interest, the overall effect of which is a panning movement from right to left across the whole village, taking in individual impressions. In this broad movement encompassing smaller actions, part of the experience of war is translated into the newsreel moment.

It was now expected of the cameramen that they record victories rather than unsatisfactory battle scenes, which also meant that they were seldom in any danger. It had been difficult to film the fighting, not only on account of the hazards and obstructive Army officialdom, but also because of the materials to hand. The cameras were clumsy; the cameramen were generally restricted to a single 50mm lens; the film stock was slow; and such action as there was took place in the distance, or was over before they could get near it. A film record, and of course it was a silent film record, could not depict the war as experienced or imagined. Recording victories was not only serving the needs of the propaganda newsreel, it was also easier to plan and execute, made greater sense as filmed news, and kept the public informed and heartened at the same time. The Battle of Amiens was reported in this fashion:

'Recent Battle-scenes and Incidents in France. Unable to resist Allied pressure the Huns burn their bullets.' Smoke on distant hillside. 'Heavy British Guns moved up to forward positions.' Artillery guns firing. 'London regiments going into action.' Troops marching. 'British cavalry got its chance with disastrous effect on the Huns.' Cavalry ride past in formation down road. 'Our gallant Italian Allies fought splendidly at the guns.' Italian troops loading shells into a large gun. 'The enemy paid heavy toll, they were meeting our men in open warfare.' Corpses lying on wooded area. 'Our losses were comparatively small. British, French and Italian wounded quite pleased with themselves.' Groups of wounded smiling for the camera. 'Germans who were glad to be captured.' German prisoners marching past. Some smile at the camera. 'British Regiments which distinguished themselves "The Devons".' Troops marching. '"The Black Watch", a famous Scottish regiment.' More troops marching.[88]

It was not possible for film of the current battle to have been filmed, processed, sent to Britain for viewing and censoring, returned to France for further inspection, returned and released while still 'news'. The material above, mostly taken by McDowell, is of earlier events and battles, yet it is only half-lies. The use of the past tense partly distances the description from the action. Even if it were a true record, it would scarcely count as a full or informative one, but that is not the point. The item offers a series of optimistic, upbeat highlights, fashioned for a home audience who had read about the battle and could sense the hope of victory. In following the army's footsteps, the cameramen and the newsreel were identifying themselves with their intended audience.

The Official naval cameraman was F. W. Engholm, who had done some commendable work for Topical in Belgium in 1914 at the start of the war. All the naval footage in the newsreel and in all the other Official films was taken by Engholm, but he was restricted by Navy censorship to general shots of the fleet at sea, usually off Scapa Flow. He was directed to avoid close shots of technical features and instead to give a broad impression of naval power. This he did by taking mostly slow panning shots of a sea filled with warships, and doing so with monotonous regularity. The naval items are among the least interesting in the newsreel.

The two cameramen about whom the least was reported, implying that they got on with their job satisfactorily, were Ariel Varges and Harold Jeapes. Varges was an American, and had been filming with the Hearst news service in Salonika when he was taken on as a WOCC cameraman in March 1918, being then moved on by them to cover Mesopotamia. His output now seems dull, though with the compensatory appeal of the exotic, and it is unclear whether the paucity of items

Harold Jeapes (seated by his Debrie camera) with batman and Egyptian servants in Egypt 1917–18.

taken by him in the newsreel was due to their routine nature or to the British audience's limited interest in the area. Harold Jeapes was fortunate in being there to accompany General Allenby's successes (see above), but he was an able cameraman who generally returned good stories, his taste for carefully composed shots of passing transport or troop lines crossing desert landscapes giving his work some individual style. Filming in the desert was itself problematic, the negative stock soon becoming unusable in the heat, and the strong light permitting images of depth and clarity but also resulting in the cameraman's shadow occasionally appearing at the foot of the frame.

Pictorial News (Official) was intended to be not just a war newsreel but also a chronicler of home front life to rival *Pathé Gazette* or *Gaumont Graphic*, and much of the newsreel's success derived from a careful balance of home and war footage, both equally entertaining. A number of cameramen, none of whom were commissioned but who all

wore uniform, were employed in Britain, and some regional cameramen took the occasional item. The usual number at any one time was
two. Apart from Bovill, the men most used were Walter Evan Davies,
George Woods-Taylor and John Hutchins. Davies and Hutchins were
fine, reliable workers, but Woods-Taylor's films show some signs of
clumsiness. There were items on recruiting, on war bonds, on protest
marches, on wounded troops relaxing at home, as well as the expected
round of standard newsreel fare: babies, animals, humorous stories. But
the dominant home subject was the royal family, to whom the newsreels
had been granted far greater access in the latter half of the war. King
George V and Queen Mary were featured almost obsessively, and
investitures in the Buckingham Palace forecourt became a regular
newsreel stand-by. It should be noted that Pathé and Gaumont,
through their international contacts and exchanges with foreign companies, were able to provide a quite reasonable coverage of the war,
even if they could not match Topical's access to Official film, but
inevitably they concentrated largely on home stories. To show that it
was now in full competition with the other newsreels for the home
market, the release pattern of *Pictorial News (Official)* was changed in
May 1918 from Wednesdays and Saturdays to the now standard Mondays and Thursdays.

The Topical Film Company was also used to produce other Official
films besides the newsreel. There was a series of films depicting individual regiments, with such titles as *The King's Own Light Infantry* and
The East Kent Regiment (The Buffs), and a short series of 'magazine'
films on the activities of the troops of the colonial and allied forces, for
example *An Egyptian Labour Contingent* and *With The Portuguese Expeditionary Force*.[89] A number of medium-length films were released
from the Admiralty Official film taken by F. W. Engholm, and the MOI
sponsored a series of short fiction films, or 'film tags', with small points
of advice for home audiences.[90] These latter were not produced by the
Topical Film Company, but did appear at the end of some issues of
the *War Office Official Topical Budget*, as well as *Gaumont Graphic* and
Pathé Gazette.

It would not be surprising if the War Office propagandists had felt a
little disappointed at the end of hostilities, simply because after so long
a period battling to produce adequate film records of the war, they had
just begun to operate with full efficiency. There were plans for expansion and new ideas for packaging and presenting films. This confidence
is shown in the newsreel itself, which towards the end of 1918 began
to break out of the rigid newsreel form which the WOCC had inherited.
The change is in the use of intertitles; previously content to offer a
simple description and only light comment, the following shows them
wanting to speak out:

THE DELIVERANCE OF LILLE BY HAIG'S MEN
'After four years of Hun rule, brutality and plunder, the joy and
gratitude of the brave inhabitants knew no bounds when they saw
their British liberators of the 5th. Army, Liverpool Irish and Lancashire troops' . . . 'A British Officer is assailed with grateful attention
and cries of "Vivent Les Anglais".'

'VIVE LA FRANCE!'
'The arrival of a French soldier occasioned a renewed outbreak of
joy' . . . 'These women of Lille had long wept, but the gladness their
rescuers brought them, restored the joy of living to their faces.'

A LESSON IN FORTITUDE
'No persecution or outrage could break the indomitable spirit of the
citizens. They knew Hun rule would end, and must have known that
British arms would destroy it, for our colours, long hidden, were
displayed in all hands' . . . 'La Marseillaise is played on the Grand
Place by a British band amid delirious enthusiasm.'[91]

The language of the Official newsreel was always more outspoken and
propagandist in tone than was generally the case with other WOCC/MOI
films, simply because this was the kind of language expected of a
newsreel. But the advance here is in the way titles cut into the item,
offering a genuine commentary to guide audience reactions. It is a step
forward in newsreel technique, springing from a desire to speak out
more and from having the confidence to do so. A review of this issue
of the newsreel indicates the enthusiasm with which the film is likely to
have been received. The description includes an earlier scene in Ostend:

Down the centre comes a laughing, waving, and gesticulating crowd,
jostling each other under the flags of all the Allies, which trail from
every window. Then a motor-lorry, packed with laughing children,
and on high a British Tommy, grinning from ear to ear – the very
symbol of victory. Everyone is smiling – smiling – smiling sometimes, it is true, through the sadness of years of suffering, but smiling
all the same. It is a picture which none could watch unmoved. Then
to Lille, with the Liverpool Irish and the Lancashires marching in,
laden with posies and all sorts of gifts, petits gamins, marching
proudly in step. More flags, more delighted smiles – joy on every
hand at the advent of the liberators. The look on the face of the
officer who rides, erect, at the head of the column is a study. Each
man's face (which master-photography has reproduced with amaz-
ing clarity) tells its tale of suffering, both seen and experienced, and
of pride in the glad honour of being among the liberators. The
'place' is thronged with a seething, swaying mass of townsfolk –
arms, hats, handkerchiefs, flags, all fluttering on high. The men-folk

are absent, but the women and children are there en masse to give the victors a greeting. The whole is a silent tribute to the glory, the worth, and, above all, the power of the kinematograph for the purposes of propaganda. The enemy may scatter broadcast his lying messages of reassurance and denial, but the kine-camera is there on the spot all the time – proof positive of things as they are.[92]

Viewed now the film certainly captures the exhilaration of the moment, the cameraman in among the excited crowd rather than viewing it from above, so that one feels a part of the celebration rather than just a witness. There is much flag-waving and smiling, and a touching moment when a child marches hand in hand with one of the British soldiers. But it is also noticeable that many of the town's inhabitants (almost all women and children, as the reviewer observes) are quite as fascinated by the camera as by the soldiers, and many turn their backs on the action described in the intertitles to make sure that they appear on the screen.

Despite hopes that the newsreel would act as effective propaganda overseas, and some attempts to distribute it in a large number of countries, the propagandists always saw their main target as the home audience. This was only sensible, since they had to offer audiences home news to be commercially acceptable, and lacked the organisation

The inhabitants of Lille as much engrossed by the camera as by their British liberators. From *The Deliverance of Lille by Haig's Men.*

necessary to adjust the newsreel to the needs of individual national markets. Moreover, there was not the potential revenue to make any such project worthwhile. The newsreel was distributed all over the world, but in very small quantities. From September 1918 a separate foreign edition was produced,[93] compiled by Foreign Editor Jasper Kemmis, but it was generally just a re-ordering of stories from one or two of the main editions, with small changes in the intertitles to explain aspects that might be unclear to overseas audiences, sometimes subtly altering the emphasis. Usually tone and import were identical for main and foreign editions. These are the titles for the foreign edition of the issue quoted above:

THE BRITISH ARMY'S TRIUMPHAL ENTRY INTO LILLE
'Enthusiastic inhabitants welcome their gallant saviours with over-flowing expressions of joy and gratitude' . . . 'The brave women of Lille, undaunted after four years of servitude, show by their faces the gladness their rescuers have brought them' . . . 'A British officer, surrounded by happy citizens, is assailed with loud cries of "Vivent les Anglais"' . . . 'The arrival of a French soldier causes renewed cries of "Vive La France".'

COURAGE THAT NEVER FAILED
'The citizens of Lille, who held out to the end, released at last. Confident in the might of Britain they display the British National Colours, long concealed, to celebrate the day of their delivery' . . . 'La Marseillaise is played on the Grande Place by a British military band amid delirious enthusiasm.'[94]

The one foreign edition would then be sent to the various countries with the titles translated into their respective languages. Whereas the titles of the main edition where white on black, foreign edition titles were reversed to black on white. There is some evidence that special editions were produced for Australian or Canadian audiences, but this may just mean the occasional single items of Australian or Canadian interest which were routinely included in the newsreel. Earlier attempts to distribute the newsreel abroad had met with little success. In 1917 a few prints were exhibited in the various British dominions, the French government handled it in France, and the Department of Information purchased copies (at 2d per foot) for distribution in neutral countries.[95] The DOI, and then the MOI, showed greater enthusiasm for handling the newsreel overseas once Holt-White's improvements had taken their effect. In April 1918 copies of the *Pictorial News (Official)* were being shown in Brazil, Canada, China, Denmark, France, Holland, Japan, Mexico, Norway, Portugal, Spain, Sweden and the United States.[96] But no more than four copies a week of any one issue were sent to any country, which meant only a token distribution was possible. Nevertheless, over the next few months copies were also sent to Argentina, Belgium, Bolivia, Chile, Cuba, the Dutch East Indies (titles in Dutch and Malay), Egypt, Iceland, India, Italy, Panama, Peru, the Philippines, Santo Domingo, and Switzerland.[97]

Sending a copy to a country was no guarantee of its sympathetic reception, or even of it being screened at all. A number of representatives wrote back to report that the contents were unsuitable for their audiences. Haiti were grateful for the films, but had no cinemas or cinematographic equipment by which to show them. Some reports were favourable however. GENERAL ALLENBY'S ENTRY INTO JERUSALEM, in its extended version, seems to have been popular wherever it was shown. One copy with titles in classical Hebrew was screened for the Jewish community at Salonika with great success.[98] A report on the work of the British War Information Committee in China stated that between September 1917 and February 1919 British Official films had been shown in 51 locations, on 593 occasions, to an audience of at least 373,537. Among the films at these shows had been the *Pictorial News (Official)* (issues had been sent from November 1917 to August 1918). Reactions were reported to be mixed, but the Allenby film, with appropriate explanations, had been received enthusiastically, audiences appreciating the significance of the entry on foot and the reading of the proclamation.[99]

In America copies were distributed in weekly editions by the Cinematograph department of the DOI, possibly by June 1917, and certainly by August. The picture is confused as the WOCC's own sales representative, W. Orton Tewson, was handling the newsreel at the same time in America and Canada. From March 1918 it was sent weekly to Official Government Pictures Inc, whose representative, Charles Urban, had been largely responsible for the effective distribution of British Official films in America. It was stipulated that 60 per cent of the resultant newsreel's content had to be British.[100] Material from the *War Office Official Topical Budget* may have already gone into the American war newsreel, *Official War Review*, which Urban also edited. In America the composite British newsreel was known as the *British War Office Official News Film*, and appears to have continued, curiously, not only after the war, but after the *Pictorial News* had lost its Official status. The last material sent to America came from issue 393–2 (10 March 1919), by which time the newsreel had become *British Government Official News* and had reached 77 in its weekly numbered sequence.[101] Probably there were no more than four copies of any one edition available for distribution in America, and as with most of the foreign exhibition that the newsreel material received, it was usually shown with other British Official films, reaching only a small audience.

Distribution abroad was valued more as publicity than for its likely effect. It was a newsreel primarily aimed at British audiences, and certainly little attempt was made to include items likely to appeal to particular Empire or Neutral audiences, as had been the declared intention. There was, however, the notable exception of Beaverbrook's native Canada. Still answering to the Canadian authorities, Beaverbrook reported on his progress:

> The Topical Budget is the film supplied twice a week to all cinematograph theatres by the War Office Committee. It is exhibited for eight minutes before the ordinary pictures are thrown on the screen, and has a world-wide circulation throughout the British Empire and allied and neutral countries. The War Records Office makes sure that a section of this film is devoted to the exploits of the Canadian Corps . . .
>
> In the work of publicity the cinematograph stands alone. It creates its own audience without effort, because men are naturally drawn to what they wish to see. And it does so because it contains that subtle admixture of art, reality, and swift and dramatic movement, which rivet the eyes and mind past all withdrawing. Many things can be presented through its medium which cannot be translated in pictures or placed upon the stage, and its appeal is not to the elect alone but to the emotions common to humanity.[102]

Probably no one else ever appreciated *Topical Budget,* or detected that subtle admixture of art and reality, that common appeal, to quite such a degree. Not only are there a fair number of items of Canadian interest in the newsreel, but also items featuring Lord Beaverbrook himself, and four on the Official war photographs. Perhaps surprisingly, no item was ever devoted to the work of the Official cameramen themselves.

The newsreel remained *Pictorial News (Official)* until three months after the war, as stated in the agreements signed by both the WOCC and the Ministry of Information. However the MOI, which closed at the end of December 1918, cancelled its agreement with the Topical Film Company on 29 November. The company took over the operation once more, although they were still owned by the WOCC and had no office accommodation of their own, being lent the nearby 80–82 Wardour Street by the WOCC.[103] When the shares in the Topical Film Company (the bulk of which were held by Beaverbrook) were offered for sale in February 1919, the company was bought by the newspaper proprietor Edward Hulton. The name became simply *Pictorial News* and remained so until May 1919. Then it became once more what it had already been referred to as for some while in the trade press, *Topical Budget.* Indeed, through all the extraordinary circumstances of the previous two years, it had retained its character. It was a more sophisticated product now, and it had a far greater audience, but it was recognisably the same Topical that in 1916 was being seen by little over half a million people. The test would now be to maintain that audience of three million.

Topical's picture of the war was an uneven one. It was a war without sound, with little sign of fighting, and little idea of death. The films were nationalistic and entirely free from doubt; they showed a war situation in existence on many fronts, then blended it with scenes of cheeriness and contentment at home. It was good newsreel coverage. If the overall picture is like the scattered pieces of a mosaic, individual pieces glitter and attract.

Topical stayed with the war long after it was over. They retained their wartime name for a period, baited Germans long into the 1920s, and made further use of their official contacts. But their last real association with the war that had seen them blossom as a newsreel, and their last appearance as the newsreel with exclusive access to the events of that war, was at the signing of the peace treaty in Versailles.

The peace negotiations took place in Versailles between January and June of 1919. Earlier events were covered for Topical (or *Pictorial News* as it still was) by Walter Evan Davies, but as the climax of the final signing approached, Harold Jeapes was sent out as Topical's representative at the finish. On 28 June 1919, the heads of the allied powers and Germany met in the Hall of Mirrors at Versailles to put their signatures to the treaty that would end the First World War, and ultimately begin the Second. Positioned inside, uniquely,[104] was Harold Jeapes:

END OF THE WORLD WAR
'Scenes at Palace of Versailles where defeated Germany signed Allies' peace terms. 28th June 1919. President Wilson, M. Clemenceau and Mr Lloyd George were given hearty reception on entering the Palace.' The leaders arrive in turn by motor car and enter the Palace; Clemenceau, French and British army officers, Paderewski, Lloyd George and Woodrow Wilson. 'Inside the Hall of Mirrors: the actual signing of the Peace Treaty, where the German Empire was proclaimed in 1871.' Various long shots of statesmen, diplomats and army officers signing the Treaty at a desk in the centre. Panning shots of statesmen and diplomats seated at long tables. Whole assembly seen standing, some still signing the Treaty. 'The scene in the famous gardens of the Palace after the signing of the Treaty.' Various shots of an enthusiastic crowd, with leaders making their way through.[105]

Restricted to a single position, with an angled view across the tables (and of course filming in natural light), Jeapes was obliged to witness history with a series of long shots and wide panning movements, showing a large crowd of people milling around in the hall. Those signing could no more be picked out than those chatting to friends or collecting autographs. An extended version was shown privately to the cinema trade on 1 July, when the visual problem was noted:

The arrival of the delegates at the entrance of the palace afforded the camera a better opportunity for securing individual portraits than, in the nature of things, could be obtained in the ensuing pictures showing the signatures being appended to the document adjusting the destinies of nations. Lloyd George, President and Miss Wilson, Clemenceau, Paderewski, and many others, all came well into view alighting from carriages and ascending the steps. Inside, looking down the long vista in the Great Hall of Mirrors, the distance between camera and subject was naturally greater, and although the effect of a vast space filled with the representatives of the signatory nations was impressive in itself, the interest in the individual figures was lessened. Aided by the kind prompting of a voice from the back the eye could distinguish the features of the history makers as they approached the table and signed.[106]

There is an obvious danger for a cameraman filming in a room full of mirrors. But it is pleasing to think that perhaps, as Harold Jeapes was panning from left to right midway through the film, he intended to include his reflection as part of the filmed record of the event: the cameraman's own signature on a document of history.

The signing of the Versailles peace treaty inside the Hall of Mirrors. Lloyd George and Bonar Law are seated on the left. From *End of the World War.*

THE NINETEEN TWENTIES
All the Pictures but no Politics

By the start of the 1920s there were around 4,000 cinemas in Britain, from the once-weekly to the super cinema, attracting up to 20,000,000 attendances a week.[1] Although lying third in production behind Pathé and Gaumont, in producing 175 to 200 copies per issue, to be shown at a total of 700 to 1,000 cinemas (assuming most took a newsreel by this time), Topical could hope to reach a quarter of the cinema-going population – that is, 5,000,000 attendances per week. Assuming that 50 per cent of the audience went to the cinema twice a week,[2] it may be calculated that *Topical Budget* was seen by 3,500,000 different people each week, or 2,500,000 per issue. Their fortunes fluctuated over the decade, and frequently they fell below this target; moreover their sales included cheaper 'runs' for newsreels long past their release date, so that they would only achieve such viewing figures for a single issue over a long period of time. Nevertheless, although this meant that several different *Topical Budget*s, of different ages, would be on release in any one week, up to 3,500,000 people would be seeing one of some description.

Distributing the Newsreel
Over the years, the newsreels had developed a complex system of hiring periods and charges, based on the idea of 'runs'. Before the war there had been a general charge of five or six pounds for the two issues that week. Then there was introduced a scale of hiring charges that decreased with each succeeding run of three days as the newsreel aged – so that the poorer the cinema the staler its news. The three day run was based, as was the bi-weekly issue pattern, on the understanding that the cinema programme would change twice a week. The newsreels were progressively forced by exhibitors to cut their charges, so that by March 1917 *Topical Budget*, advertising their 'low wartime prices', were charging two pounds for the two issues:[3]

Release	40/-	per week	2 editions
3 days old	30/-		
6 days old	22/6		
9 days old	15/-		

12 days old	10/-
15 days old	7/6
18 days old	6/-

In February 1918 the weekly charges for the two editions were:[4]

Release	£2 15 0
3 days old	£1 15 0
6 days old	£1 10 0
9 days old	£1 00 0
12 days old	15/-
15 days old	10/-
18 days old	7/6
21 days old	7/6

Alternatively, the newsreel was available for sale at a charge of 2d per foot. During Topical's Official period the newsreel was available for both sale and hire, and some exhibitors hung on to the antiquated form of direct sales long after the rest of the film trade had accepted renting. But by 1918 Topical had far more newsreels hired out than they sold, and the practice of selling had died out completely by 1920.

Throughout the 1920s *Topical Budget* was distributed by the film renters FBO, and a talk given to sales staff in 1924 by F. A. Enders (managing director of FBO and a director of Topical), at a time when the newsreel was doing poorly, makes a number of useful points. The Governing Director referred to is Sir Edward Hulton.

The next stage is Topical, which is worthy of quite a lot of discussion. With a new Organisation we have got to figure that there are many who have no experience of selling such a news reel. The Topical side is very important. It is a side which I find at the moment needs redoubled efforts.

In the past, the idea of getting Topical in, has been bunched up with the visual features etc., and there very often has been an aftermath, with the result that the whole business has been jeopardised.

I would suggest that we are perfectly capable to deal with Topical from a standpoint of selling as a separate entity. We must strengthen our talk on Topical. From the records here, I prefer to look on Topical as a bad third in the news-reel market.

I find we put out 142 copies every change-day. The first runs in the country I estimate to be about 700 to 800, so that our proportion is bad. Singularly enough, the first-run end of the Topical is the best end. After the first run we flop down, with the result that our percentage of newsreel business is bad.

Topical only pays Topical and FBO if every copy is sold thoroughly. As far as FBO is concerned, unless you sell all runs, we are losing money. We are allocating the country into areas. Cutting it into zones, and analysing where Topical should be applied.

If you are out to book Topical, boot it on its merits, and it can be booked on its merits. I have watched it closely by comparison and it doesn't have to play second fiddle to either of the others . . .

. . . We must build Topical, and we are going to build it quick. It needs a specialised study. A different angle from the other side of the business. Any run on Topical, outside first run, means full money.

It is a new angle, and very near to the heart of the Governing Director of this Company, by virtue of the fact that it touches the business he has been associated with all his life, and in my opinion there is no reason why, eventually, Topical should not be on a par with his other successful past enterprises pro rata.

Let's make a pledge among ourselves on Topical, and pledge ourselves that as soon as we can, we are going to build it.[5]

At this time Topical were charging three pounds for a first run, as opposed to Gaumont's £2 15s.[6] They were operating eight runs (that is, from first day of release to three weeks late), with further 2/6 bookings for truly obsolete newsreels. From Enders' comments, there were up to 800 first run bookings possible out of the 4,000 or so cinemas in Britain (a surprisingly low figure), and at this poor period for Topical they had around 20 per cent of the first run market. Thus from first run hire for the week's two issues, *Topical Budget* brought in £852 – £1,000 a week was considered satisfactory. Once a cinema, or a cinema circuit, had elected to book *Topical Budget* on a first run basis, it did so for a six month period. Although Enders perceived Topical to be doing badly, they were handicapped by having no control over exhibition, unlike Gaumont and particularly Pathé, whose owner Lord Beaverbrook also ran the main exhibition circuit, Provincial Cinema Theatres. Given that Topical had to rely on the independent sector, 20 per cent to a peak of 25 per cent of the market must be considered a reasonable achievement. Enders became managing director of the Topical Film Company after Hulton's death in May 1925, and greatly increased the sales of the newsreel by securing the essential lower runs, and thus the greater percentage of newsreel business.

The newsreels found it sensible to include items not tied to a specific date; these would save the newsreel from looking out of date, would prolong its marketability, and were easier to film than 'real' news. Hence the light-hearted ephemera that have come to be associated with the newsreels were as much financial good sense as proof of poor news coverage. In order to make the newsreel attractive for lower run hire, Topical, in common with its competitors, supplied many such 'out-of-date' news items; a single issue might take a number of weeks, passing from cinema to cinema, before its commercial life was over.

The Audience

Despite the above, Topical went as much for the genuine news stories as the other newsreels, and took great pride in matching or bettering its rivals. If the names of Pathé and Gaumont have remained in the public memory because of their sound newsreels, in the 1920s Topical's 3,500,000 audience made it famous and familiar. Proof of this must lie in the film parodies of *Topical Budget* that were produced. Best known of these is Adrian Brunel's eccentric *The Typical Budget; The Only Unreliable Film Review* (1925), with its spoofs of such reliable newsreel stories as the baby show, sports and Paris fashions. Brunel had earlier spoofed Pathé with his *Pathetic Gazette* (1924), and also wrote the scenario for *Topical Bonzette* (1925), one of a lively series of cartoons featuring G. E. Studdy's dog character Bonzo. Bonzo unveils a new trough, performs as Jack Bonzobbs the cricketer, demonstrates a labour-saving device for watchdogs, shows the latest fashion in hats, puts on a diving display and is shown as Joe Bonzo in training for the heavyweight boxing championship. The cameraman for the Bonzo cartoons, Pat Tobin, later found himself working as a cameraman for Topical. In 1920 the popular film comedian Pimple (Fred Evans), who specialised in film and theatre parodies, produced *Pimple's Topical Gazette*, and in 1921 a cartoon in the *Memoirs Of Miffy* series, entitled *Running A Cinema*, featured as part of its show 'The Weakly Budget'. There was even a five-minute long advertisement produced in 1926 for Colman's mustard, featuring a variety of mock newsreel stories in each of which mustard invariably made the headlines, and called *The Mustard Club Topical Budget*.

Newsreels were looked on with humour and affection. The audience survey conducted by Sidney Bernstein in 1927 reported that:

> In reply to the question 'Do you like "News" pictures?', 82¼ per cent. of the male patrons voted yes, and 87¾ per cent. of the female patrons returned the same answer.[7]

Audiences might express a liking or distaste for melodrama, comedy, mystery or adventure, but everyone enjoyed the newsreels. This is not to say that the newsreel was looked on with any great enthusiasm, or was the reason anyone particularly went to the cinema. It was there at the start of the programme, it was short, varied and aimed to please; it informed and it entertained. Most of all, the newsreel meant the magic of current events there on the screen while they were still part of everyone's thoughts.

There are few further indications of audience reaction to the newsreels. No one wrote letters about them to the fan magazines, and the newsreels instinctively avoided any sort of controversy. For their twenty-first anniversary issue, Pathé organised an audience poll to find out which of a selection of news stories from the past were the most popular. The coronation of King George V in 1911 came out on top, followed by scenes from the First World War. Next in order came the King's illness, the R101 airship flight and disaster, the investiture of the Prince of Wales in 1911, the burning of Smyrna, and the British Empire Exhibition. Least popular were 'war conditions in Ireland' and 'pictures of Soviet Russia'.[8]

The Newsreel Story

The newsreels did not make the news – they could only reflect it. The technical handicap, and consequent time delay of having to process film before screening it, meant that they naturally tended to provide pictures of what other agencies, generally the newspapers, had made into a current topic. There were other handicaps separating them from the newspapers with whom they so liked to be compared. Firstly, they could only cover a limited number of stories, and there was a widely held belief that only certain stories were suitable as 'illustrated news'. There is a striking similarity between newsreel content and the subjects selected by both contemporary photographic agencies and by newspapers for their increasingly common photograph pages. Sporting events, society weddings, royalty, celebrities, fashions, animals of all kinds – these made good pictures. Conversely, political debate, economics, all action behind closed doors, could only be conveyed by the printed word. One major difference between the popular press and the newsreels was the coverage of crime: photographs of murderers, victims, lawyers and witnesses stare out from the front pages of the illustrated papers, but the newsreels were seldom able to convey such multifaceted dramas:

OPENING SCENES IN THE 'CRUMBLES' MURDER TRIAL.
'Irene Munro the murdered London typist' . . . 'Arrival of Mr Justice Avory, the Judge' . . . 'The Prisoners – Field and Gray' . . . 'Peggy Finlay and Dorothy Ducker, Barmaids at the Albemarle' . . . 'Stoker Putland' . . . 'William Weller – the boy who found the body' . . . 'The desolate spot in the Crumbles where the body was found.'[9]

This rare murder trial item (following a murder in Eastbourne in 1920) gives some indication of how such stories might have been covered. Although all that has been filmed is the people entering the court building and an empty piece of land, the illustrated newspaper style is clear. First there is a photograph of the victim; then the various participants in the drama pass by, are named, and their place in the drama suggested; lastly the viewer is brought back to the murder, to the place where the crime took place. It is neatly dramatic, and suggestive of a more creative use of visual information than was usual for the silent newsreels. Despite talk of a good 'story', and newsreel editors instructing their cameramen to think of 'dramatising' an item, the newsreels employed little of the art of fiction film-making. A good news 'story' might begin with an establishing shot, mix together close and medium shots of the subject, then finish with a close-up, but this was not drama in the sense of a fiction film narrative. There was no progression, no revelation. The newsreels conveyed only the actuality and seldom invited audience speculation or indeed any sort of analysis of the subject. Modest in its use of the power of film, the silent newsreel trusted that a simple approach would convey the truth. The questions and doubts raised by a murder trial give some indication of how *Topical Budget* might have adopted a more critical approach.

There is more evidence of the influence of the picture papers (the *Daily Sketch* and the *Daily Mirror*) in some of the major stories covered by Topical, such as the end of Lloyd George's coalition government in 1922:

LLOYD GEORGE RESIGNS. MR BONAR LAW NEW PREMIER
'Scenes outside the Carlton Club after historic meeting of Conservative members – when Mr Bonar Law made his speech which killed the Coalition.' Crowds and traffic and men leave the Carlton Club. 'Lord Balfour, Mr Chamberlain and Mr Bonar Law leaving.' They are seen leaving the club. '"I AM NO LONGER PRIME MINISTER." Mr Lloyd George stepping out of No. 10.' Close shot of Lloyd George. 'Mr Bonar Law – who was sent for by the King to form a new government, was born in Canada.' Close shot of Bonar Law. 'FALLEN GOVERNMENT. A picture of the King with his late Ministers after the Irish Settlement, taken by "Topical" at Buckingham Palace by His Majesty's Command.' King George V and the Cabinet with Lloyd George. 'Will Mr Chamberlain who pleaded in vain for coalition, go into retirement?' Austen Chamberlain leaving the Carlton. 'Appendicitis kept Mr Churchill out of the crisis.' Winston Churchill addressing a crowd from a dais in the open air. 'What will Mr Asquith do? "Wait and see!"' Close shot of Herbert and Margot Asquith in an open carriage. 'VOICE OF LABOUR. Mr Clynes may be Prime Minister yet.' Close shot of J. R. Clynes talking to the camera. 'STILL SMILIN' THRO' "In the Wilderness" – but with one faithful friend at least.' Lloyd George stroking a large dog, then walking through a gate.[10]

This lively item, filmed by two cameramen at the Carlton Club and one at Downing Street, with the use of some library material, finds the drama of the situation in the personalities rather than the politics. The front pages of the photo-illustrated papers were given over to a collection of photographs relating to one or more stories, so that the reader's first contact with the news story was through its images, with the words coming later. Since these collections mixed location pictures with close-ups of people, it was in effect a cinematic treatment. The newsreel was, of course, in a different position, because it came out a day or two after the newspaper had covered the story; the audience for *Topical Budget* was therefore already informed, and merely wished to see the reality of moving pictures. There was no need for Topical to supply analysis or comment. However both newspaper and newsreel depended on pictures of people for their appeal. In the item above, Lloyd George looks bright and cheerful (he always performed excellently for the cameras), Bonar Law and Clynes both look awkward posing for the cameraman, and Asquith, filmed in striking close-up, looks tired and even distraught. As a drama it may lead nowhere, but it is compelling viewing.

Another constraint on the newsreels was the need to plan their product in advance. Having only so many suitable stories, it being impossible to bluff with the camera as one might with the pen, and always at the mercy of the British weather, the newsreels inevitably favoured foreseeable news – those stories with which they were familiar. They knew just how many cameramen to send to a dog show, a wedding, a football match, a horse-race, what should be shot, how much should be shot, and how they would present it.

All newsreel producers kept a calendar of social and sporting events which were covered every year at the same time and in the same way. Around one in five *Topical Budget* items could have been anticipated before any year began, and a typical year would contain most of the following:

January: The horses' rest-home at Cricklewood, New Year hunting, winter weather, winter sports at Mürren, Oxford and Cambridge crews training for the Boat Race.

February: Cambridge bumping races, the Waterloo Cup, Shrove Tuesday street football at Ashbourne.

March: Presentation of shamrocks to the Irish Guards on St Patrick's Day, National Cross Country, the Grand National.

April: The Boat Race, Blessing of the Palms ceremony at Westminster Cathedral, Bradfield College sports, FA Cup Final, Shakespeare's birthday, Maundy Money.

May: Labour Day, summer scenes at Chiswick Baths, Chelsea Flower Show, crowning of May Queen, Oak Apple Day.

June: The Derby, the Royal Tournament, Trooping the Colour, Whit Monday processions, Fourth at Eton, Alexandra Rose Day, Wimbledon, Isle of Man TT races, Ascot races, Ascot Sunday at Boulter's Lock.

July: King's Cup aerial race, Bisley, Cinema garden party, Goodwood, Port of London Authority sports, Henley, swan-upping.

August: Glorious Twelfth, cadets on HMS Worcester, Eisteddfod, Cowes regatta, Marlow regatta, hopping in Kent, Grasmere Games.

September: Whitstable oysters, Colchester oysters, start of football season, Braemar Gathering.

October: Yarmouth herring harvest, opening of law courts, Trafalgar Day, the Cesarewitch.

November: Cubbing, Schneider Cup air race, Remembrance Day, fireworks, Eton wall game, winter weather, Lord Mayor's Show.

December: Sailors at Chatham on Christmas leave, Christmas toys, turkeys, lighthouses, children in hospital, swimming in the Serpentine.

When one also considers the minor horse-races and public ceremonies, the unveiling of war memorials, students' rag stunts, weddings at St Margaret's Westminster, the Freedoms of various cities, and remembers that an event such as Wimbledon could be covered over a number of issues, then clearly little of Topical's output was the result of chance. News in this manner could be pre-sold to exhibitors; the newsreels could advertise in advance next week's news. If a company had the exclusive rights to an event, such as the FA Cup final, it would boast the fact weeks in advance – it was literally predictable news.

It was also mostly home news. Despite the widening of audience horizons by the world war, there were regular complaints about 'foreign padding' from exhibitors. Although buying stories from abroad was cheaper than filming your own news, and though they were useful to fall back on when stories were scarce, they had to be used sparingly. Generally films from abroad were novelty items – not news at all – but Topical's audience became accustomed to regular appearances from some foreign leaders and personalities. Topical exchanged material with companies abroad, and also bought from freelance cameramen: someone called Hayes supplied them with film from Paris, and a Fiorentini in Rome sent them annual pictures of Benito Mussolini and his Fascisti. In the early 1920s their American material came from exchanges with some of the smaller American newsreels: *Kinograms*, *The Selznick News*; but in 1927 an exchange deal with the Hearst Company, producers for MGM of *MGM International News*, led to an increased amount of worldwide material coming into the *Topical Bud-*

get. This coincided with a period of great financial success for Topical, but it also meant a weakening of their own production effort, and after the boom came a rapid decline. Nevertheless, Topical largely concentrated on home news, and relied on the stories they knew best. The audience was seldom surprised by what it saw.

Some tried to break the mould. The idea of the newspapers remained so strong that there were occasional attempts to emulate Will Barker's innovatory *London Day By Day* and create a daily newsreel. The producer of theatrical revues, Albert De Courville, ran such a news service between July and September 1919 at the Terry Theatre, and the *Daily Cinema News*, founded by Bertram V. May, reached a number of London halls, running between October 1919 and January 1920. Such tiny outfits, probably with just a single cameraman, offered no threat to the status quo. What did cause an upset was Pathé's introduction of a longer edition of its newsreel entitled *Pathé Super Gazette* in January 1925. Containing eight or more items, but sold at the same price as its regular newsreel, this longer, more flexible format, with stories of varying lengths, threw Gaumont and Topical completely, and led to the ten-minute format of the sound newsreels. Sound itself was of course the greatest mould-breaker of all.

Sir Edward Hulton

The newsreels worked to a rigid formula, but in the right hands they could be compelling and imaginative – good cinema, in fact. Such was the case with *Topical Budget* between 1919 and 1923, certainly their best years, when they came under the control of the newspaper man Sir Edward Hulton. He remained head of the company until his death in 1925, but illness over his last two years saw a marked lessening of his involvement. This, together with an increasing complacency throughout the newsreel world, led to a growing staleness in Topical's output. But the first four years after the war belonged to Topical, and indeed were the best of times for the silent newsreel as a whole.

Sir Edward Hulton was the son of a Manchester newspaper proprietor and the father of the owner of *Picture Post*. He founded the *Daily Sketch*, Britain's second photo-illustrated paper after the *Daily Mirror*, in Manchester in 1909, moving it to London in 1914. By the time he bought the Topical Film Company he ran a large stable of papers, which included the *Daily Sketch*, the *Evening Standard*, the *Illustrated Sunday Herald*, and a number of Manchester titles.[11] His purchase of Topical probably arose out of his friendship with Lord Beaverbrook. Concern had been expressed by Beaverbrook and the WOCC over the Topical Film Company's future once the war was finished and the official support and name were removed. The agreement had been that three months after the end of the war the shares in the company would be put up for sale. Jeapes and Wrench had sold the company to the WOCC, but Wrench had returned to the family firm, and Jeapes was understandably affronted at having to buy back the company whose services he had given over to the war effort. He may not have been in any position to purchase the company on his own, but steps were taken to ensure that Jeapes retained some control over the company he had founded. On 8 February 1919, 14,782 shares in the Topical Film Company Limited were offered by public auction; 14,382 were bought by Hulton, and 100 each by the subsequent directors of the company, James Heddle, John Theodore Goddard, William Jeapes (managing director) and W. Alfred Wilson. Beaverbrook had taken over the moribund *Daily Express* in November 1916 and had befriended Hulton, an experienced newspaper owner able to give the younger man advice and encouragement. Beaverbrook had seen some of the potential of a newsreel and had experienced some of the thrill of film production, and it appears probable that he indicated these advantages to Hulton. It is perhaps surprising that he did not consider such a move himself, as he was shortly afterwards to acquire a share in Pathé and *Pathé Gazette*. He may have seen that Topical were never going to be a great profit maker, but recognised that this new branch of journalism might make an attractive addition to the news empire of one such as Hulton, particularly as he had made his name with photo-journalism. Cameraman Ken Gordon, who joined Topical around this time, suggests that it was Jeapes who interested Hulton in the deal, but there seems little evidence for this.[12]

Hulton's first move was to do a deal with a film distributor. Topical's earlier, rather haphazard method of sale and distribution, with small cinema circuits and contacts with individual exhibitors, was clearly not suitable for a newsreel aiming for major status; an established, nation-wide network of distribution was essential. Thus in March 1919 Hulton began negotiating with a British renting firm, Film Booking Offices (FBO),[13] run by the brothers Albert and Arthur Clozenburg,[14] with an agreement signed in May. In October 1919 FBO was reincorporated as Film Booking Offices (1919) Limited, with the directorate comprising the Clozenburg brothers, Hulton, Jeapes, and managing director, F. A. Enders. FBO specialised in distributing American second features and serials, with the occasional prestige production, such as *Broken Blossoms* and *Blind Husbands*. They had offices in all of Britain's major cities, and by this one action Hulton aimed to make Topical the equal of Pathé and Gaumont. Without Hulton's involvement and financial backing it is unlikely that the company and its newsreel would have lasted long.

Under Hulton Topical were vigorous and inventive, and this brought them praise and prestige. But financially they were not particularly successful. Hulton decided that, for Topical to be competitive, a great deal had to be spent on reorganising the company and introducing new equipment. This included Jeapes' innovatory design for an automatic developing plant, built by the Vinten company. Though they went through a lean time, not showing an actual profit until 1922,[15] the rate of sales was maintained and never fell to its pre-1918 level.

Topical found themselves bound up with the *Daily Sketch*, Hulton's flagship newspaper. Between September 1922 and August 1923 the newsreel was even referred to on-screen as the *Daily Sketch Topical Budget*.[16] They featured *Daily Sketch* competitions, provided photographs for *Sketch* stories, and a number of *Topical Budget* items featured Lady Hulton's progress through society. Among Topical's directors for the period were James Heddle, former editor of the *Daily Sketch*, Alfred Wilson, another Hulton employee, and W. J. Dickenson, Hulton's private secretary.

Hulton was fortunate in his purchase, because the immediate postwar years were filled with ideal newsreel incidents. All the major sports started up again, there were threats of war in Russia and in the Ruhr, there were peace negotiations. People flew the Atlantic, flew around the world, planes flew faster and faster, airships grew bigger and bigger, catastrophes were all the greater. In the giddy years of relaxation crazes sprang up everywhere – dances, games, clothes, fads, personalities. Cameras had come closer and closer to the royal family, in King George V and Queen Mary there were two solid, dependable public servants who contentedly followed all the social routine asked of them, and in the young Prince of Wales (the future Duke of Windsor) the newsreels had their very own star. He, more than any other, was the unfailing news story of the period, and had more reason to hate newsreel cameramen than anyone else. It was a time of strikes, of Bolshevist fears, of political change and parliamentary personalities. There was civil war in Ireland, there might be civil war in England too. Ageing Lords married American showgirls, and cameras were let into London Zoo. Hollywood reigned supreme and it was great just to go the cinema.

Exhibiting the Newsreel

You arrived at the local Grand or Imperial at 6.00pm, walked through grand doors onto plush carpets, felt the welcoming warmth as you purchased your ticket (prices generally ranging from 4d to 3s 6d), passed the commissionaire and entered the auditorium. Making your way to your seat, you gazed up at the screen while the audience, perhaps as many as a thousand in an average cinema, settled down around you. The cinema programme announced the main feature, your chief reason for coming[17] – perhaps a Norma Talmadge weepie or a Harold Lloyd comedy – but first there was the supporting programme, those essential extras that made the show complete. Depending on the size of the cinema, the music was supplied by a pianist, an organist, trio, small band or full orchestra. The lights dimmed, and musicians announced with a rousing march that here was the newsreel.[18] The title came up on the screen: 'Topical Budget. The Great British News Film'.

A typical issue began by announcing the name of the newsreel, sometimes with an added slogan,[19] and the issue number, which ran, for example, 545–1, 545–2, 546–1, 546–2. The –1s were released on Thursdays, the –2s on Mondays. The issue number was no longer repeated on the titles of the individual items as had been the case up to mid-1919. This opening title would last for 10 feet or so, during which time the musicians usually played a march. The silent newsreels became so associated with this musical style that it was natural that the sound newsreels should adopt the same when they came to be obliged to supply their own music. However musicians' efforts were principally directed towards accompanying the feature film, and a short item such as a newsreel received little special attention – frequently only a pianist would play. The newsreels could be relied upon to provide a regular round of stories and there were a regular set of tunes to match:

If I were a manager engaging a pianist, I think I would test them on a 'Pathé Gazette' or 'Gaumont Graphic', for such topical pictures test the memory and the quickwittedness far more than the 'drama' or 'comedy'. I very seldom play a straight march to one, although I have heard this done, and even waltzes. When I was staying in London some few years ago, 'The King and Queen' visited the East End one day, and the picture was shown the same night at the New Cross Empire, when the band played 'Hearts and Flowers'. Would

Main title for issue 867–2 (9 April 1928).

you believe it? . . . National Anthems and folk songs of all nations should be memorised . . . 'Land of my fathers' for Lloyd George, 'Ap Shenkin' or 'Jenny Jones' for other Welsh scenes. I used to play 'Men of Harlech', but you can't do it in Wales now, as the kids have a very vulgar parody on the words . . . I was playing 'The Star-spangled Banner' to any American scenes of patriotism or military and Navy events long before the war . . . 'Stars and Stripes' march is good, too, if the scene is long, but it is very well known, and a big encouragement to the 'chirpers'. For Royalty – our own, I mean – 'War March of the Priests'. A scene where Queen Mary or Princess Mary are alone or in the foreground is best suited by the song, 'Mary' ('Kind, kind, and gentle is she').[20]

Weddings were accompanied by Mendelssohn, hunting scenes by 'D'ye Ken John Peel?', marches by marches. Contemporary audiences could expect news stories to be matched with obvious, popular tunes or a quite incongruous light air. Often the pianist would play just the single piece throughout the whole newsreel.

Following the main title came the first item. There was seldom much thought put into the order of items in *Topical Budget*; unless they wanted to emphasise one in particular by placing it first, the order was usually that in which they were printed up by the labs. Certainly the contents of the newsreel were not arranged or edited with any overall effect in mind – such sophistication did not come to the newsreels until E. V. H. Emmett became both editor and commentator for *Gaumont-British News* in the 1930s. It was not uncommon, however, for one item to be placed after another as a comment on its predecessor, usually to score a political point. It may have been only coincidence that an item on the death of Lenin was followed by one on the new Labour Government,[21] but Topical were fond of following items on disarmament talks with scenes of military manoeuvres. Issue 678–1 (release date 21 August 1924) juxtaposes an item on the Inter-Allied Conference, entitled WILL DISARMAMENT COME TRUE?, with tank manoeuvres at Aldershot; issue 649–1 (release date 31 January 1924) pairs an item on the French occupation of the Ruhr with one on the Prince of Wales unveiling a war memorial in London, 'GIVE US PEACE IN OUR TIME O LORD'. But unconscious, often ludicrous, clashes between adjoining items were also common. Thus THE FLAME OF FANATICISM (scenes of the civil war in China) was followed by CANINE SAGACITY (a dog show in Ipswich).[22] The titles of some items might also be a humorous comment on the story that preceded them: thus the arrival of the new American Ambassador is followed by an item on radio broadcasting, ANOTHER GREAT AMBASSADOR – WIRELESS!,[23] and LONDON'S OWN CROSS-WORD PUZZLE (an item on the fog) is followed by 'FOG' OF COURSE (on the new craze for crossword puzzles).[24] Topical seldom gave thought to thematic unity. There were five stories, barring a major event, and their topicality was theme enough.

Each item opened with its own main title, and underneath were the descriptive titles that predated the sound commentary. Before 1918 it had been uncommon for there to be any further intertitles cut into the actual film story, save for the occasional longer item.[25] By 1920, with growing confidence in the newsreel form, this practice was becoming increasingly common, sometimes giving plain information about location or personalities, sometimes commenting on the scene. The tone was generally light-hearted; it made the occasional attempt towards populism, and in the presence of royalty became obsequious:

FIXING FIDO'S FACE
'Super-Shampoo and Beauty-parlour for Dogs, opened in London' . . . 'Bath first!' . . . '"Vacuum drier – Oh, Lor!"' . . . '"Do they think I'm a pudding?"' . . . 'Manicure!' . . . '"Teeth filing – this is too much!".'[26]

THE DERBY 1927
'Epsom the "Mecca"' . . . 'Many drunk deep at the Well of Prophecy – Alas!' . . . 'From the ashes of the past emerges a structure worthy of old associations' . . . 'His Majesty arrives to share with his people the thrills of The World's greatest race' . . . 'I gotta 'norse!' . . . 'Messrs. George F. Allison and Geoffrey Gilbey who broadcasts a description of The Race to the World' . . . 'They're off!' . . . 'A brilliant race won by "Call Boy" (E. C. Elliott up) who led from start to finish. Hot Night . . . 2 Shian Mor . . . 3.'[27]

PRINCESS MARY WEDDED TO VISCOUNT LASCELLES, D.S.O., AT WESTMINSTER ABBEY
'Still "Our Princess"! Amid unforgettable scenes of love and loyalty the King's daughter marries an English nobleman thereby enabling H.R.H. – in her own sweet words – to "remain in her native land"' . . . 'Glorious was the day – the bride sets forth with her father from Buckingham Palace' . . . 'Wonderful Whitehall' . . . 'At the Abbey' . . . 'Queen Alexandra arrives' . . . 'Queen Mary and her sons' . . . 'Arrival of the bridegroom' . . . 'Princess Mary arrives at the Abbey' . . . 'The ceremony in the Abbey' . . . 'Man and wife' . . . 'A thunderous oration' . . . 'The roar of Piccadilly. "Shout after shout to greet the bridal pair"' . . . '"And from the balcony, hearts glowing, they did bow the people gracious thanks"' . . . '"And kindly thoughts, as myriad as angels' wings in heaven, go with them". Princess Mary starts for her honeymoon: King and Princes pelt Bride and Lord Lascelles – with confetti.'[28]

The main title of an item could be matter-of-fact, obscure, arresting, humorous, misleading, misspelled, witty, or simply dull:

THE GREATEST MENACE WE HAVE EVER KNOWN (Coal strike)
PRINCE BOARD'S THE LIFEBOAT (that is, boards)
ARE TOWN GIRLS PRETTIER THAN COUNTRY GIRLS? (Daily Sketch competition)
SWEET (SCENTED) ARE THE USES OF ADVERTISEMENT (Scent fountain in Paris)
NO HEAT NO LIGHT NO HOPE! (Scenes in the Soviet Union)
'MEE-OW! MEE-OW! WE HATE THE MOVIES!' (Cat show)
IS MISS DOROTHY KNAPP THE 'PERFECT WOMAN'? (American model)
'BIFF!' ALSO 'BANG!' (Boxing)
AND NOW YOUR FOOD WILL COST YOU MORE! (Dock strike)
WHO WILL WIN NEXT YEAR'S BOAT RACE?
WIERDEST FINANCIAL PROBLEM IN HISTORY (that is, weirdest)
'T'COOP' GOES NORTH (Sheffield United win FA Cup)
'SUZANNE! SUZANNE! WE LOVE YOU TO A MAN!' (Tennis player Suzanne Lenglen)
M. CAILLAUX OR M. CAILL-I-O-U-? (French finance minister)
HOME SECRETARY PRAISES ONE-ARMED MOTORISTS[29]

For a major event taking up the whole of one issue, up to a quarter of the total footage (or 75 out of 300 feet) might be taken up with descriptive titles, although a story with plenty of action (such as the Derby) would have far less. The item below, 132 feet in length, is almost 50 per cent titles:

ANOTHER GREAT AMBASSADOR – WIRELESS!
'The eve of the New Year, was the eve of a new era when millions in Britain "listened in" to America'(11) . . . (15)'In this little hut at Biggin Hill was first heard the voice of a man speaking at Pittsburgh U.S.A.'(23) . . . (30)'Capt West of the B.B.C. who first heard the voice from America – a voice which proclaims the beginning of a new bond between the two English speaking nations'(41) . . . (46)'The nine-valve set which picked up America on a 100 metre wave length'(52) . . . (61) 'Tuning up for America'(63) . . . (71)'Here they are! America talking' (73) . . . (80)'Switching through the voice of America to broadcasting station'(88) . . . (92)'From Biggin Hill runs a connecting line to the broadcaster'(97) . . . (100)'The broadcaster'(101) . . . (106)'"Hello! Uncle Carectacus! Can you put me onto Mars?"'(112) . . . (117)'And all over the country, people "listened in" to "Big Ben" '(122) . . . (132).[30]

The longer the titles took to read, the longer they had to stay on the screen. The line beginning 'Capt West of the B.B.C. . . .' lasts for 11 feet, the line 'The broadcaster' one foot. The style is both informative and informal.

It is not possible to judge the influence the intertitles had on the audience's perception of the images. Intertitles were avidly read in the silent era of course (sometimes out loud), and absorbed, but they could not have had the commanding effect of sound. What is vital is that words and pictures were separated: the viewer read, then saw. Until 1918 the opening titles would describe the whole action. If two events occurred within an item, then they were divided up to indicate two separate subjects:

ARMCHAIR COOKERY
'Mr W. Lawton the barrister-chef straps up his right arm and demonstrates how disabled soldiers can cook their own dinners. Preparing an omelette, peeling potatoes, which are cooked on a collapsible gas stove.'[31]

It was the great discovery of the last few months of the war, put into full use by 1920, that titles could comment as well as describe – that it was advantageous to cut further titles into an item, and that these actually made the item more watchable. A few static shots of Dusseldorf locations during the French invasion of the Ruhr in 1923 could be greatly enlivened by some inflammatory comments:

MORE CAMERA PEEPS AT RUHRITANIA
'Snapshots of Gen. Degoutte who has a "way" with Brother Boche' . . . 'This mighty building in Dusseldorf is for an Exhibition. Will the exhibits include a lump of coal?' . . . 'The Germans are building enormous Banks. Does the paper money take up so much room?' . . . 'Rhineland, bursting with tears, is in flood and – ' . . . ' – the Cologne "penny steamers" have struck!'[32]

Titles did not only brighten up poor footage. They could be used to complement and entertain, as in this item on the opening of the oyster season at Whitstable, which carries its amusing conceit very well:

FIRST VICTIMS OF A SHELL-FISH PLEASURE
'Only satisfaction of doomed Whitstable "Natives" is that they will cost consumers more this season' . . . 'Dragged from their beds at dawn' . . . 'Into captivity' . . . 'Sorting the prisoners' . . . 'Interned.'[33]

Thus although the strength of an item depended on the camerawork, the silent newsreel reached its peak as an art form and news vehicle when it best deployed its silent commentary. Hence this item from 1921 on Lloyd George at Chequers, skilfully filmed by Fred Wilson (one of Topical's most able cameramen), and well served by the choice and placing of titles:

David Lloyd George and daughter Megan at Chequers in 1921. From *Downing Street in Buckinghamshire.*

DOWNING STREET IN BUCKINGHAMSHIRE
'Mr Lloyd George's visit to the "Chequers" given by Lord Lee as country residence to British Premiers for ever.' General shot of house. Lloyd George and party come onto the lawn. 'Lady Hamar Greenwood takes a snapshot.' Lloyd George and Lord Reading walk down path. Lady Hamar Greenwood photographs them. 'India? A word with Lord Chief Justice Reading who – ' Lloyd George and Lord Reading talking with third man. ' – becomes Viceroy of India.' Close shot of Reading lighting a cigarette. Shot of the whole party, posed for the camera. 'Miss Megan Lloyd George thinks it is nicer than Downing Street.' Megan Lloyd George talking to her father.[34]

This deftly produced item shows the silent newsreel at its best. Wilson's camerawork is conventionally good, beginning with an establishing long shot of the location, then mixing medium and close shots of the personalities involved. But more than that, it invites the audience into its subject; the shots do not merely get closer, rather the camera comes closer by stages to the people as they move away from the building. These people are both on show and yet relaxed; there is no awkward posing for the camera. The item concludes with Lloyd George and his daughter, a popular figure of the time, both of whom made appealing newsreel figures. The titles follow a similar movement towards the audience. There is the opening, establishing line, and then the subsequent titles equate with the closer shots – the cheeky splitting of titles, during which Lord Reading becomes Viceroy of India, is not only amusing and confident, but shows a facetious attitude that prefigures the sound newsreel commentaries. Lastly, Megan Lloyd George actually looks like the titles' description of her. Together, editor and cameraman have produced a relaxed, informal portrait, which humanises the politicians.

Topical sought to make their product as attractive as possible. Apart from the stories chosen, and the informal manner of presentation, use was made of decoration and colour. Topical's opening titles were characterised by some highly ornate and attractive designs. Mock-Greek columns, for example, decorated by objects connected with the subject of the item, surrounded italicised titles. Items on strikes featured a policeman, perhaps with the Houses of Parliament in the background. The title of Topical's coverage of the 1921 FA Cup Final is superimposed over live action from the game, and in 1928 they were employing an elaborate title sequence in which the words 'FBO presents' would appear in front of curtains, which would then draw back to reveal the words 'Topical Budget. The Great British News Film' and the issue number. The man who designed many of Topical's titles during the 1920s, Alf Skitterell, was held in high esteem within the industry. Like the language of the titles, they helped to characterise *Topical Budget* as a pleasing, friendly product, in sympathy with its audience.

The use of colour was widespread in the silent cinema. Crude methods of colouring had been in use since the earliest days, and Charles Urban's Kinemacolor process had been used for topicals to notable effect, but the most common method was tinting, by which a whole scene or film would be dyed in one colour. Individual items could be presented in their own individual colours, just as certain scenes were given in particular colours in fiction films. The main colours used in newsfilms were red, blue, green, mauve, amber and yellow. Sometimes the colour would be used to match the subject: horse-races and cricket matches were in green, fires in red, aerial and marine pictures in blue. But this was not rigidly adhered to, and often the whole newsreel would be tinted with just one colour. The use of such colour was selective; only a certain number of *Topical Budget* items or whole newsreels were tinted, but audiences were accustomed to seeing the news in this manner. There was also the more elaborate method of stencil colouring, by which a number of colours were applied to the individual frames of film. This was time-consuming and expensive, as the work had to be sent over to Paris, and Pathé and Gaumont both reserved it for fashion items, often with beautiful effects. Topical had neither access or means to employ stencil colouring, and this is presumably not unrelated to the fact that they produced remarkably few fashion items as compared to their competitors.[35]

The average length of a whole issue was 300 feet, or five minutes at silent film speed. Commonly there were five items, each around 50 to 60 feet (including titles). Variations were played on this formula, and items could be as short as 15 feet or take up the whole of the issue. Newsreel producers still harked back to the days of the topical, and those stories they favoured the most, and in which they took the greatest pride were of topical length, 300 feet or more. Topical's longest single issue was 609–2 (release date 30 April 1923), which was 687 feet long, comprising the main title (10 feet), the wedding of the Duke of York and Lady Elizabeth Bowes-Lyon (328 feet) and the FA Cup final (349 feet). In general, the whole issue passed by in around five minutes, an amalgam of music, colour, humour, light comment and visual information, watched by 3,500,000 people a week.

Producing the Newsreel

Between thirty and forty people worked for the Topical Film Company in the early 1920s. At the head was Sir Edward Hulton, although he took little part in day-to-day operations after the company offices moved from Shoe Lane (where the *Daily Sketch* was based) back to Wardour Street in September 1919, and still less after 1923, when illness led him to retire to the south of France. The directorate was made up of managing director William Jeapes (with overall reponsibility for the running of the newsreel), James Heddle (formerly editor of the *Daily Sketch* and with the *Evening Standard*), W. J. Dickenson (Hulton's private secretary, replacing Alfred Wilson as a director in 1923), and John Theodore Goddard, long-time associate of Jeapes and solicitor to the company since at least 1913. Heddle resigned as a director in August 1924 and was replaced by F. A. Enders of FBO. The affairs of the company were discussed at weekly meetings (usually on a Thursday), following screenings in FBO's Soho Square viewing theatre of the three newsreels' two issues for the week, Pathé and Gaumont lending them copies for this. The newsreels tended to consider the bi-weekly issues as two parts of a single edition. The management made their comments on length, photographic quality and contents, judging which they thought the best. Matters relating to the running of the newsreel were aired, and Captain Holt-White, head of the editorial department, would report on the week's work and expenditure. All matters of policy and expense were referred to Hulton for his approval.

Topical's operations were divided into three sections, as they had been under the WOCC: editorial, technical and sales. The editorial department comprised its head, Holt-White, his news editor, Charles Heath, the cameramen, and the various office staff involved in collating the material required to form the newsreel. Holt-White, the former journalist and novelist, seems to have held a position unique in the newsreel world, a result of his successful work during the war period.

Then he had been called in to co-ordinate the various strands of an inefficient organisation, overseeing the path of production from selection of material to filming, processing and exploiting the product. He gave purpose and vision to an organisation previously content with survival and then suddenly required to compete on the highest level and to produce government propaganda. His role as link between management and staff continued into the 1920s, and he reported to all directors' meetings. His duties were to control the editorial expenses, organise the movements of the cameramen, report on the use and state of camera equipment, deal with film material from outside sources and exchanges, see that all film used and all costs were accounted for, and finally to guide the newsreel in its choice of subject-matter and the way in which this was to be sold to exhibitors.

The uniqueness of his position lay in the relation between his role and that of the news editor. The news editor of a newsreel commonly directed the cameramen, viewed and selected the material shot, wrote the titles, and generally oversaw production before the newsreel was handed over to be printed. Holt-White's duties obviously would have overlapped with those of Charles Heath, Topical's news editor throughout the 1920s, and it is unclear how the work was divided between them. For instance, it was normally the job of the news editor to write the titles and intertitles, hence the preference for former journalists in this post. Heath had worked as a writer and photographer in Fleet Street before the war, but Holt-White had been a journalist for many years, had written a number of books, and surely, as the author of *The People's King. A Short Life of Edward VII*, would have been entrusted with some of Topical's more patriotic items.

Holt-White's overall purpose was to ensure that the *Topical Budget*, in its selection of material and efficient operation, was sufficiently attractive to exhibitors for it to build on its wartime success. Heath it was who carried out his directions, instructing the cameramen, viewing the film shot, and dictating its physical editing. The flexibility of this arrangement meant that Heath could also operate as an additional cameraman when required (unusually, he possessed his own camera and was paid extra job-by-job for this work).

The number of cameramen working for Topical varied. At the start of the decade there were four regulars, but by 1922 this had increased to six. There was always a demand for freelance workers, some of whom filmed for Topical on a fairly regular basis. Others would turn up at the offices on the chance of an assignment, or there were those living out of London who could be called upon for regional material. Usually, however, cameramen in the regions would take material they thought of interest, and then hope to sell it to any one of the newsreel companies.

Using the busy period October to December 1922 as an example, six cameramen were employed by Topical on a regular basis: Fred

TABLE II

Cameramen's assignments:
October–December 1922 (issues 579–2 to 592–1)

Cameraman	Used	Unused	Held
'Bunny' Hutchins	25	8	5
Frank Danvers Yates	25	10	5
'Taxi' Purnell	16	6	7
Fred Wilson	26	6	12
Norton Gardner	20	11	3
Jimmy Taylor	22	1	3
Edward Tassie	10	6	1
Charles Heath	3		1
Oscar Bovill	5		
Monty Redknapp	4	1	
Alvin Willis			1
Edward Grant	2		
Bert Bloomfield	1		
J. B. McDowell		1	
Charlie Crapper		2	
Thomas	2	1	
Best	1 (cartoon)		
Supplied	2		
Library	16		
Companies			
The Selznick News	21		
International News	3		
'La Community'	3		
First National Pictures	4		
Granger's Film Service	1		
Green's Film Service	1		

Wilson, Frank Danvers Yates, 'Bunny' Hutchins, Jimmy Taylor, Norton Gardner and 'Taxi' Purnell. During this period Topical released 26 issues containing 128 items, three of them part of regional issues only. For this they made use of the services of 17 cameramen all told, plus film from five outside companies and their own library of negatives. Of the main cameramen, Hutchins went on 38 assignments, for eight of which his film was not used, and on five occasions his film was held for future use. For the others, Yates went on 40 assignments (10 not used, 5 held), Purnell on 29 (6 not used, 7 held), Wilson on 44 (6 not used, 12 held), Gardner on 34 (11 not used, 3 held) and Taylor on 24 (1 not used, 3 held). Of the other cameramen used, news editor Charles Heath went on 5 assignments (1 held), and regular freelance operator for Topical, Edward Tassie, went on 17 (6 not used, 1 held). There were eight other cameramen used, each working on only a handful of items. From outside sources, they used 21 items from *The Selznick News* (around Christmas it was customary to use more American material than usual), three from *International News* and three from 'La Community', a company supplying them with occasional stories from France. There were single items from other companies and two items supplied by unnamed freelance cameramen. Topical were involved in a 'find a film star' competition at this time in conjunction with First National Pictures, who supplied them with four stories. Finally, they used 16 items from their library of negatives.

This was a remarkable period for Topical; they were greatly involved in the film star competition, Lloyd George's coalition government collapsed and there was a general election; they managed to get cameras into 10 Downing Street to film Bonar Law's new cabinet (after the end of the coalition but before the election), sent two cameramen (Taylor and Yates) to Doorn in the Netherlands to film the wedding of the ex-Kaiser, and dispatched Hutchins to Rumania to film the coronation of King Ferdinand I. There was Armistice Day, the State Opening of Parliament, the Lord Mayor's show, and Christmas. The figures in Table II are taken from Topical's issue books, which were used to record what was filmed and what was released. It is not known what records were kept by Topical in the early years, but certainly when the WOCC took them over and Captain Holt-White took charge of the editorial department, he found the information kept to be inadequate and the first issue sheets to survive come from this period, covering issues 301–1 to 376–2 (30 May 1917 to 11 November 1918). These are the editor's records of the newsreel as it would probably be released, with main title, intertitles, length of item (excluding titles), the issue number and date of release. The titles and intertitles on the actual films often differ slightly. These sheets also record the separate foreign edition produced from September 1918. All succeeding records were kept in handwritten issue books by the news editor. The first such issue book is the largest and the most detailed. Covering the period between issues 393–1 and 638–1 (6 March 1919 to 15 November 1923), though with gaps between issues 400–1 to 429–2 (24 April 1919 to 17 November 1919) and 524–1 to 574–2 (8 September 1921 to 28 August 1922), these give the subject and location, the names of the cameramen, the amount of film they took, the amount used in the newsreel, what film was held over or rejected, and the expenses incurred. These were records of the cameramen's actions rather than the newsreel as released, and if they were kept up after issue 638–1 they have not survived. Records of release were kept in a series of issue books, nine of which survive[36] between issue 541–1 (5 January 1922) and 1019–2 (9 March 1931), with a large gap between 856–1 and 910–2 (19 January 1928 to

TABLE III

Details from subject index cards – letter 'F'

Subject	Number of items
FAIRBANKS, Douglas	2
FAIRS	18
FARMING AND FARM LABOURERS	10
FASCISTI	7
FASHIONS	53
FELIXSTOWE	1
FENCING	3
FERRYS	2
FÊTES	32
FIELD, Admiral	1
FIREMEN	28
FIRES	56
FIREWORKS	19
FISHERMEN ('see also trawlers')	1
FISHING	2
FLAGS	7
FLAX SPINNING	1
FLOODS	37
FLORIDA	5
FLOWER SHOWS	11
Marshal FOCH ('see also Marshal')	2
FOG ('see also Lord Mayor Show')	4
FOLKESTONE	1
FOOTBALL (ASSC.)	230
'FORESTERS' SOCIETY	1
FOXES ('see also Hunting')	3
FRANCE ('see also Paris')	83
FREEMANTLE [sic], Admiral	1
'FROTHBLOWERS'	2
FRY, Commander C. B.	1
FUNERALS	51
FURNACES	1

Note: The numbers of items include some stories held in Topical's library which were not released. One item might encompass more than one subject, of course, so for instance not all the FASHION entries are for fashion stories, and many of the FIREMEN and FIRES entries overlap.

4 February 1929). These give the newsreel as released, with a descriptive title (seldom the actual title used on the film), the length of the main title, intertitles and picture, the issue number and release date, and separate items intended for regional issues. These books also sometimes give the times for films as they were handed in for printing, but do not

give the names of the cameramen.

Topical also kept up a subject index, covering issues 500–1 to 1017–2 (24 March 1921 to 23 February 1931). Handwritten on 6 × 4 inch cards, these give, under each main subject heading, a description of the individual item, the month and year, length of the item (excluding titles) and the issue number (omitting the –1 or –2). They also indicate where an item had made use of earlier material from the library of negatives, and there is a separate section for featured personalities. As with other newsreel subject indexes, the choice of subject headings and the method of classification is idiosyncratic. The entries for the letter 'F' give an idea of the range and style.

A library of negatives was essential to a newsreel. Topical held material going back to at least 1916, but some film may have been lost in the 1924 fire, possibly from the 1919–20 period. The holdings in the library that was retained by Brent Laboratories after *Topical Budget* finished in 1931 ran largely from 1921. Shots were reused in later items, compilations were made (such as the 1928 *Our Leader* on Stanley Baldwin), and by 1931, when the newsreel was winding down and there were few cameramen left, a fair proportion of the newsreel was actually constructed out of old material. After all, film of last year's snow looks very much like film of this year's snow. Also in the library were 'portrait' shots of personalities of the day, used for stock shots of people liable to be featured regularly in the newsreel but not always available to be filmed.[37] Topical regularly exchanged material with newsreels from abroad, usually America, and most notably agreed a deal in 1927 with *MGM International News*, which led to a large amount of largely ephemeral American stories being featured in *Topical Budget* in the late 1920s. Exchanges of material were of two kinds. The most common method was to send surplus prints of individual items (a rash experiment in sending negatives to Germany in 1924 was abandoned when they were returned in poor condition), but during 1922 and possibly at other periods the cameramen were directed to shoot extra footage for American consumption, thus producing two different negatives for the same story.

A single issue of *Topical Budget* might be produced in the following manner. For issue 580–1, to be released 5 October 1922, eight stories were filmed, with five eventually going into the finished newsreel. The main story was the Prince of Wales' visit to a meeting of ex-servicemen at Crystal Palace. Two cameramen were assigned: Hutchins, who filmed 221 feet, of which 23 feet were used in the newsreel and 56 feet were destined for America, and Tassie, who filmed 129 feet, 20 feet for Britain and 52 feet for America. With 8 feet of title, this first item in the newsreel was 51 feet long. The second item, on a new bomber aeroplane, was filmed by Yates, who took 144 feet, of which 56 feet were used in the newsreel, and 23 feet were intended for America. With 14 feet of title, the full-length item was 70 feet. The third item focused on an indoor golfing school in Kensington. Wilson took 338 feet, of which 55 feet were used in the newsreel – quite a high rate of wastage for a cost-conscious company such as Topical; Wilson's expenses of £3 10s are also surprisingly high. The item with title came to 69 feet. The fourth item was supplied by Granger's Film Service, and showed scenes in Turkey of Sultan Mehmed VI, shortly to be dethroned. The rather uninformative footage, 28 feet, needed 21 feet of titles to liven it up. The last item was of a dog show at Crystal Palace, for which Yates took 235 feet, of which 41 feet were used in the newsreel, together with 7 feet of titles. Thus only the first two stories were selected for American sales. The Prince of Wales story and the bomber story were delivered to the printers on 2 October (the day of the previous issue), the golf story and the last two stories the day after, and the newsreel was released on 5 October, a Thursday. With 10 feet of opening title, the full issue was 297 feet long, of which 74 feet were titles and 223 feet were picture. Three other stories were filmed but not used: Yates took 137 feet of a shoe leather fair, and Hutchins took 91 feet of a diamond sale and 85 feet of a story given in the issue books as 'Prince's Day'. None of these was kept for further use. Thus a total of 1,380 feet of film was taken, of which 223 feet went into the newsreel and 131 feet were sold to America. 1,054 feet of film were unused. 75 per cent wastage was a usual figure, even without the American material. Issue 593–1 (4 January 1923) saw 896 feet shot and 206 feet used, for issue 593–2 (8 January 1923) it was 849 feet and 234 feet.

A low nationwide distribution per issue was 140, a high number 200. During their Hulton period, Topical averaged around 175. From July 1922, as well as the main edition, Topical also began producing occasional regional issues, instituting a full 'territorial scheme' in February 1923. A regional issue usually simply meant that one item from the main edition would be dropped to be replaced by one of local interest. In addition some items of local interest which were nevertheless part of the main edition might be given in extended form. 'Local' usually meant of interest to regions centred around Birmingham, Cardiff, Leeds, Liverpool and/or Manchester, as well as Scotland. Thus issue 680–1 (release date 4 September 1924) had five items in the main edition: Ramsay MacDonald leaving for the Fifth Assembly of the League of Nations at Geneva; the arrival of the 'All Blacks' touring team; a wrecked cargo liner off the Cornish coast; and two items on matches from the opening of the football season – West Ham United against Preston North End, and Tottenham Hotspur against Bolton Wanderers. The Birmingham edition (nine copies sent out) included an extra match between Chelsea and Coventry City, and the Manchester edition (eight copies sent out) had instead an extra match between Arsenal and Manchester City. The Scottish edition (thirteen copies sent out) featured the Ramsay MacDonald item and items on the visit of the Duke and Duchess of York to Glasgow, and on the Braemar

Gathering. Averaging out the figures available for February to September 1923, a distribution of 175 copies might have comprised 14 copies to Scotland, 36 to Yorkshire, 37 to Lancashire, 14 to Birmingham, 6 to Cardiff, and 68 to London. *Topical Budget* would only have been seen abroad as the British footage in a foreign newsreel with which Topical had an exchange deal. It was not distributed in any country except Britain after 1920.[38]

'Men Who Film the World For You'

The star figures of any newsreel were the cameramen.[39] Newspapers and film magazines carried articles on the daring exploits they undertook, and though there was a good deal to the job that was routine, it meant varied and lively employment for the lucky few. The usual route to the career was through an early interest in photography. Journalistic experience was not sought in anyone except editorial staff, and the qualities looked for and displayed by the best cameramen were stubbornness, patience, ingenuity and an easy rapport with people.[40] The newsreel cameraman was a generally welcome figure, and many of the most watchable *Topical Budget* items are engaging precisely because the subjects know that they are on show and are happy to be seen performing. The importance of the camera and cameramen themselves as a focal point is clear, not merely creating the news story in a mechanical sense but being the object of the participants' interest. One of the most noticeable things about the silent newsreels is just how much people look at the camera, how often they are seen peering at us down the years.

It has been possible to trace seventy-six cameramen whose work went into *Topical Budget*.[41] They range from the polished expert with years of experience to the most hapless freelance, one item shot out of focus and never employed again. There were others, particularly for the years 1911–17, whose names are now lost, but it is possible to calculate most of Topical's main cameramen year by year (see Table IV).

There was some glamour attached to being a cameraman, and a great camaraderie and fellow-feeling between them. They have been well described as:

. . . fun-filled, large-overcoated and bibulous men with loud voices and connections as close to Gatty's Music Hall as to any technical union.[42]

Many of them had, of course, begun working when films were shown in the music halls, and William Jeapes himself had put on shows at Gatti's in Villiers Street and Westminster Road. There was no cameramen's union at this time, but there was the Kine Cameramen's Society, a 'social organisation' founded in December 1918. Its first meeting, at Emile's Restaurant in Wardour Street, featured Bert Bloomfield, Billy

TABLE IV

Main cameramen

1911	Davies? Engholm? H. Jeapes Ward? Woods-Taylor
1912	Davies? Engholm? H. Jeapes Ward? Woods-Taylor
1913	Davies? Engholm? H. Jeapes Ward Woods-Taylor
1914	Davies Engholm H. Jeapes Ward? Woods-Taylor
1915	H. Jeapes Woods-Taylor?
1916	H. Jeapes Woods-Taylor?
1917	Bovill Engholm H. Jeapes McDowell Malins Raymond Varges
1918	Bassill Bovill Buckstone Davies Engholm Hutchins H. Jeapes McDowell Raymond Varges Wilson Woods-Taylor
1919	Cotter Gemmell Gordon Hutchins H. Jeapes Tassie Freelance: Davies
1920	Cotter Gemmell Gordon Heath Hutchins H. Jeapes Parry Purnell Tassie Wilson
1921	Heath Hutchins Parry Purnell Wilson Freelance: Tassie
1922	Heath Hutchins Purnell Taylor Wilson Yates Freelance: Gardner Redknapp Tassie
1923	Benson Heath Hutchins Purnell Taylor Wilson Yates Freelance: Bloomfield Bool Gardner Grant Redknapp
1924	Benson Gardner Heath Hutchins Purnell Yates
1925	Benson Gardner Heath Hutchins Jones Plowman Purnell
1926	Benson Harris? Heath Jones Plowman? Purnell
1927	Benson? Harris? Heath Jones Plowman? Purnell
1928	Benson? Harris? Heath Jones Plowman? Purnell?
1929	Benson? Harris? Heath Jones Plowman? Purnell?
1930	Benson? Harris Heath Jones? Plowman? Purnell? Tobin
1931	Benson? Heath Jones? Plowman? Purnell? Tobin?

Note: These are all the traceable cameramen, regular employees and freelance, who worked with some frequency for *Topical Budget* in the above years. Where a question mark is given, it is likely that they did work then, but there is no paper evidence to confirm this. Names for years such as 1915 and 1916 are clearly missing. Figures for the years 1917 to 1923 are certain as records survive, but the 1917–18 period is unusual because of the number of Official cameramen, and not all of the men given as working during the early 1920s did so at the same time. Names for the final years are probable, but it is unlikely that there were many cameramen working for Topical by the time of its demise.

Bool, Walter Evan Davies, Jack Wiggins and George Woods-Taylor, all Topical Film Company employees at one time or other. Never a true trade union, but still a precursor of the ACT and the ACTT, the Kine Cameramen's Society soon grew to include virtually every newsreel and studio cameraman either working or hoping for work. At its first annual dinner in November 1919 nearly sixty attended.[43] The purposes of the Society's weekly meetings were partly social, partly educative, and 'tended to uplift the status of the cameraman generally'. Virtually every cameraman who ever worked for Topical was a member. The Society folded in 1928 when the bank holding their funds collapsed.

Whatever glamour a cameraman might boast, to the company they were merely employees with a part to play in the chain of activity

Cartoons of *Topical Budget* cameramen in 1918 drawn by Walter Evan Davies for the *Kinematograph and Lantern Weekly*. Clockwise from top left: John 'Bunny' Hutchins, George Woods-Taylor, Frank Danvers Yates and Davies himself.

involved in producing the newsreel. Topical's attitude towards the cameramen may be seen from the comments made at one directors' meeting about their supposed negligence:

> The Board accepted Mr Jeapes' report and the recommendations it contained, and gave instructions for the work to be carried out forthwith. It was suggested and the Board agreed, that that part of the report which dealt with the neglect of the camera men, should be specifically put to those men from the Board. Capt Holt-White was instructed to do this . . . It was also decided that no camera man was to be allowed to tamper with his camera etc. and that in the event of anything going wrong, it was to be handed to Mr Jeapes immediately for him to deal with.[44]

Topical gave little mention in the newsreel of a cameraman having been responsible for it, save for occasional references to 'our intrepid operator', and still less made them the subject of an item in the American manner. Two exceptions are an item on an outing of the Kine Cameramen's Society and one in which Topical's cameramen are featured climbing the radio mast at Daventry.[45] Topical's review of the year for 1923, PEEPS AT THE PAST, features a live-action cameraman turning the handle of his camera on each of the intertitles.[46]

Pay for a regular cameraman could vary quite widely. Ken Gordon wrote that around 1910 darkroom staff were paid 30/- a week (most cameramen doubled as darkroom staff at this period), and in 1912 a cameraman could expect from 35/- to £3, which later fell to £2.[47] When the first Official cameramen were sent out to the Western Front in 1916 they were considered well-paid at £1 a day.[48] By February 1919 the Kine Cameramen's Society was recommending a minimum £5 10s weekly wage, but reported that some cameramen were getting as little as £2 10s.[49] In May 1919 they quoted £3 10s as the least some cameramen were getting, adding that, 'bricklayers and carmen get far higher wages – and belong to trade unions'.[50] Cameraman Paul Wyand wrote that he got £4 a week on joining American Pathé's British branch in 1927, £5 a week when he moved to Fox's British branch in 1928, £9 a week when he joined *Pathé Gazette* in 1929, and £10, rising to £14 after six months, when he joined *British Movietone News* the same year.[51] Hence wages were unregulated and subject to large variations. For comparison, an average cameraman in the British feature film industry could expect £15 a week, a top class cameraman £50.[52] For further comparison, agreements with the National Union of Journalists for this period had fixed the pay of a qualified newspaper reporter or sub-editor with three years' experience at a minimum of nine guineas a week, an ordinary journalist or reporter of equal experience a minimum of six guineas a week, and provincial journalists aged twenty-four and with three years' experience could expect anything from £4 7s 6d to £5 15s a week depending on the circulation of the newspaper.[53]

There is less information about pay for other staff. Topical's news editor before Charles Heath, Patrick McCabe, revealed in a court case against his former employers Pathé that as news editor he had been paid £7 a week on joining them, rising to £9 by the time he left them in November 1917.[54] Women laboratory staff (cutters, repairers and so on) earned around £3 to £3 10s.[55] When Topical took on a 'circulation manager' in December 1924 to improve sales, a Mr Dudman, he was paid £8 a week, to rise to £10 once the net revenue had reached £1,000, with an increase or decrease of £1 for every rise or fall of £50 thereafter.[56] In 1921 William Jeapes was earning £600 per half year plus commission.[57] When he left Topical in May 1925, his replacement as 'general manager', Clemence Winterman, started on £15 a week, plus 5 per cent commission 'of printing profits'.[58]

Cameramen were adequately if not well-paid, but most found claims for expenses a handy additional income. Expenses for a normal story were counted in shillings, but a story away from London meant hotel and travel bills. On the rare occasions that a cameraman was sent abroad for a story, the expenses could rise to £30 or more, and he might be expected to film a number of possible further items prior to his return. The highest single example of expenses, £111 10s 1d for Wilson when he filmed the funeral of the ex-Kaiserin Auguste Victoria in Germany in April 1921, was all the more extraordinary since he was back that same week to be part of the team filming the FA Cup Final. More usual was his trip to Switzerland in January 1921, when he filmed a number of items at St Moritz; returned via the Riviera, filming at Monte Carlo and Nice; and came back to Britain in February only to be sent out again to cover the British army in occupation in Dusseldorf, filming a carnival in Paris on his way there.

For the more run-of-the-mill stories at home, astute claims for expenses and ruses such as this described by Pathé and Movietone cameraman Paul Wyand were a common part of a cameraman's life:

Since cameramen in those days depended upon their expense accounts for the luxuries of life, there was great consternation when [Topical Budget], anxious to effect economies, instructed its staff: 'No more travelling by taxi. Go by tube.' There is, of course, a law forbidding the transport of inflammable film by Underground, so a Topical Budget cameraman promptly lugged his gear to Piccadilly and said to the ticket collector: 'Give me your name and number.'

'What the devil for?' asked the man.

'You're permitting me to break the law. I have inflammable film here, and it's not allowed to be transported by tube.' When the ticket collector hesitated the cameraman persisted: 'Either give me your name and number or throw me out.'

The ticket collector willingly acceded to this last request, and the

cameraman returned triumphant to his office. The order was res-
cinded, and thereafter (although there may have been cases of men
travelling by Underground and charging for taxis) no one was
specifically instructed to use this plebeian form of transport.[59]

Cameramen were generally treated with indifference. Such a charge
applies to the *Topical Budget* management, who were for the most part
newspaper or film distribution men. The only director of Topical to
have worked within the newsreel industry, or to have had any experience of camerawork, was William Jeapes, and he was notably more
sympathetic towards the cameramen. But they were there to fulfil their
part in the production of the newsreel. The news editor decided how
long an item was going to be, and then instructed the cameramen to
take just so much footage. If more than one cameraman was assigned
to a story, each had his specific instructions for covering a particular
aspect of the story. Within these limitations, the cameramen were free
to decide how they would go about the filming. Tight control was
exerted over the amount of footage shot. Average figures are difficult
to calculate, as the situation varied widely for different stories, but a
single cameraman aiming to shoot 40 feet of material for a regular story
might take 150 feet all told, and a ratio of 1:3 to 1:4 seems common.
Sporting events naturally led to greater wastage. With a major event like
the 1923 Cup Final, 2,411 feet were shot by eight cameramen, 243 feet
ending up in the newsreel.

The great fears were mechanical failure and the weather. Topical's
issue books contain many stories that were never filmed due to camera
breakdown, pictures out of focus, the film jamming and so on. The
weather was a still greater worry, and newsreel editors dreaded the
winter months. A London before the Clean Air Act was misery to
cameramen with slow film stock and only natural light on which to
depend. A number of opening intertitles for *Topical Budget* mention the
poor weather by way of an apology for the gloomy pictures that follow.
Artificial lighting was used on occasion, but arc lights had to be hired,
and the trouble and expense prevented their use for all but special
events (such as election night in Trafalgar Square). Topical referred to
their few items filmed at night as being lit with 'potted sunshine'. The
limitations of film stock, cameras and lighting meant that newsreel
stories of the period were almost invariably shot out of doors. It was
fair weather news, and the climate was as important a factor in the
selection of news stories as any news editor.

Roughly speaking, a cameraman went on three or four assignments
per week, half of them teamed with other cameramen. This was in
contrast to the war period, when only major social or sporting events
would be covered by more than one man. Their cameras were mostly
hand-cranked, and there were special lightweight models for newsreel
work. The accepted running speed for silent filming was sixteen frames

Fred Wilson filming comedian Alfred Lester in Switzerland, for issue number 492–2 (*'I've Got a Motter'*, 31 January 1921).

per second, and the normal turning speed for the handle two turns per second, exposing one foot of film. An experienced cameraman could naturally keep to this speed. Among the popular makes of camera in use by the newsreel companies were the Pathé, Moy, Bell & Howell, Vinten and Williamson. An unusual design was the Akeley, with its circular body and unique tilting facility, allowing the eyepiece to remain level while the camera could be tilted for 270 degrees. This proved very useful for filming aeroplanes taking off, or processions passing below a high camera position. One of the most popular and reliable makes was the Debrie, which Ken Gordon suggested was introduced into the country by *Topical Budget*.[60] Certainly it was a favourite of the Jeapes brothers, and choice of camera was largely a matter of individual taste. Few cameramen attached to a newsreel owned their cameras, however, which were usually the property of the company. Freelance cameramen were of course obliged to use their own cameras.

There were some automatic cameras in the silent era, including the extraordinary Aeroscope, which was driven by compressed air and charged by a foot pump. Although temperamental, its portability proved popular in the war, where Geoffrey Malins in particular made much use of it, and it stayed in regular use into the 1920s. The first electrically driven camera in common use by the newsreels was the Newman of 1922. There was also the clockwork-driven Debrie Sept, a tiny camera invaluable to 'pirating' cameramen wishing to snatch illicit footage.

The film they used was 35mm nitrate stock, employed by the film industry until the 1950s, and highly inflammable. A nitrate fire was a real and constant danger, and indeed a small fire broke out at the Topical Film Company's premises in June 1920, and a serious one in October 1924. Film processing took place in the laboratories at 76–78 Wardour Street. There were fifteen or more 'editorial staff': joiners, negative cutters, repairers (all posts usually taken by women) and graders, under the supervision of Jack Wiggins, who was responsible to William Jeapes. The film, once delivered by the cameraman, was wound on wooden or pin frames, developed, rinsed, washed, dried, printed, the titles added, the negative rejoined, then the exposed positive developed and treated by the same process. If colour tinting was required, the film would be dipped into a bath of dye before drying. Such was the hurry in which a newsreel was produced that it was quite common for the news editor to have the negative screened before selecting the sections required and writing the titles. The hurry, and the large number of prints required in that short time, led William Jeapes to invent an automatic developing plant after the First World War, which permitted the production of multiple copies from the one negative. It was a matter of some pride for Topical that they were the first newsreel to employ such printing machines.

On an assignment a cameraman would take with him his camera, a tripod, the film magazine, a take-up magazine, the camera handle and tripod handle, and also maybe an exposure meter and an extra lens. Cameras had twin magazines, either on the outside or inside of the body, which held on average 400 feet of film. For a hectic event such as a Cup Final, with several cameramen sending in multiple dispatches of film, the cameraman might put his name and the time of the shot on a board; he would then film this, in the manner of a present-day clapperboard, before taking film of the action. A cameraman had to be dexterous: there was a handle for filming, a handle for panning the camera left or right, and a third for tilting it up or down. A cameraman was a man of many talents, having to be diplomat, journalist, photographer, technician and artist, and not merely display bravado and nerve. It was the cameraman who saw the news story in film terms, and although increasingly imaginative editing had done much to improve *Topical Budget*, the creative figure was the cameraman, the artist behind the art of the newsreel.

Exclusive Rights

Much of what the newsreels covered was dispiritingly routine. No newsreel cameraman reminiscing about the past has ever given much mention to what must have been the deadly round of cattle shows, dog shows, baby shows, unveilings, launchings and parades. What lifted them out of the rut, set their pulses running, and saw them at their most competitive and inventive, were the big stories, and with them the opportunities offered both by the tradition of exclusive rights and the consequent practice of 'pirating'.

The idea of a newsfilm company being able to purchase the exclusive rights to an event had begun in the earliest years of the industry, when Barker, Jeapes and Urban fought first to buy up the rights, then to ensure that their rivals respected these. They never did – equal vigour was put into securing pictures despite the ban and the watchful eye of the rights-holder. Harsh words were exchanged, even blows, and the film trade decided it wisest to organise ballots for major sporting occasions, with winning companies being awarded the shared rights.

With war restrictions and all big events such as the Derby and the FA Cup shelved until after 1918, such contests were forgotten; with the coming of peace, the three newsreel companies still in existence went into the attack all the more vigorously. If the 1920s were recalled as a golden age for newsreel cameramen, it was largely because of 'pirating'. The one company having purchased the rights to an event, the others showed remarkable ingenuity and determination in securing their own footage. Despite regular threats of legal proceedings in advertisements and newsreel intertitles, no such action was ever taken. Outwardly hostile, the newsreel companies implicitly acknowledged both the fun of the competition and the indication it gave of the healthy state of the industry.

For Topical, with their weaker market position and smaller profile, it became a demonstration of their strength as a newsreel that they were able to purchase the exclusive rights to events and to produce impressive results. It was not necessarily a more profitable course, since such absurd sums of money were involved (Topical paid almost £1,000 to film the 1923 FA Cup Final), that even if the number of copies printed was more than doubled Topical would make less than for a standard issue. Indeed they often advertised their exclusive pictures of major sporting events free for any exhibitor who became a regular subscriber. During the Hulton period, Topical came to be characterised by their enthusiasm for exclusive coverage and special events, and part of their comparatively dull state during the latter half of the decade is due to a marked drop in such activities (though, notably, with a marked increase in overall sales).

Thus they purchased the rights to the FA Cup Finals in 1921, 1922 and 1923, plus the British Empire Exhibition in 1924, though they appear to have been less lucky with major horse-races. However there were comparatively few events for which the rights could be bought, or indeed were worth buying, and tales of cameramen forever snatching pirated footage from rights-holders must be tempered with the knowledge that such escapades were infrequent. The FA Cup, Test matches, the Derby and the Grand National were the regulars, and though major royal events were naturally excluded, large sums of money still had to be paid for camera pitches. But beyond these standard newsreel stories, Topical sought the unusual or striking exclusive. Two strands characterise *Topical Budget* in the 1920s: the ordinary routine of most newsreel stories, light-heartedly but skilfully presented, and a remarkable sequence of major single stories and story-series following that greatest exclusive of all, the First World War. Thus in 1919 they had a cameraman inside the Hall of Mirrors for the signing of the Treaty at the Versailles Peace Conference and also a cameraman accompanying the British Expeditionary Force in North Russia. In 1920 they covered the Prince of Wales' Empire tour and in 1921 the Duke of Connaught's tour to India. Three years in succession they got exclusive coverage (of varying kinds) of visiting film stars to Britain: Douglas Fairbanks and Mary Pickford in 1920, Charlie Chaplin in 1921, the Talmadge sisters in 1922. These were the stories in which Topical took greatest pride, and they are seen at their best when being at their boldest.

The converse of exploiting an exclusive was pirating. Horse-races were harder to pirate, or 'pinch', than football matches, as 'Bunny' Hutchins points out:

> Of all the big races the Grand National Steeplechase is easily my favourite, especially as . . . the exclusive rights were always granted to one firm, and naturally the other newsreels wouldn't stand for that, so they had to 'pinch' it, and I was generally on the 'pinching' side. All sorts of schemes and manouevres were resorted to by both sides to outwit each other, and disguises of all sorts were assumed. It was all good fun but perhaps a bit nerve-racking as the time of the race drew near, because it was only necessary to be put out of action for a few seconds as the horses passed your section for all your labours to be in vain. But I was never caught at Aintree and always got away with it. 'Pinching' a Football Cup Final at Wembley is easy in comparison, because, if you get rumbled, your camera is merely kept under lock and key until the match is over. You consequently walk out of the ground looking very downhearted, proceed to an appointed place and pick up another camera and ticket, held in reserve for such an emergency, and in you go again![61]

Topical made something of a speciality of their coverage of regular horse-races. Harold Jeapes had been a teenage jockey before becoming a cameraman, and Sir Edward Hulton owned a number of racehorses. But they usually found themselves pirating the Derby or the National. The issue book entry for issue 604–2 (release date 26 March 1923) tells eloquently the story of Topical's efforts to pirate the 1923 Grand National. A remarkable sixteen cameramen were used, the high number essential because it was expected that several would be unable to secure any pictures or would be caught. There were Topical's four regular cameramen at the time, Hutchins, Taylor, Yates and Purnell, along with news editor Heath; some of the usual freelance men, Bloomfield, Taylor, Woods-Taylor, Gardner, Jones, Bool and Redknapp; two new names, Matthewson and Hawkins and the mysteriously named 'A. Stranger' and 'B. Stranger'. Of the 879 feet shot, Hawkins took the most with 250 feet, only to have it confiscated by the police; Purnell shot the next largest amount with 133 feet; the Strangers shot only 16 and 28 feet each; and Woods-Taylor, Bool, Redknapp and Gardner were all unable to obtain any picture. Thus only eleven cameramen's work was actually used, 186 feet eventually being used in the newsreel (excluding titles).

Almost 10 per cent of all *Topical Budget* items were horse-races. Today they appear to be among the dullest newsreel stories because of the advances in televisual presentation, and the ground-level positions chosen for the cameras now seem to give a rather unsatisfactory impression of the action. Paradoxically, some of the shots in pirated versions, where the cameramen were at a distance and therefore obliged to position themselves higher up, now appear the more effective. But horse-racing was of great importance to Topical and to the silent newsreel as a whole. What is often held to be the first ever newsfilm was a horse-race, Paul's short film of the 1896 Derby, which, by being screened the following night, qualifies as the first attempt to film a current story and present it while it was still news.[62] By 1898 Biograph were able to screen the Derby on the same day,[63] and William Jeapes always claimed that he was the first to film the Grand National and screen it the same day, in 1903. The very first issue of *Topical Budget* included the Ebor Handicap. The 1913 Derby was notable for two events, both of which Topical filmed. First was the suffragette Emily Davison throwing herself in front of the King's horse 'Anmer', albeit only caught in long shot.[64] Second was the 'bumping' that went on between the leading horses, leading to the disqualification of the first horse home, 'Craganour'. Newsreel release patterns at this time meant that the Derby fell on what was a release date for Topical but not for the other newsreels. They were therefore obliged to produce their film that night (it was in fact usual for a newsreel to issue a rough cut to some cinemas on the evening of such an event, then to produce a tidied-up version for subsequent release). Owing to the unavoidable hurry, Topical had the wrong horse in triumphant close-up at the end of the film. However, theirs were the only cameras, still or cinematograph, to capture the 'bumping', and frame stills from *Topical Budget* appeared in the evening papers as proof of the illegality.

It could be a hazardous task for a cameraman to secure any shot more exciting than the usual routine panning with the horses as they rode past, as Hutchins recalls:

I had one narrow escape at Epsom some years ago. I was instructed to get what we call a 'ground shot'. I found a spot just above Tattenham Corner and lay down full length with my hand-cranked camera on the ground just outside the rails. As the horses thundered by I felt something whizz past my head. My assistant told me afterwards it was a horse's hoof. I took measurements and found the nearest hoofmark was exactly 18 inches from my camera! My picture was O.K., but I have never repeated the experiment. Nowadays such shots are obtained by automatic cameras.[65]

Pinching a picture meant eluding the efforts of the rights-holder. The police were under instructions to confiscate the film or camera of any cameraman without a permit, and the company's own minders might be used to hustle them away. Failing that, smoke bombs might be let off, mirrors shone into the pirates' lenses, or banners advertising the name of the rights-holders waved in front of the expected camera position of the pirates. Ken Gordon alleged that on one occasion when Topical were pirating a race and filmed Pathé's banners, they merely scratched them out on the negative, and ugly scratch marks were clearly visible on the release print.[66] Great effort was put in by both sides, and it is a sign of Topical's weakening status as a newsreel that for both the 1924 and 1925 Grand Nationals they were obliged, or found it preferable, to buy a negative from Pathé.

For three years in succession, as noted above, Topical secured the exclusive rights to the FA Cup Final, and in the first of those years in particular, 1921, fully demonstrated the advantages of the privilege. From 1920 to 1922 the Cup Final was held at the Stamford Bridge ground, considered at the time an unsuitable venue, which resulted in some dull matches with disappointing crowds. The best of them, and the best attended, was 1921, when Tottenham Hotspur beat Wolverhampton Wanderers 1–0. Topical's coverage of this game is outstanding, one of the finest newsfilms of the silent era.

They used nine cameramen: these were their four regular cameramen at the time, 'Bunny' Hutchins, 'Taxi' Purnell, Fred Wilson and news editor Charles Heath, plus the freelance men John Parry, Edward Tassie, former Official cameramen Walter Evan Davies and Oscar Bovill, and Bill Arch. What is striking about the film is its imaginative use of camera positions. Ordinary football matches were covered by only one or two cameramen for the usual one-minute long item. Such coverage could only give a brief impression of the match, and notoriously seldom included a goal being scored. Film stock was expensive, cameras held only so much film, and overall it was impossible for them to cover a match in the manner of television today. But Topical's 1921 Final shows them in remarkable control of their subject, manipulating it towards their own ends.

The film begins with the main title superimposed (a sophisticated touch) over action from the game, followed by a title to remind everyone that this is the only coverage worth watching. The following description gives each sequence, with camera location, action and length of shot. 'Main shot' refers to the key camera position behind each goal, which gives an angled view down from the right. Not all of the game is shown in sequence, as is made clear.

1. [Titles] CUP FINAL 1921 GREATEST EVENT IN FOOTBALL HISTORY. (6)
2. [Titles] 'The Topical Budget presents Exclusively the pictures of the great match taken on the Stamford Bridge ground.' (15)
3. [Titles] 'Any other films shown are without the consent of the F.A. Authorities.' (21)
4. [Titles] 'Topical Budget. Greatest Cup Final. Tottenham Hotspur defeat Wolverhampton Wanderers by 1 goal to nil.' (28)
5. [Titles] 'All roads led to Stamford Bridge.' (32)
6. People crowding onto a train. (37)
7. View down at crowds walking down street filmed from vehicle moving towards them. (46)
8. View down outside stadium as crowds enter through the gates. (51)
9. Section of the crowd seated on the ground at the edge of the pitch. (58)
10. Close-up of enthusiastic Tottenham Hotspur fan. (64)
11. [Titles] 'When his Majesty arrived unexpectedly the vast throng sang "God Save The King".' (72)
12. Car arrives outside the stadium (King just visible). (78)
13. Shot from position within the crowd of people cheering and waving hats. (84)
14. [Titles] '"Wolves" Take the Field.' (87)
15. Wolverhampton Wanderers team filmed face-on coming out of the tunnel. All go past the camera followed by the referee and linesmen. (102)
16. [Titles] '"Spurs" Take the Field.' (105)
17. Tottenham Hotspur team all come out and pass by the camera. (114)
18. [Titles] 'The teams were presented while the King stood in the pelting rain.' (119)
19. Medium shot from edge of pitch of the King shaking hands with the players in driving rain. (125)
20. Close shot at the centre of the pitch of the toss and the two captains shaking hands. (133)
21. [Titles] 'A terrific storm marred the first portion of the play.' (138)
22. Main shot behind Spurs goal of play in the rain [First half]. (143)
23. [Titles] 'It was practically impossible for the players to keep their feet.' (149)
24. Ground-level shot from centre pitch, looking towards Wolves goal, of players falling over in mud [First half]. (153)
25. [Titles] 'The Australian cricketers watch the game.' (157)
26. Close-up of the touring Australian cricketers, with jump-cut [Second half]. (164)
27. Panning shot from main position going right to left of stadium, behind Wolves goal [Second half]. (190)
28. Main shot behind Wolves goal of Spurs attack, with keeper saving and a foul in goal-mouth [First half]. (199)
29. Ground-level close shot from left-hand side of Spurs goal as keeper saves [Second half]. (204)

30. Main shot behind Wolves goal as Spurs attack is cleared [Second half]. (214)
31. Medium shot of King watching game [Second half]. (219)
32. Closer shot of the King [Second half]. (223)
33. [Titles] 'Half Time – "Spurs" 0. "Wolves" 0.' (228)
34. Main shot behind Wolves goal as they clear an attack [Second half]. (236)
35. Main shot behind Wolves goal of Spurs attack [Second half]. (238)
36. [Titles] '"Wolves" Goal In Peril!' (241)
37. Main shot behind Wolves goal of Spurs attack, Wolves keeper saves and clears [Second half]. (248)
38. Main shot behind Spurs goal as Wolves attack [Second half]. (260)
39. Main shot (slightly closer) of Spurs attack [Second half]. (266)
40. Main shot of section of the crowd [Second half?]. (269)
41. Main shot behind Wolves goal as Spurs attack is cleared [Second half]. (276)
42. Ground-level medium shot directly behind Wolves goal as keeper clears [Second half]. (280)
43. Ground-level close shot to right of Spurs goal as keeper clears [First half]. (282)
44. Main shot behind Spurs goal of Wolves attack, with brief jump-cut [Second half]. (296)
45. Ground-level medium shot to right of Wolves goal as keeper and a defender clear, with appeals for a foul [Second half]. (301)

Tottenham Hotspur on the attack in the 1921 FA Cup Final. From *Cup Final 1921 Greatest Event in Football History.*

46. [Titles] 'Dimmock – outside left – scored for the Spurs five minutes after the interval.' (308)
47. Main shot behind Wolves goal panning to goal-mouth as Dimmock approaches and scores. Keeper picks ball out of net [Second half]. (321)
48. [Titles] 'Goal!!' (322)
49. Close shot face-on of people cheering [Second half]. (326)
50. Ground-level medium shot from behind Wolves goal of ball going in and keeper picking it up [Second half]. (335)
51. Main panning shot of cheering crowds behind Spurs goal [Second half]. (340)
52. Identical shot of cheering crowds behind Wolves goal [Second half]. (348)
53. Ground-level medium shot to left of Wolves goal as they clear a Spurs attack [First half]. (352)
54. Identical position as Wolves clear attack [Second half]. (358)
55. Main shot behind Spurs goal of Wolves attack cleared [Second half]. (369)
56. Ground-level medium shot to right of Wolves goal as shot goes over the bar [Second half]. (372)
57. Medium shot as King drops his stick and a neighbour picks it up [Second half?]. (383)
58. Closer shot from main position behind Wolves goal of Spurs attack [Second half]. (390)
59. Panning shot from left to right from main position behind Spurs goal on action in middle of pitch [Second half]. (412)
60. Ground-level medium shot to left of Wolves goal as Spurs attack is cleared [First half]. (419)
61. [Titles] '"Wolves" constantly hard-pressed.' (422)
62. Ground-level medium shot to left of Wolves goal. Keeper saves and foul in goal-mouth [First half – same action as shot 28]. (435)
63. Jump-cut from previous shot to corner taken and defender heading the ball away [First half]. (440)
64. [Titles] 'Cleared!' (441)
65. Ground-level medium shot to left of Wolves goal of action in goal-mouth as a cross goes over [First half]. (445)
66. [Titles] 'There was a tremendous rush to see the King present the cup.' (450)
67. Main shot behind Wolves goal as crowds rush over the pitch towards the main stand. (469)
68. Panning shot from left to right from main position behind Spurs goal of crowd movement. (476)
69. Medium shot of King presenting cup to Spurs captain, obscured by policeman's head. Jump-cut after policeman has been asked to move out of the way. (492)
70. Jump-cut to Wolves team receiving losers' medals. (502)
71. Jump-cut to King and officials leading the crowd in giving three cheers. (505)[67]

The film is all the more exceptional when one realises that it was almost without precedent. Filming of pre-war Cup Finals was done with four cameramen at the most, usually positioned at ground level, and surviv-

103

ing examples scarcely serve as adequate records of the games. Topical are known to have filmed the Cup Final in 1913 and 1915. There were no further finals until after the war, and for the 1920 match, between Aston Villa and Huddersfield at Stamford Bridge, Gaumont secured the rights, using around six cameramen to produce a reasonable record of a quite uninteresting game. Topical made no attempt to pirate footage, instead offering exclusive coverage of a Georges Carpentier boxing match. Ordinary football games were not covered with as great a frequency as later in the decade, so Topical were working largely without prior example or experience when they covered the 1921 Final.

The success of Topical's coverage, and its innovation, are the key shots taken from positions behind each goal and offering an angled view on the action. Cameramen can be seen on the film in various positions around the pitch for closer shots, but the editor always goes back to these main positions. The use of such angles is not only attractive but imparts a sense of momentum, involving the audience in the game. Then there is the remarkable instance of two cameramen actually capturing film of the goal! The main shot of this follows Dimmock as he approaches the goal and scores; the second, from a position behind the net, only just gets the shot as the ball goes in, but it may nevertheless count as the first ever action replay.

What is also striking about the film is its apparent dishonesty. Of the nine shots depicting action in the first half, six are actually from the second, and of the twenty-seven shots depicting action in the second half, six are taken from the first. One goal-mouth foul from the first half is seen in long shot in the film's first half, then in medium shot from a different angle in the film's second half. The distinctive layout of the Stamford Bridge stadium and the atrocious weather in the first half make such identification easy; why Topical acted in this way is harder to work out. If it were simply because the weather ruined most of the first-half footage, then why include scenes from that half in footage of the second? Were audiences fooled? Are Topical admitting to an impressionistic picture of the game rather than an exact record by showing so much footage between the start of the second half and the goal, which they acknowledge took place only five minutes later? Confusion caused by a large number of reels of film coming in, and the need for rapid production no doubt contributed, but the notion of an impression of the game seems the best answer. The film shows Tottenham Hotspur dominant and Wolverhampton Wanderers on the defensive. It is satisfying as film narrative. The newsreels were accustomed to reporting sporting events (other than horse-races) in a small number of shots, which in no way could count as a full record of the game. Topical's film is an expansion of that idea, as honest an account in their terms as any television final today.

The other companies' pirated records of the game show the value of purchasing the exclusive rights. Half of *Gaumont Graphic*'s coverage is devoted to scenes outside the game, with crowds entering the stadium, and individual close-ups of all the players and the referee taken before the day of the Final. Fleeting shots of players coming onto the pitch are from other matches. Their shots of the Final are lamentable, snatched from between a jostling crowd's heads and shoulders. Pirated film was often of greater interest as bar tales between cameramen than as a record of the event.

Topical's film of the 1922 Final,[68] also at Stamford Bridge, does not survive, but the match has a reputation as one of the dullest finals ever played. Huddersfield Town beat Preston North End 1–0. The *Bioscope*'s account of Topical's coverage is moderate in its enthusiasm:

> A remarkable record of the much-discussed Preston foul which won the day for Huddersfield is contained in the Cup Final edition of the 'Topical Budget', which acquired exclusive rights of this event. The essential features of the whole match, very cleverly put together to form a continuous 'story', are represented in the film, which was mainly taken from a standpoint immediately behind the goal posts. In addition to these vivid scenes of the actual game, there are good pictures of the vast crowds of spectators at Stamford Bridge, and of the presentation of the Cup by the Duke of York, accompanied by Prince Henry. The photographic quality is remarkably fine.[69]

The reference to 'a continuous story' interestingly suggests both that Topical now saw the game in terms of narrative, and that this was apparent to the spectator. Clearly they had learned from the previous year's experience, but camera positions directly behind the goal would not have been as effective. However, all the action on the day took place off the pitch. A *Daily Mirror* news photographer later described the day:

> The Cup Final of 1922, the last of these matches to be played at Stamford Bridge, was made memorable by an extraordinary 'war' between rival cinema organizations, one of whom had paid a large sum for the exclusive rights to film the match.
>
> I saw the battle from the top floor of a high building overlooking the ground, from where I had hoped to obtain some photographs with a long-focus camera, but as I was sharing the position with the well-known film man, Frank Bassill, on this occasion a 'pirate', I was handicapped by the efforts of the defenders.
>
> They used heliographs to deflect the sun's rays into our lenses and let up a huge sausage balloon in front of our window, where they did their best to anchor it. This was only partly successful, however, for the clumsy thing swung about in the wind and left us clear at times. Also one of Bassill's assistants managed to hide behind some chimney pots and work above it.

At the sound of the referee's whistle starting the match there came a terrific noise of hammering and crashing at a point away to our left, and we saw the corrugated-iron roof of a building alongside the ground fly off in all directions.

A moment later there appeared, rising through the aperture, two heads which I recognised through my glasses as those of Tommy Scales and Leslie Wyand, pioneers in the production of movie news reels.

Steadily they rose higher and higher, turning their handles as they came, as the telescopic tower ladder upon which they stood was wound up by friends in the room below.

This happening brought into action the defenders' large mobile 'stand by' force, members of which, armed with double-poled banners and flags, dashed off to meet the new attack. They soon blotted out Scales and Wyand, but the matter did not end with them.

Inside the ground there were a number of pirates who had escaped the gate watchers, the most notable being Jack Cotter, who had got in disguised as a half-witted football fan.

He had arrived in a charabanc wearing a large false moustache and a flaring suit of the colours of one of the teams. Over his shoulder he carried a huge mallet, also 'done' in club colours, a vicious-looking weapon in the head of which was concealed his camera.

In the end the attackers got a very presentable film, and the incident did much to prove that it was not profitable to pay big money for exclusive rights of such events. If the invaders are really determined they nearly always win.[70]

Scales, Cotter and Bassill were all filming for *Pathé Gazette*, Wyand for American Pathé. Only Wyand had not worked with Topical previously: Bassill had been an Official cameraman; Scales worked for the WOCC as an Official cameraman to the New Zealand forces (though nothing of what he took appeared in the *War Office Official Topical Budget*); and Cotter had worked for Topical between 1919 and 1921. In virtually all anecdotes of pirating in the 1920s, Topical and Pathé are the great rivals, the efficient but uninteresting Gaumont scarcely being mentioned. The description of Cotter in the above account may have been confused with his guise the following year, which is when he dressed up as a West Ham United fan, complete with giant hammer with camera concealed inside. Pathé then filmed him as part of their coverage of that game, but contrary to some claims, Topical did not do so as well out of ignorance. The picture of Cotter turning the handle of his hidden camera is the most familiar image of the pirating cameraman.

The defensive actions described, such as balloons, flashing lights and banners, were all common, as were such responses as scaling ladders and trees. What are not described are the heavy tactics also employed, which led to the event being labelled by the press as 'The Battle of Stamford Bridge'. Whether it was the cameramen themselves, or just 'minders' hired by Topical is unclear, but certainly blows were exchanged and pirated film snatched. 'A good scrap ensued with several casualties, but with honours even', recalled Jock Gemmell, formerly with Topical but at this time working for Pathé.[71]

To avoid the attention of the minders, pirating cameramen were often accompanied by wives or girlfriends.[72] First the cameraman would 'snatch' his film. Since cameras, even the lighter newsreel models, were bulky objects and hard to disguise, the clockwork-driven Debrie Sept, though it took only 17 feet of film, became popular, as it could easily be hidden in a coat pocket. Pathé's Paul Wyand recalled:

> These snatches were often worked with a woman accomplice. An outsize handbag or sandwich basket made an ideal hiding-place for a camera or cans of film, and since we always passed each roll of film to the accomplice as it was used, only the film actually in the camera would be confiscated if we were caught, and the accomplice could slip away and rush the other spools to the laboratories.[73]

If film was confiscated, or if the cameramen were led out of the ground, it was traditional for the rights-holders to treat the captured pirates to a drink afterwards, so that the whole exercise became a curious mixture of fierce rivalry and jovial fellowship.

With film cans carefully labelled, dispatch riders hurtled through the streets of London, riding along pavements until this particular practice had to be banned. All the newsreel companies were based in Wardour Street, and everyone there stood on the pavements or leaned out of the windows, anxiously waiting to see who would be the first to arrive. Lookouts were posted on the roof, and if Pathé were first back with film they hoisted a flag with their symbol, a cockerel. If Topical beat them to it, they announced the fact by hoisting a dead chicken![74] The competition was, of course, to get the results processed and onto the screens as fast as possible, and the newsreels were immensely proud of their achievements in this vein. Although *Topical Budget* was released regularly every Monday and Thursday, it was a point of honour to have the coverage of a football final, horse-race, the Boat Race or a royal wedding on the cinema screens that evening, and as far afield as possible. It was possible to have a few copies ready for distribution within two hours of the last piece of film coming in. A re-edited version would then form part of the usual issue. For the production of regular release prints for an event such as the 1922 Cup Final, laboratory staff would work non-stop from Saturday evening until Monday afternoon, producing up to 500 prints (nearly three times their usual figure) for nationwide distribution.[75]

In 1923, the FA Cup Final was played for the first time at a far more suitable venue, the new Wembley stadium. Once again Topical secured the rights to the game, though the price of nearly £1,000 caused some concern within the film trade. Topical's advertising showed them in confident mood:

> In spite of film Pirates' boasts, this will be exclusive to the 'Topical Budget', and the exclusive rights will be maintained to the utmost limits of the law. Do not put on a film which the Courts might compel you to withdraw. Can the Pirates guarantee to give you this game from start to finish on release date? Of course they can't. We can![76]

The Final itself was to prove a newsworthy story, if not quite in the manner that Topical would have wished. Events on 28 April 1923 are well known. As many as 200,000 people attempted to fill 126,000 places. Crowds clambered over barriers, filled the stadium literally to the point of overflowing, and spilled on to the pitch. It was only thanks to the great patience shown by the crowd, and careful police guidance, including the celebrated policeman on a white horse, PC George Scorey, that the pitch was cleared and the match finally started, forty minutes late. Bolton Wanderers, who were playing West Ham United, won 2–0.

The chaos naturally ruined all of Topical's plans and privileged camera positions. Topical employed eight cameramen: the regulars, Benson, Gardner, Hutchins, Taylor and Yates, and freelancers Bovill, Ford, and Woods-Taylor. It would seem reasonable to expect that they would want to keep to the successful 1921 formula, but the main camera positions were almost directly behind the goals, and the cameramen were presumably in place before the crowd trouble. This is a disappointing rejection of the angled key shots from 1921, or else ignorance of their worth. But it was the positions on the pitch that were lost. Topical made the most of the situation, with some fine footage of the crowds climbing fences and pouring into the stadium, and the fact that they had men on the ground meant good shots of the scene on the pitch, including a close shot of PC Scorey in action. However, the crowds standing around the edge of the pitch prevented any ground-level filming of the play, and all of Topical's coverage of the actual match was filmed from positions in the stands, with results little better than those pirated by Gaumont and Pathé. The latter's plan for the Final included hiring an aeroplane, since Topical would be hard-pressed to block aerial shots. Topical's reply was simple – they had their name written in giant letters on the roof of the stadium. Having hired the plane, Pathé had to make the most of the expense, which they did by ensuring that the only aerial shots in their version gave the letters upside down. Topical's film is a fine record of the event, but not the record of the game they might have wanted. A copy of their film was

From *Pathé Gazette's* pirated footage of the 1923 FA Cup Final, showing the name 'Topical Budget' displayed on the roof of Wembley Stadium.

presented to the West Ham United football club.[77]

There was no coverage by any newsreel of the 1924 Final. As a protest against the increasing fees being demanded by the Football Association, the three newsreel companies put in a joint bid of £400, which was turned down. For once the newsreel companies had decided that it was to everyone's advantage for all three to have access to the major sporting events. The experiment failed, and the temptation of exclusive coverage proved too great. Topical found themselves pirating the 1925 Cup Final and never held the exclusive rights to any Cup Final thereafter.

Film Stars

In September 1921 the world's most popular man, Charlie Chaplin, decided to make a trip to his home country. His arrival at Southampton, then Waterloo, and his subsequent stay in London, saw him greeted by vast crowds and (to use the newsreels' favourite phrase) 'scenes of unparalleled enthusiasm'. He recorded his experiences of the trip in a curious, frank manner in *My Wonderful Visit*.[78] Among other impressions, the book records Chaplin's weary forebearance of the press, with their continual questions – 'Mr Chaplin, why are you going to Europe?', 'What do you do with your old moustaches?' and 'Are you a Bolshevik?', and in particular his battle with one persistent newsreel cameraman. The man's name is not known, but certainly he was filming for *Topical Budget*, who had managed to get the only cameraman on board the Olympic on its journey from New York to Southampton.

Chaplin has been pursued by the press before his departure, and finds that even on board he is not to be left alone:

> The camera man and many of his brothers are aboard. I discover him as I turn around. I did not want to discover anyone just then. I wanted to be alone with sky and water. But I am still Charlie Chaplin. I must be photographed – and am.
>
> We are passing the Statue of Liberty. He asks me to wave and throw kisses, which rather annoys me.
>
> The thing is too obvious. It offends my sense of sincerity.
>
> The Statue of Liberty is thrilling, dramatic, a glorious symbol. I would feel self-conscious and cheap in deliberately waving and throwing kisses at it. I will be myself.
>
> I refuse.[79]

Settling into life on board ship, Chaplin seeks escape from the children with autograph books and the curious crew pointing him out to one another, finding repose in reading and the gymnasium. He describes the first-class passengers as snobs and is happier with the greeting from the ship's firemen and stokers. Seeing a game of baseball being played on deck, he is invited to join in:

> I am invited timidly, then vociferously, to play a game. Their invitation cheers me. I feel one of them. A spirit of adventure beckons. I leap over the rail and right into the midst of it.
>
> I carry with me into the steerage just a bit of self-conciousness – there are so many trying to play upon me. I am looked upon as a celebrity, not a cricket player. Suddenly a motion-picture camera man bobs up from somewhere. What leeches! He snaps a picture. This gets sickening.
>
> One of the crew has hurriedly made himself up as 'Charlie Chaplin'. He causes great excitement. This also impresses me. I find myself acting a part, looking surprised and interested. I am conscious of the fact that this thing has been done many times before. Then on second thought I realise it is all new to them and that they mean well, so I try to enter into the spirit of the thing.[80]

Spotting the first-class passengers watching him perform, he decides to leave, but he encounters further persecution from the curious in a Turkish bath. Later, having dressed for dinner, he goes into the smoking-room:

> I meet the demon camera man. I do not know him, as he is dressed

up like a regular person. We get into conversation. Well, hardly conversation. He talks.

'Listen, Charlie, I am very sorry, but I've been assigned to photograph you on this trip. Now we might as well get to know each other and make it easy for both of us, so the best thing to do is to let's do it fully and get it over with. Now, let's see, I'll take to-morrow and part of the next day. I want to photograph you with the third-class passengers, then the second-class, and have you shown playing games on deck. If you have your make-up and your moustache, hat, shoes, and cane, it will be all the better.'

I call for help. He will have to see my personal representative, Mr. Robinson.

He says, 'I won't take "No" for an answer.'

And I let him know that the only thing he isn't going to do on the trip is to photograph me. I explain that it would be a violation of contract with the First National exhibitors.

'I have been assigned to photograph you and I'm going to photograph you', he says. And then he told me of his other camera conquests, of his various experiences with politicians who did not want to be photographed.

'I had to break through the palace walls to photograph the King of England, but I got him. Also had quite a time with Foch, but I have his face in celluloid now.' And he smiled as he deprecatingly looked up and down my somewhat small and slight figure.

This is the last straw. I defy him to photograph me. From now on I have made up my mind that I am going to lock myself in my cabin – I'll fool him.

But my whole evening is spoiled. I go to bed cursing the motion-picture industry, the makers of film, and those responsible for camera-men. Why did I take the trip? What is it all for? It has gotten beyond me already and it is my trip, my vacation.[81]

The rest of the journey proceeds more smoothly, with Chaplin reading and socialising, and finding himself less of a curiosity. He makes no further mention of cameramen until the last day on board, when the ship is off Cherbourg:

The lighter is coming out. The top deck is black with men. Somebody tells me they are French and British camera men coming to welcome me . . .

. . . Suddenly there is an avalanche. All sorts and conditions of men armed with pads, pencils, motion-picture cameras, still cameras. There is an embarrassing pause. They are looking for Charlie Chaplin. Some have recognised me. I see them searching among our little group. Eventually I am pointed out.

'Why, here he is!'[82]

All the expected questions are asked: 'Why are you going to Europe?', 'What do you do with your old moustaches?', 'Are you a Bolshevik?' He retires, shattered, and spends the night worrying about how he will deal with his arrival in England. In the morning he is greeted by the mayor of Southampton, signs autographs, meets old friends and ponders on the strangeness of returning to England. Taking the train to London, he arrives to an ecstatic reception at Waterloo:

> Immediately I get out of the train, however, we somehow get disorganised and our campaign manœuvre is lost. Policemen take me by each arm. There are motion-picture men, still-camera men. I see a sign announcing that motion pictures of my trip on board ship will be shown that night at a picture theatre. That dogged photographer of the boat must have gotten something in spite of me.[83]

Cameramen continue to pursue him, and crowds to throng round him, on his car journey to the Ritz hotel. One cameraman attempts to film him from a moving car, and he instructs the driver to put down the top. Nearing the Ritz, he is led by policemen through the dense crowd into the hotel. As he escapes, his last sight is of a newsreel cameraman:

Charlie Chaplin performing for the camera on board the Olympic. From *Charlie on the Ocean*.

I can see one intrepid motion-picture camera man at the door as the crowd starts to swarm. He begins to edge in, and starts grinding his camera frantically as he is lifted into the whirlpool of humanity. But he keeps turning, and his camera and himself are gradually turned up to the sky, and his lens is registering nothing but clouds as he goes down turning – the most honourable fall a camera man can have, to go down grinding. I wonder if he really got any pictures.[84]

Chaplin's remarkable tale of press persecution is one of the best accounts there is of a famous figure's relations with the newsreels. But despite his irritation with the cameraman, and declared wish to avoid him, the evidence of Topical's issue-length item on the story would seem to indicate that he was both more patient and co-operative than his account seems to suggest. The veracity of his report is shown by the closeness between what he relates and what Topical filmed:

'CHARLIE' ON THE OCEAN
'Exclusive pictures of the voyage home of the great little man who has spread sunshine and laughter round the whole globe.' Chaplin on deck with the Statue of Liberty in the background. Medium shot looking down at people on deck; Chaplin enters, shaking hands. People lift him onto their shoulders and show him to the camera. 'The only cine operator to accompany the best loved man in the world from New York to Southampton . . . was from the Topical Budget.' Short sequence from Chaplin's film *The Champion* (Chaplin sharing his last sausage with his pet bulldog). Close-up of Chaplin on the boat. 'Au revoir to Mary and Douglas.' Chaplin with Mary Pickford and Douglas Fairbanks. 'Goodbye to New York; only a few years ago "Charlie" landed here a poor and unknown lad.' SS Olympic steams out of New York harbour and Chaplin waves farewell. 'Showing them how to do it.' Face-on view as Chaplin demonstrates his walk and gestures. He directs members of the crew as they attempt to imitate him in turn. He gives another demonstration, gives a tip [?] to one of them, walks off and waves goodbye. 'Keeping fit.' View down at Chaplin pitching and catching a baseball in front of a group of people. Close shot of Chaplin helping a man wearing a bowler hat and moustache in imitation of him. 'Adoration.' Close shot of Chaplin talking to a small boy. Close shot of him signing his autograph for a girl. 'Charlie's Circus.' View down at people playing on deck dressed as animals, including two as an elephant, walking over upturned pails. '"Greets his home-kin at Southampton"'. The SS Olympic approaching Southampton harbour. View from quayside up at Chaplin, who doffs his hat to the camera. Chaplin and others coming down gangplank. 'A terrific welcome at Waterloo.' Car carrying Chaplin with men clinging to its sides, and headed by two mounted policemen, drives away from the

station through large crowds which follow behind. Sequence filmed from moving car ahead of Chaplin's. Chaplin seen sitting in open section at the back of his car, filmed from vehicle overtaking; he waves to the camera. 'Scenes at the Ritz.' Medium shot looking down at car moving slowly through a mass of people, with Chaplin standing at the back. Close shot from within the crowd as Chaplin stands and acknowledges the greetings of the crowd from a now stationary car. Reverse view angled down at the same scene with people looking up at Chaplin. Medium shot looking down at police struggling as they guide Chaplin through the crowd to the barriers in front of the doors of the Ritz hotel. Chaplin looks through hotel window and throws money [?] to the crowd below. 'Charlie's wireless message to the British Public through "TOPICAL". S.S. Olympic. Editor. <u>Topical Budget</u>. I wish that I could be capable of expressing my sincere appreciation for the manner in which I have been welcomed by my Kin in the Homeland. All that I can say is that I have been deeply touched, and my gratitude will be everlasting. It is all too wonderful to think about, it is like a dream. Faithfully, Charlie.' Final close-up of Chaplin.[85]

Chaplin's participation helped to make this one of Topical's most attractive items. His comment that the film of him would be shown in the cinemas that evening was of course correct. Topical would have had prints ready for the evening shows, and possibly their cameraman on the voyage had disembarked at Cherbourg (other cameramen would have covered the arrival at Southampton and Waterloo) and rushed his film to London. After this hurried release on 10 September, the date of Chaplin's arrival, the fully edited and titled item was issued on 12 September.

Topical's coverage of the visit had begun on 5 September with an item entitled 'CHARLIE' – BEG PARDON! MR CHARLES SPENCER CHAPLIN which they used to prefigure their major coverage and which was probably footage supplied to them by an American company. Having arrived, Chaplin seems to have largely escaped their cameras, as Topical covered the rest of the visit with only two more routine items. Issue 525–1 (15 September 1921) contained an item on the visit entitled 'SANTA CLAUS' WITHOUT HIS WHISKERS.[86] Then on 13 October (issue 529–1) they released an item entitled BACK NEXT YEAR, showing Chaplin leaving Southampton, and in the company of British film actresses Alma Taylor (a meeting which Chaplin recounts) and Chrissie White (according to Topical's records).

Film stars were a unusual subject for Topical since Britain could boast hardly any, and the rare visits by true Hollywood stars were a major event. It is not known how many cameramen covered the Chaplin visit, as there are no credits for cameramen in the issue books at this time, but the previous year four cameramen had been used to film

114

the arrival in Britain of Mary Pickford and Douglas Fairbanks, 251 feet of film being used in the newsreel.[87] One of the four, 'Bunny' Hutchins, showed the typical mixture of ingenuity and persistence that was the mark of a good newsreel cameraman:

I must just tell you about the first visit of Mary Pickford and Douglas Fairbanks to this country. It was during Ascot week. I returned from the races one evening and as I had been doing the Paddock etc., I was all dressed up in morning dress, spats and silk hat complete. As soon as I came into the office the Editor yelled at me: '5 o'clock train, Southampton – scoop story' – and away I had to go (I did manage to borrow a mackintosh and another hat!). Reading my instructions in the train, I found I had to get on board the Red Star Liner 'Lapland' in mid-channel and get my stuff before the ship arrived at Southampton. A 'Sketch' and 'Standard' press photographer went with me. We went off in the pilot's cutter and after a very bumpy night at sea we eventually scrambled up the Jacob's ladder of the 'Lapland' and then our troubles started. We had no authority to be on board! As soon as we got on board we darted into a bathroom and locked ourselves in. Looking through a porthole we could see the pilot's boat still alongside, and officers were heard scurrying about looking for us. At last the boat pushed off and the liner got under way again. Our cameras had been hoisted aboard with the pilot's luggage. Well, out we came – straight into the arms of an officer – 'The old man wants you two on the bridge'. We duly appeared before the Captain, a real old salt, who proceeded to chew up the English language into little bits. It was against all Emigration regulations ..... Mary Pickford's manager had arrived on the scene by this time, and between us we quietened the old mariner and proceeded to do our stuff with 'Mary and Doug'. A plane was waiting at Southampton, and within half-an-hour of the ship's arrival I was back in London with films and plates, still wearing my Ascot kit. The films were on view, and the Evening Standard full of pictures was on sale, before the famous couple arrived at Waterloo.[88]

Here clearly are the advantages of Topical's association with Hulton: benefiting from the Hulton press's news-gathering service, collaborating with a Hulton photographer, and having films flown back to London. There was presumably not too much displeasure at Hutchins' exploits, as during his stay Douglas Fairbanks visited FBO and saw Topical's coverage in their viewing theatre.

It was Hulton who was also responsible for an extraordinary competition in which Topical, FBO and the *Daily Sketch* were all involved. On 11 September 1922 it was first announced in the *Daily Sketch* that Norma Talmadge, then one of Hollywood's pre-eminent stars, was looking for a new British film star to appear alongside her in her next feature film, *Within the Law*. Film star competitions were quite common, the usual prize being a screen test, but this was a competition on an altogether grander scale, and 80,000 would-be British film stars entered. Thanks to a brilliantly organised campaign by Hulton and the American company First National Pictures, the whole nation was engrossed by the topic for over two months.

On 2 October the competition was first mentioned in *Topical Budget*, and thereafter there were regular items, with such titles as WHO WILL BE THE NEW BRITISH FILM STAR? and RUSH FOR FAME, as the competition grew and grew. Photographs and details of entrants were published in the *Daily Sketch*, but a greater prize was an appearance in the newsreel. *Topical Budget*'s items for the competition featured groups of lucky contestants from the various regions nationwide striking suitable poses for the camera.

Norma Talmadge and her equally celebrated actress sister Constance arrived in Britain on 7 November to an ecstatic welcome. The number of contestants had been whittled down to what was labelled 'The Lovely Hundred', and a lengthy process of screen tests began. First National had brought their own cameramen, and Topical were obliged to use the footage the Americans took of the final stages of the competition, and of the selection of the winner, Margaret Leahy from Marble Arch.

She was taken on a rapid tour of the country, followed all the while by Topical, and greeted by enthusiastic crowds wherever she went. She left for Hollywood on 25 November 1922. At a hectic time for the newsreel (the Lloyd George coalition government fell, bringing about a general election) they had devoted seventeen items over nine weeks, or 20 per cent of all their news items for the period, to the *Daily Sketch* competition. Margaret Leahy was fêted by America as she had been at home, but by the time she arrived on the set in Hollywood it was realised that she had not the least talent for acting and could not be allowed to jeopardise the film or the Talmadge name. Given all the advance publicity, and with the possible threat of legal action if they just sent her home, something nonetheless had to be done with Leahy. A solution was found within the family. Natalie Talmadge, the least known of the three sisters, was married to Buster Keaton, then about to direct his first feature film, *The Three Ages*. Joe Schenck, chairman of First National and married to Norma Talmadge, told Keaton to take Leahy as his leading lady, 'because comic leading ladies don't have to act'.[89] Keaton proceeded to do his best, and though many good scenes were wasted during the production, the resultant film, premièred in Britain in July 1923 and distributed by FBO, turned out to be a success, with many going to see the film purely on the strength of 'that nice English girl who won the contest'. Margaret Leahy returned to Britain for the première, then went back to California, married and settled down. She did not act again.

116

Norma Talmadge (left) congratulating the '*Daily Sketch* girl', Margaret Leahy. From issue 586–1.

The Chaplin and Margaret Leahy episodes show a different kind of exclusive to the single coverage of a major event – the extended exclusive, with an obvious appeal to audiences and exhibitors alike. Both kinds were meant to make *Topical Budget* seem a worthwhile newsreel to book, and to be a draw for audiences who might be expected to show some loyalty towards a single newsreel. The episodes also show the newsreel borrowing some of the glamour of the fiction film: Chaplin puts on a performance and would-be film stars are tempted with an appearance in *Topical Budget*. The newsreel was the humble relation, but it shared the same screen as the feature film, and geared itself to appeal to the shared audience. Lastly, the Margaret Leahy extravaganza in particular shows Hulton's use of the newsreel as a part of his larger newspaper interests; not as a further news source, but as a kind of moving picture supplement, sharing the same person-alities, competitions, methods and generally benign attitude towards the news of the day.

Royalty
In May 1919 H. G. Wells let it be known that he declined to go to the cinema because of the snobbery of the newsreels.[90] Royalty were the newsreels' favourite subject, the aristocracy a regular feature. Photo-graphy and cinematography, in the popular press and cinema, had brought the royal family close to the British public in a way never known before. British society had yet to shake off a faith in titles which

117

permeated the feature film industry, for whom all too often a character's earldom or similar ennoblement was thought of as being of sufficient interest in itself, and it supplied the newsreels with a reliable type of story, naturally to their liking. An event, however minor or static, was topical if a lord attended it. Society weddings at St Margaret's Westminster were invariably covered; hunts with the Quorn and the Duke of Beaufort were regular items.

Topical were royalists, probably to a still greater degree than the other newsreels. From 1917, when they were able to cover the movements of royalty freely, two or three items of some issues could be devoted to the activities of the royal family. It was only after the WOCC take-over that they were able to keep up such coverage. Events such as the silver jubilee and funeral of Queen Victoria, the coronation of Edward VII, the latter's funeral, the investiture of the Prince of Wales, the coronation of George V, and the Delhi Durbar were the great topical events of their day, vitally important factors in forming and promoting the early British newsfilm industry. However, regular access to the royal family was denied to the newsreels. They were officially obliged to keep their distance, although reports of figures of 100 yards or 50 yards do not match the evidence of some items in which the cameraman was obviously only a few feet away. It was the protractedness of the war that changed matters. In 1916 King George V appeared in five *Topical Budget* items; in 1918 he appeared in thirty-six. The gradual realisation, as people grew weary of the war, that a home propaganda campaign was needed, the desire for positive images, and the eventual official awareness that the cinema was both a popular and an apparently controllable medium, brought royalty and cinema together. Permits were granted, glances were offered at the camera, and from 1917 onwards royalty made more and more public appearances. By the end of the war, expediency had turned into habit. It was now a part of royal life that they be constantly featured in the illustrated papers and newsreels; the newsreels in their turn sought royal stories, came to be characterised by their fondness for them, and had an audience which expected them.

The stars were King George V and Queen Mary, their five children, the Prince of Wales, the Duke of York, Princess Mary and, to a lesser extent, Prince Henry and Prince George, and Queen Alexandra (widow of Edward VII). Of these, the dominant figure was the Prince of Wales, aged twenty-four at the end of the war, whose evident popularity was exploited in a series of mammoth Empire tours and continual public engagements in Britain. He became the newsreels' favourite subject-matter, and though his nervous look and manner can seem unappealing now, it was certainly not the case then: the extraordinary worldwide enthusiasm generated by his presence came in large part from constant exposure on cinema screens. His apprehension in front of the cameras was understandable. On duty at home, relaxing, on holiday, or touring the Empire once again, newsreel cameras followed him everywhere. He retained a particular dislike for British newsreel cameramen, and they responded in kind. The Prince was an enthusiastic, but accident-prone horseman, and Topical habitually sent half a dozen cameramen to cover his horse-racing activities. What particularly irritated him was the cameramen's habit of setting up position around the first fence, waiting for him to fall off:

> Although fond of riding, the Prince was not a good horseman, and when he rode in army point-to-points at Hawthorn Hill, Maidenhead, as he often did, the newsreel cameramen always gathered at the first jump. This was where the best pictures were to be had, for it was there he almost invariably fell from his horse. One day he climbed to his feet and shouted: 'Can't you b———s go to the second jump for a change?'[91]

Eventually, after a succession of accidents from racing and hunting, and a broken collar-bone, he was requested to refrain from any further racing.

The Prince of Wales' tours of the Empire were also covered by the newsreels, and for his tour to Australia from March to October 1920, Topical secured the exclusive film rights from the Admiralty. William Jeapes called Will Barker out of retirement (which he had announced immediately after the Armistice) to be official cinematographer to the tour. His various films were sent back to Britain as they were taken, Barker developing them himself with makeshift equipment, and released as regular items in *Topical Budget*, with a time delay of generally a month. This was a positive piece of action from Topical following a rather fallow period after the exciting events of 1919, and once again can be seen to confirm the value of the extended exclusive, not only as a means of convincing exhibitors that a regular audience would be attracted to such a series, but in declaring Topical's continuing strong position as a newsreel after the war. Thus Topical's audience saw the Prince visit the West Indies, Panama, San Diego, New Zealand, Australia and the islands of the Pacific. Shortly after the tour was over, Topical released a feature-length compilation of the material taken by Barker, entitled *50,000 Miles with the Prince of Wales*, and shown to the trade in November 1920. Such compilations were to become a common way for the newsreels to re-market old material, though the results tended to be tedious. But *50,000 Miles with the Prince of Wales*, 5,900 feet long, is not as wearisome as it might have been, thanks to some bridging material between the obvious news items. There is a great deal of parading and handshaking, but in between there are shots of Aborigines, Maoris, animals, a sequence filmed from the front of a moving train, and the film ends with a lengthy (and unchronological) coverage of the on-board 'Crossing the Line' ceremony. Nevertheless, it is hardly compelling viewing in this form, a clear indication of how the newsreel story, for all the talk there was of the newsreels lengthening their coverage if only the exhibitors would let them, had come to depend on brevity.

Topical declined to learn their lesson, and between December 1920 and May 1921 Harold Jeapes and the American cameramen U. K. Whipple (from Universal) covered the Duke of Connaught's tour of India. The tour had been originally designed for the Prince of Wales, but he was pulled out owing to exhaustion from the previous one. Again, the results were dispatched to Britain in sequence for regular showings in the newsreel, then packaged togther as the feature-length *Across India with the Duke of Connaught* (6,400 feet), a private showing of which was given (with much pride on Topical's part) to Queen Mary and guests at the West End cinema. Topical featured this in issue 506–2 (release date 9 May 1921).

King George V was not, on the face of it, ideal newsreel material: unanimated, often ill, and dull. Yet in his way he was a better performer than his eldest son. His devotion to the royal routine made him a perfect subject for the newsreels; he positively enjoyed opening things. But newsreel cameramen found that he also provided them with attractive informal moments: smiles of pleasure, asides to his companions, chats with members of the public. On film he comes over as a natural, genial performer. For the 1921 FA Cup Final, Topical had a camera directed towards the King for the whole match, being rewarded with a short sequence in which he drops his stick, two or three neighbours bend to pick it up, and he jokes with one of them about it. It may seem a foolish incident, but it gave just the right touch for the newsreel. The King and Queen co-operated with the cameramen, who consequently thought well of them from a professional point of view.

Queen Mary had less in the way of a discernible newsreel personality, but was as devoted to her duties as her husband, and as understanding of the requirements of the cameramen. Queen Alexandra made no concessions at all towards the cameras, but the Alexandra Rose Day, an annual charitable event, was a newsreel favourite, with young women dressed in white pelting Queen Alexandra's open carriage with roses as it passed down the street. Topical's three items covering her death in November 1925 typify their style and sentiments when dealing with royalty:

QUEEN ALEXANDRA

'It is with profound regret that "Topical Budget" records the death of the Queen Mother at Sandringham. The passing of the beloved consort of Edward VII and the mother of our King plunges the whole Empire into mourning. Pictures which recall the gracious personality of the adored Queen. 1865. The first portrait of Her Majesty taken after her arrival in England' . . . 'A portrait taken in

1867; King George is on her knee' . . . 'The public always crowded to welcome her on Rose Day' . . . 'At Farnborough in war-time' . . . 'Shamrock Day with the Irish Guards' . . . 'Empire Day: salute from 10,000 children in Hyde Park' . . . 'At the wedding of Lord Louis Mountbatten' . . . 'The last portrait of the beloved Queen.'

PASSING OF THE 'GENTLE LADY'
'Sad scenes attend Queen Alexandra's death at Sandringham House' . . . 'The stricken mansion' . . . 'To the aged inmates of Trinity Hospital she was a true friend' . . . 'The face she loved' . . . 'King and his sons at Sandringham Church' . . . 'Mourning tenants' . . . 'At rest' . . . 'The King and Queen's wreath bore this moving inscription: "For darling mother dear from her sorrowing and devoted Georgie and May"' . . . 'St George's Chapel, Windsor, where Her Majesty will be laid beside King Edward.'

QUEEN ALEXANDRA
'Nation's tribute of tears as the beloved lady passes to her rest. The sad little cortege leaves Sandringham' . . . 'In London the people crowned her death with their grief and the heavens sent her a white shroud' . . . 'Four monarchs followed the gun carriage: King George, King of Norway, King of Denmark, King of the Belgians' . . . 'Whitehall: Through an avenue of sorrowing friends' . . . 'At the Abbey' . . . 'The endless queue of homage.'[92]

The very wordiness of these items shows Topical not just wishing to speak, but admitting that the pictures they showed could not sufficiently express their feelings.

Princess Mary was a popular figure, and her marriage to Lord Lascelles was probably the biggest newsreel story of the decade. Topical's preparations were reported in *The Times*:

Careful arrangements have been made to obtain films of the wedding of Princess Mary to-morrow. To secure, for example, an adequate series of pictures for 'The Topical Budget', one of the moving picture 'newspapers', preparations were begun as soon as the news of the engagement was announced. In order to provide good positions along the route for photographers employed by the firm, it was necessary to pay nearly £3,000, and to-morrow there will be 15 film photographers taking pictures for the Budget. In addition, six photographers will be employed to take 'still' photographs.

Between them they will take over 10,000 feet of film, though only one-tenth of this will be shown to the public. As soon as the photographs are taken they will be carried to the headquarters of the organisation and developed at once. In this way a great part of the

121

Queen Mary, Lady Elizabeth Bowes-Lyon and the Duke of York on the balcony at Buckingham Palace. From *The Royal Wedding*.

film will be ready before the ceremony is finished. After all the films have been assembled a careful selection will be made, and about 1,000 feet will be shown for exhibition. Sub-titles and explanations will be added, and an hour after the last picture has been taken the film will be ready for distribution. Except in a few cases in the extreme North, it will be shown in the big towns throughout the country the same night.[93]

The completed film was actually 518 feet long including titles, but even allowing for newsreel hyperbole, £3,000 for camera positions is a colossal amount. However, the figure for the cameramen is confirmed in the *Bioscope*, which reported sixty cameramen from all the newsreels covering the event.[94] The other major royal wedding of the period, that between the Duke of York (the future George VI) and Elizabeth Bowes-Lyon in 1923 was covered by nineteen cameramen in what must have been a hectic week for Topical since the same issue contained their exclusive coverage of that year's FA Cup Final.[95] All eight cameramen covering this second event had also filmed the wedding. The royal family, and their correct presentation, were of the greatest importance to Topical. The mixture of deference and informality that they achieved came from the royal family's greater tolerance and use of the news media, and the newsreel's increased confidence and immense enthusiasm for the subject: it was a case of unacknowledged co-operation between the two.

Politics and Politicians

It was held to be one of Sir Edward Hulton's virtues as a newspaper owner that he had no particular party allegiances. His entry in *The Dictionary of National Biography* is condescending, but accurate as far as it goes:

> Hulton's interests as a newspaper proprietor were purely commercial. In an age when the political influence of large press syndicates is so marked this limitation may perhaps be considered to his credit than otherwise. His newspapers, if they were without literary merit, were at least free from the charge of political interference. He recognised that the public wanted news, and set himself to supply it in its simplest form, garnished with prize competitions, puzzles, serial stories, and other harmless aids to popularity.[96]

Hulton's papers could certainly boast little literary merit, but such was scarcely their purpose. Their merit and message lay in pictures – and it was just so with his newsreel. During the 1924 general election it was found necessary to declare Topical's lack of political intentions:

To the Editor of THE BIOSCOPE

DEAR SIR. – It has come to my knowledge that some apprehension exists among exhibitors that news films may be used for the purpose of disseminating Party views during the General Election campaign.

In view of the dangerous nature of this suggestion, I should be grateful if you would allow me, through your columns, to give exhibitors the assurance to which they are entitled, by stating as formally and clearly as possible, the policy of the 'Topical Budget' in this matter.

Our view has always been, is to-day, and always will be, that political propaganda should find no place in a newsreel. In pursuance of this policy, we decided at the outset of the present campaign, that no political messages whatever should be included in the 'Topical Budget'. The whole of the branch managers of FBO (1919) Limited were written to, asking them to convey this assurance to exhibitors, immediately the dissolution was announced, with the further promise that our pictures of the Election would deal fairly with all parties.

In order further to emphasise the impartiality of the 'Budget's' election news, we have issued a poster reading 'Political Crisis, <u>all</u> the Pictures but no Politics', in the belief that, by displaying it at their doors, exhibitors may be able to allay any public uncertainty existing on this point. A similar message appears as a title in the 'Budget' itself; which, in its issue for to-day (Thursday) contains news photographs of the leaders of all parties.

I am, Sir, yours faithfully,
EDITOR, 'Topical Budget'[97]

The accusation had been levelled at all the newsreels, and Topical's letter is more self-publicity than self-defence, but they believed in their impartiality just as they believed in the integrity of the film medium. Certainly there was no wish to preach, or much thought given to a viewpoint.

However, politics could be entertaining enough, and this was especially true in the case of politicians. The turmoil that was British politics in the first half of the 1920s threw up both dramatic situations and plentiful characters, the latter being needed by the newsreels most of all. The Asquiths, Balfours and Curzons of the world were lofty, uncinematic figures, but Lloyd George and the new era of the common man brought in popular performers, who paused for the cameras, whose faces filled the newspapers and mouthed silent words to the newsreel cameras. By demanding that such figures came before the cameras, the newsreels helped transform David Lloyd George, Ramsay MacDonald and Stanley Baldwin into popular figures. Their looks engaged the audience, and it was better still that they had wives or families. If Asquith's star had fallen, Margot Asquith was still popular, and Topical devoted much attention to the activities of Megan Lloyd George, Ishbel MacDonald and Lucy Baldwin.

British politicians only gradually came to discover the power and popularity of the cinema; likewise the cinema took its time to make use of politicians. The first people with political intent to exploit its potential were the suffragettes, who collaborated with topical film-makers as they did with some newspapers. In 1908 William Jeapes' Graphic company had great success with a film of a suffragette rally, for which they were able to purchase the rights, from the suffragettes' own special platform.[98] With the evidently growing popularity of the cinema in the years after 1910, politicians made their first tentative steps towards exploiting it for their own ends. Before the war Cecil Hepworth filmed speeches given by Bonar Law and F. E. Smith using his 'Vivaphone' system, a method of synchronising film with a gramophone recording, and in 1916 Hepworth became involved in a charity project to film what became known as 'The Cabinet Film'. The intention was to film the Cabinet in session, to which Hepworth would add individual portrait shots of the ministers which he had been in the process of gathering together anyway. The cameras and lights were apparently all set up and ready at 10 Downing Street, but the project was abandoned, according to Hepworth because the Cabinet members feared potential ridicule.[99]

No such fears remained in 1922, when shortly after Lloyd George's resignation as Prime Minister, but before the general election that soon followed, the new Prime Minster Bonar Law invited Topical into 10 Downing Street. This was a straightforward party political ploy, which the newsreel happily fell for, since they secured the first pictures ever to be taken there.

Within only a few years, to be featured in the cinema was no longer ridiculous, but actually advantageous. Lloyd George was the first politician to appeal to the public through his appearances on screen. As Minister of Munitions and then Prime Minister, his cheery, ebullient nature came over well, and crucially he acknowledged rather than merely tolerated the cameras. More than that, he realised that a good film performance depended on movement, and took care to appear both natural and animated. Public persona was determined as much, if not more, by how one looked as by what one said or did, as the royal family had also discovered, and both Lloyd George and King George V showed an early, instinctive appreciation of the difference between a newsreel shot and portrait photography. In Topical's film of the Cabinet in session at 10 Downing Street,[100] the different attitudes shown towards the presence of cameras are quite marked. The whole event was staged; a press release had to be issued afterwards denying that an actual Cabinet session had been filmed:

Bonar Law's cabinet in session. From left: Sir Philip Lloyd-Graeme, the Marquis of Salisbury, Andrew Bonar Law, Stanley Baldwin and Leopold Amery. From *The New Government*.

The Press Association is authorized to deny the statement that a film was taken on Wednesday of the Cabinet at work. A film was taken of members of the Cabinet some time after the Cabinet meeting.[101]

Nevertheless the film gives the impression of just such a meeting, with the full co-operation of the participants. The camera is placed at one end of the room looking down the table as Bonar Law leads in ten ministers, who then take their places around the table. A close shot follows of Law reading an announcement, with the Marquis of Salisbury and Stanley Baldwin sitting either side of him. A medium shot across the table shows Sir Philip Lloyd-Graeme, Salisbury, Law, Baldwin and Leopold Amery. Then comes a close shot of the Duke of Devonshire and Viscount Peel, according to the intertitles discussing a point; both men are posing very stiffly for the camera. Clearly filmed later on, as the seating arrangements have changed, there then follows a close shot of Lloyd-Graeme talking with Amery and Peel. Another close shot, with a slight panning movement, shows Law talking to Viscount Curzon, Baldwin and Viscount Cave. Finally there is, in the words of the intertitles, 'a fine study of the quiet and yet steadfast dignity of the new Prime Minister', with Law in close-up seated at the table and offering a smile to the camera.

Several of the ministers look awkward, as might anyone in such artificial circumstances. But the most assured performance comes from Stanley Baldwin (he manages to turn up in three close shots). His look of what may well be amused contempt is nonetheless a confident look at the camera, not a stare into the middle distance or a nervous pose in obedience to the instructions of the cameraman. Law looks relaxed when sharing a joke at the table, and seems reasonably assured for the final close-up. The film itself (taken by two cameramen, Jimmy Taylor and Oscar Bovill) is deferential and a little dull. Some comment in the intertitles, however light-hearted, would have created greater interest in some rather stiff characters.

The newsreels were helping to dramatise political news simply by their dependence on characters. Politicians could not, of course, be heard in a silent newsreel, and Hepworth's efforts had involved compiling portrait shots with extracts from speeches in the intertitles. In 1919 Maurice Elvey produced *The Victory Leaders* and, presumably in ignorance of Hepworth's earlier efforts, declared in the opening title, 'This film is the first attempt at Cinema interviewing'. However, all he could show were close-ups of famous personages 'in a pose of characteristic and typical movement',[102] with brief messages in the intertitles. All that the politicians had with which to project themselves to the audience was their appearance and camera manner. Some indeed do mouth words to the camera, an action which presumably did not seem quite so ridiculous as it can do now.

Thus the characters had their appeal, but issues had to be approached with caution. The silent newsreel was in any case hampered by its very silence: the intertitle could reveal bias but it could not persuade in the manner of a sound commentary. Also there was a great deal of pressure from the film trade to keep politics out of the cinemas. When Lord Beaverbrook bought a controlling stake in the Provincial Cinema Theatres chain at the end of 1919 and then a half share in British Pathé in February 1920,[103] the film trade reacted with alarm. Their fears were expressed by the *Kinematograph Weekly*:

> . . . That the newspaper as a factor in the life of the people has long since been relegated to second place in importance by the kinema theatre is nowhere realised more keenly than at the headquarters of the various newspaper trusts, and at the political organisations closely allied with them. An institution which gets into direct touch with 20,000,000 people or more every week makes even a modern circulation insignificant by comparison. Can you wonder if the mouths of the newspaper owners water as they regard the infinitely greater public reached by the film? And can you wonder if they attempt to secure control of that medium also? Personally, we are surprised neither that the Press boss has discovered the film theatre nor that he should desire to control it; we are, however, anxious that the probable use he would make of his power shall be realised, and that the public, as well as the trade, should have its eyes open to the real danger that some of its film material may eventually show the same signs of doping as the 'news' it gets . . .[104]

When Hulton had entered the film industry a year before, the film trade had been flattered and had duly welcomed him. Although he controlled a newsreel and a renting firm, his lack of government connections and any avowed political persuasion made him acceptable. But Beaverbrook was already a far more dominant figure, intimate with the most powerful in the land, and a former politician himself; moreover, he had acquired a large stake in exhibition. The newsreels were quiet on politics and issues of the day out of personal preference, partly because these subjects lacked visual interest and so seldom made good news stories, but also because of the independent exhibition sector. They were continually obliged to please – if an exhibitor did not like one newsreel for whatever reason, he could always hire another. A newspaper was a private purchase, selected according to the buyer's own preferences; but a newsreel was part of a cinema show, and the audience went to see the main feature, not the newsreel. To please everybody, the newsreel challenged nobody. Nor did it wish to influence its audience with a viewpoint, for those who ran the newsreels had always seen them as a means of recording an event without having to interpret it. Of course on occasion they had to express an attitude, but the line they unquestioningly took was that of common, public prejudice.

The *Kinematograph Weekly*'s fears about Beaverbrook were not re-alised. His greatest use of joint ownership of the *Daily Express* and *Pathé Gazette* seems to have been to announce in the paper that the newsreel would be smuggling cameras into London Zoo to break a current ban on filming there. To both Hulton and Beaverbrook, the newsreel became just another part of their news empires, an occasion-ally handy source of pictures and a reasonably profitable sideline. Both men knew that there was no money to be made in British film produc-tion or in handling British feature films, and they entered renting and exhibition for the profits, even for the fun of it, but not to exert any influence on the news as it appeared in the cinemas. Indeed, it is disappointing that they did not try. Hulton had no especial political bias, and even Beaverbrook was more interested in the plain wielding of power than in wielding it in any particular direction. An injection of argument or criticism into the newsreels at this early stage in their development might have saved them from their supine stance of later years. But it is unlikely that Beaverbrook or Hulton ever saw the newsreels for any more than what they were, rather than what they could be. The newsreels were accepted as reportage and entertainment, a part of the cinema world rather than a new part of the newspaper world. The newsreels were silent, and it may simply have been accepted that they had nothing to say.

The *Kinematograph Weekly*'s comments about the impressiveness of the 20,000,000 cinema attendance figure when compared to newspaper circulations are misleading. As has been calculated, such an attendance figure represented 14,000,000 people going to the cinema once or twice a week. In the mid-1920s the sales of some popular British newspapers were: *Daily Mail* 1,750,000, *Daily Express* 1,100,000, and *Daily Mirror* 950,000, while the actual readership would be around four times these figures. At the time of the article, Beaverbrook's *Daily Express* was selling some 750,000 copies a day, providing a readership figure of 3,000,000, which roughly equals *Topical Budget*'s weekly attendance.[105] There can only be a vague correlation between a newsreel seen once or twice a week and a newspaper read daily, just as it would be unwise to see one as an alternative to the other: each served its own function. Beaver-brook's *Pathé Gazette*, the most popular British newsreel, had an audi-ence figure per issue of 7,500,000, or 10,000,000 attendances per week.

On the matter of party politics, Topical were as good as their word. Their coverage throughout the 1920s seems largely even-handed, with a natural bias towards whoever was in power at the time. The emer-gence of the Labour Party was noted for its curiosity value, but was never seen as a threat. If in 1928 they could produce a laudatory compilation of Baldwin stories under the title *Our Leader*, it was be-cause they were seeking to make fresh use out of old material, not to suggest Conservative sympathies (even if they held them). Neverthe-less, in 1920 Topical's favourite politician was Lloyd George, and eight years later it was Stanley Baldwin. The shift is from the politically engaging to the conservatively secure, an indication not of political allegiance but of how, as the decade progressed, the newsreels gradually lost their commitment to news of the day.

If they were fair to personalities (since all sides could provide equally attractive screen figures), then their attitudes could only be expressed in the intertitles. Here there is some doubt, for we cannot be sure of the contemporary audience's understanding of the images delivered to them. How much did Topical depend upon assumed audience reactions? The first known intertitles delivering political comment come with the First World War. The word 'hun' for a German occurs as early as October 1914,[106] and when the WOCC took over the newsreel it took on board the accepted language, so that the growing propagandist tone was as much natural to the newsreel as it was War Office policy. However, there is sometimes a puzzling lack of comment:

DISSATISFIED TEACHERS
'Trafalgar Square demonstration for increased salaries.' Teachers at a rally in Trafalgar Square, many of whom are women. A show of hands.[107]

What is a teachers' strike doing in a propaganda newsreel if it is not to be commented on? A matter-of-fact description such as this, although a newsreel commonplace, seems to imply some kind of acceptance of the action, but it is more likely that Topical took the audience's reactions as read – they had only to present the images. Newsreels were always late with the news, of course, being released just twice a week, and could depend on an already formed audience attitude. The teachers' strike was yesterday's news, but the newsreel revealed what it had actually looked like. This is not to say that they refrained from making comment where comment was scarcely needed:

PACIFISTS ROUTED AT BROTHERHOOD CHURCH
'A pacifist meeting held at Kingsland was broken up by the forces of loyalty and patriotism. The crowd breaking into the church.' Crowd, with two policemen, watches as small group of men break windows of church and try to force their way in.[108]

The strikes of the immediate post-war period saw little comment from Topical. Two whole issues were devoted to the transport strike of October 1919, but the titles are purely descriptive. The titles below are for a complete issue:

RAILWAY HELPERS
'Peers, V.C.s, Bishops, Generals, Tommies and Tars, all lend a hand to load and unload trains.'

'Messrs Henderson, Clynes, Gosling and Mr Robert Williams, Secretary, leaving after the conference at Caxton Hall.'

AT TOWER HILL
'Mr Thomas, supported by Mr Bromley, addressing a mass meeting of railwaymen.'

HUSTLING HOUNSLOW
'Parcels, passengers and mails dispatched with speed and safety.'

SAVING THE HORSES
'Lady Volunteers assist in exercising the railway van horses.'

AGAIN AT DOWNING STREET
'Interested crowds watch the N.U.R. delegates arrive to meet the Premier.'

THE NAVY ON THE LINE
'Sailors from H.M. Submarines keeping the track in order on the L. and S.W. Railway.'

GUARDING OUR SUPPLIES
'Mounted police escort convoys leaving King's Cross.'[109]

This moderate tone, describing in plain terms the emergency measures being taken and how ordinary people were coping, seems admirable. The coal strike of 1921 saw Topical in a far more outspoken mood:

THE GREATEST MENACE WE HAVE EVER KNOWN
'Opening scenes in the historic Coal War of 1921. While the mines were flooding miners watch Cardiff play Notts Forest' . . . 'Even the colliers have to search the slag heaps for fuel' . . . '3,000 gallons a minute pouring in at Llwynpia, but 25 men have been permitted to pump' . . . 'Types of the Pit ponies which were left to drown in some of the Mines.'[110]

This seems merely foolish: the greatest menace known requires stronger images than a crowd at a football match or the plight of the pit ponies (no newsreel, least of all Topical, could resist the animal angle to any story). Other main titles over the next few issues show the same tone being maintained:

IN THE SHADOW OF DISASTER (503–1)
EVEN THE BABIES GO ON STRIKE (503–2)
TO MAINTAIN THE NATION'S LIFE (503–2)

The general strike threatened in 1921 became a reality in 1926, but by now moderation, or perhaps caution, had returned:

BRITAIN'S FIRST 'GENERAL STRIKE'
'Miners leave the pits and Greatest Industrial Upheaval Begins.' Group of miners walking away from pit head up slope towards camera, smiling as they pass. 'Scenes in Downing St.' Medium long shot of large group of men being moved away from Downing Street area by policemen (view looking towards Whitehall). Close shot of Winston Churchill and another man standing outside 10 Downing Street. 'Mr Arthur Henderson.' Close-up of Arthur Henderson. 'Mr Ramsay MacDonald.' Shot of Ramsay MacDonald. '"A State of Emergency". Volunteers for National Service crowd Whitehall.' Long queue of men entering wooden building in Whitehall area. Closer shot of a group of them smiling for the camera. 'Hyde Park – becomes the Milk Depot of the Metropolis.' Medium long shot of fleet of vans lined up at Marble Arch. Medium shot of van (else-where) with sign "Food Only" at the head of a long line of such vehicles curving into the distance. 'Mr A. J. Cook (Miners' Secre-tary).' Close-up of Cook. 'Mr Ernest Bevin ("Dockers' K.C.").' Close-up of Bevin standing outside the Houses of Parliament. 'Mr J. H. Thomas.' Shot of Thomas. 'How London went to work.' People on foot and on bicycles criss-crossing London street. Some motor vehicles in background. Camera pan. 'London Bridge.' View from South Bank side of large numbers of people crossing London Bridge. Camera pan. 'To Feed the People. Sir W. Mitchell-Thom-son, Postmaster-General, becomes Chief Civil Commissioner.' Close-up of Mitchell-Thomson. 'The Prime Minister's Message – "Steady!"' Close-up indoors of Stanley Baldwin at a desk writing and smoking a pipe.[112]

Here is a fair mixture of issues at hand and personalities involved. The opening sequence with the miners is staged, and dramatically is a good beginning, just as the closing shot of a steady Stanley Baldwin is a fine conclusion, intended to be reassuring. The moderate tone is note-worthy, reflecting the general wish at the time for it all to be sorted out amiably, quickly and quietly. Topical devoted almost all of four issues to the strike, reserving themselves throughout to showing the major figures from each side and to carrying descriptive comment on safe scenes from the emergency. It is reasonable and responsible reporting, but uninvolving. Somewhere between the prejudice of 1921 and the

Main title of *Topical Budget*'s first item on the General Strike of 1926.

moderation of 1926, a change actually in parallel with Topical's decline in vitality, there was room for a newsreel with a reasoned position.

A bizarre example of the occasional disparity between titles and action, and a notable example of unintentional political ambiguity, is an item from September 1921 (the year Topical seem to have been most prone to strong comment) entitled FARCICAL 'REVOLUTION' WHICH MAY BE SERIOUS IF IT SPREADS. The Labour council of the London Borough of Poplar, headed by George Lansbury, had refused to levy the rate demanded by the London County Council, and council members were arrested and sent to prison. Topical's item is so cheerful, and the subjects are so willing, that it is hard to decide just who is exploiting whom. The intertitles all feature a picture of a policeman with the Houses of Parliament in the background:

FARCICIAL 'REVOLUTION' WHICH MAY BE SERIOUS IF IT SPREADS
'Poplar's Labour Council prefer Gaol, to levying rates to pay L.C.C. for Services Rendered. "Queue up for Black Maria!"' . . . 'Mr Geo Lansbury, Poplar's Benevolent "Bolshie" Boss' . . . 'Alderman John and Mrs Councillor Scurr hope to enjoy their rest cure' . . . 'Mrs Alderman "Minnie" Lansbury gathers a nosegay for Holloway' . . . 'Mr and Mrs Councillor Cressall and a few of the "little things" they have to leave behind them' . . . '"<u>Do</u> go down to Brixton Daddy!" Councillor Rugless has taken the advice of his 7 weeks old "Red"'

. . . 'Alderman "Sam" March J. P. Mayor of Poplar. Off to the Brixton Beano!'[113]

The Cressalls and Ruglesses are shown with their children; the Scurrs are seen seated contentedly in a garden; Minnie Lansbury (George Lansbury's daughter-in-law) picks flowers; and Sam March waves goodbye to a group of colleagues. Clearly Topical's title-writer is out to ridicule their actions, although only the main title is admonitory. But what of the pictures themselves? The cameraman would have been under instructions to film each of the major figures and probably to get the shots of the children. Yet the councillors put up a great performance, appear attractive and in fact gained publicity for their actions. Might this have been with the cameraman's complicity? He did what was required of him by both sides, and both sides would have been quite satisfied with the outcome.

Topical therefore paraded, to fluctuating degrees, the conservative prejudices of the day. They worked best when they simply recorded the safe line, the personalities rather than the issues. When they tried to make comment, they were more flippant than observant. Their role, and their duty, was to provide moving pictures. If what they filmed can be said to have helped reinforce the status quo, either in their taste for safe subjects or for the uncontentious angle, this was to some extent determined for them. In the wish just to be topical and to film the stories of the day, they bowed to the choice of stories and pictures selected by the illustrated newspapers, and of course to those from whom they had to secure permission to film. Furthermore they had to please a heterogeneous cinema audience: there is some evidence that that the newsreels' fear of controversial subject-matter was borne out by adverse audience reactions. The poll conducted by *Pathé Gazette* in 1931 and referred to at the start of this chapter showed 'war conditions in Ireland' and 'pictures of Soviet Russia' as being the least popular among a selection of newsreel subjects. The audience were presumably reacting to the idea of the films rather than the images themselves, but that is of course the whole point: the people in the cinema had not come to see the news – if anything they had come to escape from it. They wanted a programme of entertainment, and although it might be expected of a newsreel to show current stories, the newsreels were not expected to draw attention to themselves by being challenging – by being attractive or appealing certainly, but not by provoking. There is no evidence that the newsreels were not wholly content with this state of affairs.

However, Topical's coverage of both Ireland and Russia is of particular interest. In 1919 the recently demobbed Ken Gordon was sent by Topical on a semi-official basis to accompany the British Expeditionary Force in North Russia. The first item made from the material returned by Gordon on his arrival in Russia is typical of those that followed:

OUR TROOPS IN BOLSHEVIK RUSSIA
'First battle-scenes on the Archangel Front. Exclusive pictures taken by the "Topical Budget" operator on the Dvina' . . . 'Our men attacking "Bolshies" on the Dvina. They are fighting for the cause of our loyal Russian friends' . . . 'Scenes in a captured village, where our soldiers made a haul of the "Red" snipers' . . . 'The liberated inhabitants enjoy the soothing strains of British music' . . . 'The children are delighted.'[114]

In all Topical carried fifteen items between June and October 1919 on the disastrous and unpopular North Russia campaign. Conditions were poor for filming and the surviving footage is mostly out of focus. At least two other private cameramen also filmed with the BEF at Archangel, and reviews of such films mention the poor focusing and the difficulties of filming in the extreme cold and with so little daylight. But what footage from Gordon that does survive is off-cut material; had the film been of poor quality, Topical would have made some kind of apology for it in the intertitles and would presumably not have made so great a use of it over so long a period. It showed considerable initiative to send Gordon to North Russia, but as a bold exclusive for a newsreel seeking to assert itself after the war it was something of a misfire with a war-weary public. The enterprise was partly intended to show Topical's strength as a newsreel after the war and in this it succeeded, but the subject-matter was out of keeping with *Topical Budget* in peacetime. Their only subsequent extended exclusives abroad would be of royal tours.

Topical's coverage of Ireland in the early 1920s, which saw the creation of the Irish Free State and the civil war, is impressive because of its thoroughness. One of their most notable items in the pre-WOCC period had been THE DUBLIN REBELLION,[115] which showed scenes in Dublin following the Easter Rising. The 'troubles' of the post-war period would have been difficult to report without betraying some kind of position, and the evidence does indicate that Topical, rather than attempt to adopt a disinterested stance, put their faith in an equitable peace settlement and the validity of the Irish Free State. This they combined with as wide and varied as possible coverage of the visual stories that were yielded up by the situation. From the time of the unrest following the death of Terence MacSwiney in October 1920, to the death of Michael Collins in August 1922, around 10 per cent of all *Topical Budget* items were devoted to Ireland, rising to 20 per cent at high points in the crisis. It was costly to support a cameraman or cameramen for so long a period, and Topical's coverage is praiseworthy therefore in extent and kind. It is reasonable to take the main titles employed by the newsreel as statements of attitude and intent, and the following are titles for the majority of the items covering the Irish situation from De Valera's negotiations in London to Tim Healy's appointment as the Governor-General of the Irish Free State:

IS IT THE DAWN? (515–2)
'I WANT PEACE' (516–1)
'ULSTER WILL NOT YIELD' (516–1)
'GETTING ACQUAINTED' (516–2)
IRELAND'S FATE DECIDED IN THE HIGHLANDS (524–1)
IS IT PEACE? (529–1)
GOVERNMENT'S ANSWER TO VALERA (529–2)
WILL THERE BE PEACE IN IRELAND? (533-?)
'FORGIVE AND FORGET' (537–1)
'IRISH FREE STATE' (537–1)
PEACE COUNCIL AT THE PALACE (537–1)
FURTHER PICTURES OF IRISH PEACE (538-?)
(SINN FEIN MEMBERS MEET AT DUBLIN PARLIAMENT HOUSE) (538–2)
THE SURRENDER OF DUBLIN CASTLE (543–1)
BRITISH EVACUATE IRELAND AFTER HUNDREDS OF YEARS OF OCCU-PATION (543–2)
THE GREAT TREK (544–1)
HUNTING IN FULL SWING IN IRISH FREE STATE (544–2)
PEACE IN IRELAND MEANS 'BUSINESS AS USUAL' AT ALDERSHOT (545–1)
BATTLE OF BELLEEK (564–1)
(IRELAND REFUGEES) (564–1)
IRISH FREE STATE TO MAINTAIN THE CONSTITUTION (564–2)
ASSASSINATION OF F. M. SIR HENRY WILSON BY GUNMAN (565–2)
CIVIL WAR IN IRELAND (566–2)
DUBLIN. HEMMING IN THE REBELS (567–1)
DUBLIN'S CIVIL WAR (567–2)
ULSTER DAY THE TWELFTH (568–1)
FALL OF LIMERICK (570–1)
IRISH NATIONAL ARMY SWEEPING ON (571–1)
FIRST IRISH NATIONAL TROOP SHIP (572–1)
PASSING OF MR ARTHUR GRIFFITH (573–1)
(MICHAEL COLLINS) (574–1)
(MICHAEL COLLINS) (574–2)
'LET THE DUBLIN GUARDS BURY ME!' (575–1)
REBIRTH OF A NATION (589–2)[116]

Two of the above items are particularly striking, demonstrating the varied approach of Topical. IS IT THE DAWN?[117] is entirely titles: that is, no pictures at all, only a message to Topical's audience from Eamon De Valera, and (bizarrely enough) some poetry:

135

'Though refusing all interviews De Valera asks "Topical", Exclusively, to issue his peace message to the whole world.

THE MESSAGE
"Ireland is fighting solely for the right to live her own life in her own way. She loves equally all her children and she needs them all.

_ _ _ _   And Oh! it were a gallant deed
To show before mankind,
How every race and every creed
Might be by love combined –
Might be combined, yet not forget
The fountains whence they rose.
As, filled by many a rivulet,
The stately Shannon flows.

[Signed] Eámonn de Valéra July 4 1921.'

It is not easy to say what one should make of this. A statement from De Valera prior to his talks with Lloyd George, together with a portrait shot of him, would have been reasonable, though still remarkable, but bad verse is strange. This is the only occasion Topical ever had an item without pictures[118] and shows quite a strong sympathy for De Valera – while he was taking part in talks and a lasting peace settlement seemed possible.

Another kind of reporting, and one likely to appeal more to the audience, was to show pictures of the fighting. An item such as THE BATTLE OF BELLEEK,[119] showing safe artillery fire and following troops into an empty village, is disappointingly unexciting, but one item at least is far more dramatic:

CIVIL WAR IN IRELAND
'Mr Michael Collins' desperate fight against "Irregulars". These remarkable pictures of the bombardment of the Rebels' Stronghold in the Four Courts, Dublin, were taken by "Topical's" operator lying on his back under fire.' Medium long shot of the Four Courts building. 'A Sniper's nest.' Long shot from position by a wall of the top of the Four Courts. 'Free State guns in action.' Military vehicles in street. 'Shells bursting on the Four Courts.' Shell fire and smoke between two buildings to the left of the Four Courts. Rear view of Irish Free State troops manning large gun in street. View of gunfire and smoke through window. Return to shot of clouds of smoke between two buildings. Sandbags in position beneath broken windows. View through window again. 'Snipers emptied the Streets.' Man looking down empty street spanned by an arch. 'Homeless!'

Adults and children seated on pavement. 'RORY O'CONNOR Commandant of the Rebels and defender of the Four Courts [title features still of O'Connor]. Later. The Four Courts go up in Flames' [title accompanied by picture of the building on fire]. Crowd in street by bridge to the right of the Four Courts. Ruined frontage on building. Medium long shot of smoke rising between Four Courts and adjoining building [to the left] seen from over the river. Long shot of Dublin with the Four Courts on fire and much smoke over the area. Medium long shot of building to the left of the Four Courts with smoke rising from behind it. Medium shot of great clouds of smoke pouring out between this building and the Four Courts.[120]

It was often dangerous for the cameramen to report the civil war, and an item of this kind, with the operator apparently under fire, is remarkably modern in manner. Certainly nothing in the *War Office Official Topical Budget* took the cinema audience quite so near the fighting. Overall, Topical's coverage of this whole period seems engaging in every sense, a good example of the newsreel during its finest period, at its best.

The Phenomenon and the Thing Itself

Topical Budget referred to themselves as 'the Great British News Film'. Other slogans used by them during their time emphasised their Britishness, and were straightforward jibes at the French-based Pathé and Gaumont. The intertitles for their coverage of the 1922 election night in Trafalgar Square indicate their attitude:

'TOPICAL' TRIUMPHS AGAIN
'By permission of the Authorities we transform Trafalgar Square on Election Night – into the World's greatest Cinema Theatre. 50,000 cheering people watch us show 50,000 feet of pictures and all Election results wirelessed by Marconi to our screen' . . . '"Topical's" reporters receiving the Wireless results' . . . 'Others filmed this unique scene by our 3,000,000 candle-power lights – But we don't mind – 'TOPICAL' IS BRITISH We Lead – Others Follow!' . . . 'The Soul of England still.'[121]

The films were supplied by FBO, the arc lights were hired, and the Soul of England is Nelson. This insular attitude not only determined their view on the world, it was the final governing factor behind their choice of stories. Their allegiance was to the rituals of society. The newsreel's year was made up of anniversaries, traditions, parades, memorials, ceremonies, the customary and the familiar. They filmed society reaffirming itself; all other incidents, irruptions or upsets were presented, albeit implicitly, as deviations from the norm. This was not, of course, merely a matter of attitude, since it was also one of cost and convenience. As noted above, many factors, from the limitations of film stock to the independent cinema exhibition sector, governed the choice of newsreel subjects. But probably Topical would not have wished it any other way: they substituted habit for commitment. John Grierson eloquently pinpointed what he saw as the limitations shared by all the newsreels, silent and sound:

> Among the foundation stones, the pompous parades, the politicians on pavements, and even among the smoking ruins of mine disasters and the broken backs of distressed ships, it is difficult to think that any real picture of our troubled times has been recorded. The newsreel has gone dithering on, mistaking the phenomenon for the thing itself, and ignoring everything that gave it the trouble of conscience and penetration and thought.[122]

It is difficult to counter this, except to query just what 'the thing itself' means. But today we need not be so harsh; rather we should be grateful that so much was recorded by the newsreels, and with such skill. It is wonderful that in this century we can look back at Emily Davison at the 1913 Derby, women haymakers, soldiers on the Western Front, the celebrations of the delivered inhabitants of Lille, Lloyd George or Charlie Chaplin acting for the cameras, the Prince of Wales scowling at them, Dimmock scoring the winning goal for Tottenham Hotspur, PC Scorey on his white horse, the dog shows, the cattle shows, the beauty shows, the launches, the parades, the crowds, the places, the incidental, accidental happenings captured inadvertently, and everywhere people passing by or staring at the camera. This is as close to 'the thing itself' as may be reasonably expected. It is probably misleading to pay too great attention to the word 'news' in such a newsreel – their intention was to be, as the original word for the newsfilm had it, topical. As time passed, and the newsreels grew more sophisticated, and most importantly acquired sound, topicality was not enough. But by that time *Topical Budget* was no more.

Topical Budget, having increased in stature and vitality from the start of the First World War, reached a peak of achievement under Sir Edward Hulton's management between 1919 and 1923. Three events, coming close together, spelled the end of this era. On 23 October 1924 a fire broke out at the 76–78 Wardour Street premises. Originating in a tank of celluloid in the Topical labs, and possibly set off by a fused wire, the explosion and subsequent fire blew out the windows and set a car ablaze on the opposite side of the street. The stairs between the Ideal Film Company on the ground floor and the Topical Film Company above caught fire, and a number of the women laboratory staff were cut off and had to jump down from the first-floor windows. Four were hospitalised, and one, Julia Ginsberg, who was originally reported as having only injured her foot, died a month later. The Ideal premises were undamaged.

It is unclear how much was lost in the fire, though the essential library of negatives appears to have survived largely intact, but Topical had to transfer their printing work to an outside firm and had troubles with discontented staff and the poor quality of the laboratory work. Despite such a calamity, the next issue came out on time, and it is rather surprising that they did not devote an item to themselves, since the fire had been widely covered in all the newspapers. William Jeapes oversaw the rebuilding of the printing works at 76–78 Wardour Street, but then caused further shock in May 1925 by announcing his resignation as managing director. The Topical Film Company had been to some extent the Jeapes family firm, but William Jeapes had been discontented ever since being obliged to sell the company to the wocc in 1917. Hulton's purchase of the company, and the introduction of a number of newspaper men into the running of the newsreel, can only have increased the sense of insult, and it was probably only because Topical was his creation that Jeapes stayed with the company for so long after. Having announced his resignation on 11 May,[123] he left with six months salary, then started all over again. On 3 May 1926 the first edition of *Empire News Bulletin* was released, William Jeapes' new newsreel produced by a new production company, British Pictorial Productions. This venture was to prove as successful as all his others and led eventually to the sound newsreel *Universal Talking News*. Jeapes valued independence above power, and with his two newsreels after *Topical Budget* rediscovered a product that was humbler than its rivals, yet over which he could exercise complete control. *Universal Talking News* (which used silent cameras and added on sound in the studio) carried the ethos behind Topical on into the sound era.

Just twelve days after Jeapes' departure from Topical, Sir Edward Hulton died. His personal influence on the newsreel had not been great, but his money and position as a newspaper proprietor had ensured its strength and creativity. It had been of some concern to Hulton that this part of his news empire was comparatively unsuccessful, and he even gave F. A. Enders, Topical's new managing director, permission to call on his estate should he need the money to improve Topical and FBO's performance. There was also a suggestion from Beaverbrook that he himself buy Topical and FBO from Hulton, or at least offer help to improve results.[124] Enders purchased a majority shareholding in the company in November 1925.

What few references there have been to Topical in past accounts have assumed that the company did not survive long after the fire. In fact, under Enders' lively and purposeful management (and without recourse to the Hulton estate) they were more successful than they had ever been before, but they cease to be of interest as a newsreel. *Topical Budget* was still entertaining, skilfully put together, and popular with audiences. The items and issues from this period are fun to watch, valuable for the archival material that they represent, and still on occasion they display creative camerawork or imaginative editing. What is missing is any progression or distinctive character. The years 1925 to 1931 were years of formula, in which *Topical Budget* became indistinguishable from *Pathé Gazette*. In the words of the Adrian Brunel parody, it became the Typical Budget.

Topical Budget ran from September 1911 to March 1931. Over that period some 2,000 issues were produced, or 10,000 individual items. If all survived (and around 80 per cent do), and they were run continuously at silent film speed, they would last for seven days. Assuming an average of twelve hours daylight over the year, that represents fourteen days of that period in history captured on film, eleven days of which survive. That fact alone, no matter where they pointed the cameras, or with what level of skill, is something to be treasured. That they made these films with some discretion and care, that they were imaginative and innovative, is to be celebrated. The three aims Topical always held – entertainment, good photography and topicality – ensured their vitality as a newsreel, and our resultant pleasure as recipients of this visual heritage.

In conclusion, the words of Lord Beaverbrook again, talking about the newsreel's role as a propaganda tool, but expressing sentiments which anyone associated with *Topical Budget* would have shared:

> In the work of publicity the cinematograph stands alone. It creates its own audience without effort, because men are naturally drawn to what they wish to see. And it does so because it contains that subtle admixture of art, reality, and swift and dramatic movement, which rivet the eyes and mind past all withdrawing. Many things can be presented through its medium which cannot be translated in pictures or placed upon the stage, and its appeal is not to the elect but to the emotions common to humanity.[125]

NOTES

Abbreviations used:
BBK Papers   Beaverbrook Papers
BLMB   Brent Laboratories Minute Book
HLRO   House of Lords Record Office
PRO   Public Record Office

Introduction

1. John Barnes, *The Rise of the Cinema in Great Britain* (London: Bishopsgate Press, 1983), p. 28. This contains much further information about the film activities of the Wrench firm at the turn of the century, as do Barnes' *The Beginnings of the Cinema in England* (Newton Abbott: David & Charles, 1976) and *Pioneers of the British Film* (London: Bishopsgate Press, 1983).
2. *Bioscope*, 12 February 1914, p. 613.
3. Henry E. White (ed.), *The Pageant of the Century*, (London: Odhams Press, 1933), p. 147.
4. *London Day By Day* appeared at the Palace Theatre in July 1906, and again at the Empire Theatre in January 1907. *Kinematograph and Lantern Weekly*, 12 December 1918, p. 56.
5. Nicholas Pronay, in Paul Smith (ed.), *The Historian and Film* (Cambridge: Cambridge University Press, 1976), p. 97, says of archetypal newsfilms that 'they set out to interest a *specific* audience by reporting an event which had *news value* not because of the inherent pictorial interest of the subject, but because the audience was already interested, had already been *conditioned* to be interested in it'.
6. Ken Gordon, 'Forty Years with a Newsreel Camera', *The Cine-Technician*, Mar–Apr 1951, pp. 44–50; *Kinematograph and Lantern Weekly*, 10 April 1919, p. 64.
7. This is the likely release date. The issue was reviewed in a weekly trade paper [see note 8 below] on 7 September. One of the items, the Ebor Handicap, took place on 30 August. Topical's tenth anniversary issue fell on 1 September 1921 (issue number 523–1). From all these it appears probable that the first issue came out on 1 September (a Friday), or just possibly 31 August.
8. *Kinematograph and Lantern Weekly*, 7 September 1911, p. 969.
9. There were occasional experiments with other issue patterns. In mid-1913 *Pathé's Animated Gazette* was coming out three times a week.

10. Cameraman Harry Raymond claimed to have founded the *Topical Times* in 1912 when he was with Jury's (*Kinematograph and Lantern Weekly*, 16 October 1919, p. 107); if this was a newsreel it did not last long and was not a success. During the First World War Charles Urban edited *Official War Review* in America and after the war co-founded the American newsreel *Kinograms*.
11. F. A. Talbot, *Moving Pictures. How They Are Made and Worked* (London: William Heinemann, 1912), pp. 277–86.
12. Raymond Fielding, *The American Newsreel 1911–1967* (Norman: University of Oklahoma Press, 1972), pp. 87–8. The earliest reference to the term and to *Topical Budget* is in 1917; HLRO, BBK Papers E/2/13, 16 November 1917, Tewson to Beaverbrook.
13. Talbot, *Moving Pictures*, p. 278.
14. Ibid, p. 277.
15. BLMB, 1913–1947, p. 31.
16. *Bioscope*, 5 December 1912, p. 711.
17. The other major newsreel story of the period, the coronation Delhi Durbar of 1911, was not filmed by Topical. Two key newsfilm events, the coronation of King George V and the investiture of the Prince of Wales, occurred just before *Topical Budget* was founded.
18. Valentia Steer, *The Romance of the Cinema* (London: Arthur Pearson, 1913), pp. 86–7.
19. Advertisement in the *Bioscope*, 28 November 1912, p. 620.
20. See Kevin Brownlow, *The War, the West, and the Wilderness* (London: Secker & Warburg, 1979), pp. 8–21, 55–8.
21. The notable exception was Pathé.
22. A. J. P. Taylor, *Beaverbrook* (London: Hamish Hamilton, 1972), p. 144.
23. This was issue number 339–2, released on 23 February 1918, and the first time the newsreel was known as *Pictorial News (Official)*. Allenby entered Jerusalem on 11 December 1917.
24. Movietone's American parent company, Fox, had been running a sound news show at a London theatre for a few months up to this date.
25. Issue number 928–1, release date 6 June 1929, length 431 feet. In the *Bioscope*, 12 June 1929, p. 25, extensive coverage is given to Movietone and Gaumont's efforts, which is then followed by: 'F.B.O. were also out in record time with an excellent sound picture of the race . . . creditably executed'. The comparative brevity of this notice, and the absence of any information in Topical's own records, would seem to suggest that they resorted to some simple sound effects so as not to be outdone by their rivals on this occasion. The experiment does not appear to have been repeated.
26. *Kinematograph Weekly*, 19 March 1931, p. 38.

The World War

1. *Bioscope*, 27 September 1917, p. 23. This press notice was put out four months after the take-over by the WOCC. So poor had been the performance of the Official newsreel up to this date that it was felt necessary to readvertise the scheme as if it were a fresh initiative. The first steps towards distribution overseas had already been taken. Also, *Topical*

Budget was actually released on Wednesdays and Saturdays at this time.

2. *Bioscope*, 13 August 1914, p. 645.
3. *Bioscope*, 17 September 1914, p. 1025.
4. Evan Strong, 'War and Cinematography', *Bioscope*, 20 August 1914, pp. 737–9.
5. *Bioscope*, 3 September 1914, p. 864.
6. Quoted in the *Bioscope*, 20 August 1914, p. 701.
7. Details from cinema handbills and other papers held by Mr Clifford Jeapes, and from renters' advertisements in the *Bioscope*, 10 December 1914, pp. 1065 and 1085, and *Bioscope*, 7 January 1915, p. 56. The two missing titles appear to be *The King of the Belgians with his Troops* and *With the Belgian Army* (640 feet), but it is not known which was released first. Another possible title in the series is *The Devastation of Termonde*.
8. But as the film was taken on 20 September and released three days later, it was a remarkably quick transaction.
9. Nicholas Hiley, *Making War. The British News Media and Government Control, 1914–16* (PhD thesis, Open University, 1985), pp. 382–3. These figures are based on an analysis of newsreel exhibition taken from trade returns in the *Bioscope* from January to June 1915.
10. The examples range from issue number 250–1 (7 June 1916) to issue number 268–2 (14 October 1916).
11. BLMB, 1913–47, p. 44.
12. 'Running the Topical Films', *Cassell's Saturday Journal*, 29 May 1915, p. 2.
13. Issue number 192–1, release date 28 April 1915, length 52 feet.
14. Issue number 197–1, release date 2 June 1915, length 51 feet.
15. Issue number 204–1, release date 21 July 1915, length 50 feet.
16. Issue number 218–2, release date 30 October 1915, length 35 feet.
17. Issue number 238–1, release date 15 March 1916, length 60 feet. Grammatical errors and spelling mistakes were not uncommon in *Topical Budget* at this time.
18. Issue number 239–1, release date 22 March 1916, length 56 feet.
19. Issue number 194–1, release date 12 May 1915, length 102 feet.
20. Issue number 194–2, release date 15 May 1915, length 85 feet.
21. Issue number 268–1, release date 12 October 1916, length 48 feet.
22. For example, an item showing WAACS tending graves in France, WHERE OUR HEROES SLEEP, issue number 346–2, release date 13 April 1918, length 38 feet.
23. CHANGING QUARTERS, issue number 193–1, release date 5 May 1915, length 58+ feet.
24. For example, BELGIAN ENGINEERS IN THE FIELD, issue number 221–1, release date 17 November 1915, length 58 feet.
25. Issue number 255–1, release date 13 July 1916, length 53+ feet.
26. Issue number 268–1, release date 12 October 1916, length 57+ feet.
27. As witnessed by George Pearson in *Flashback. The Autobiography of a British Film-maker* (London: George Allen & Unwin, 1957), p. 29.
28. Issue number 206–1, release date 4 August 1914, length 51+ feet.
29. Issue number 268–2, release date 14 October 1916, lengths 42+ feet

and 77 feet.

30. Issue number 274–1, release date 22 November 1916, length 64 feet.
31. Issue number 247–1, release date 17 May 1916, length 57 feet.
32. Issue number 270–1, release date 25 October 1916, length 52 feet.
33. Issue number 269–1, release date 18 October 1916, lengths 71 feet and 55 feet.
34. Issue number 267–1, release date 4 October 1916, length 57 feet.
35. Issue number 228–1, release date 5 January 1916, length 40+ feet.
36. The Topical Film Company were agents for Official films from Saloni-ka before they were taken over by the War Office Cinematograph Committee. HLRO, BBK Papers E/2/1, 30 October 1916. From July 1916 the Official cameraman to the British was reported to be Ariel Varges of William Randolph Hearst's International Film Service. Var-ges can probably be credited with the bulk of the film from Salonika and of the forces in Serbia in *Topical Budget* at this time. He later became the Official cameraman in Mesopotamia. Hiley, *Making War*, p. 438.
37. Issue number 272–2, release date 11 November 1916, length 67 feet.
38. Issue number 278–2, release date 23 December 1916, length 57 feet.
39. Issue number 227–2, release date 1 January 1916, lengths 34 feet and 73 feet.
40. Taylor, *Beaverbrook*, p. 89.
41. Hiley, *Making War*, p. 424.
42. S. D. Badsey, *British Official Film in the First World War* (1981), p. 10.
43. Hiley, *Making War*, pp. 423–4.
44. See S. D. Badsey, 'Battle of the Somme: British war-propaganda', in *Historical Journal of Film, Radio and Television* vol. 3, no. 2, 1983, pp. 99–115; Brownlow, *The War*, pp. 61–5; Hiley, *Making War*, pp. 439–53; Nicholas Reeves, *Official British Film Propaganda During the First World War* (London: Croom Helm, 1986), pp. 157–64 passim.
45. Hiley, *Making War*, pp. 456–7.
46. General Charteris and Colonel Hutton Wilson. HLRO, BBK Papers E/2/5, 9 May 1917, Beaverbrook to Charteris; E/2/5, 14 May 1917, Beaverbrook to Hutton Wilson.
47. These were *Battle of the Ancre and the Advance of the Tanks* (released January 1917) and *The German Retreat and the Battle of Arras* (released June 1917).
48. Issue 10 of *Annales de la Guerre* was available at the same time as the first issue of the *War Office Official Topical Budget*. A regular exchange deal was set up between these two official newsreels.
49. HLRO, BBK Papers E/2/14, 20 April 1917.
50. HLRO, BBK Papers E/2/14, 12 April 1917.
51. HLRO, BBK Papers E/2/5, 8 May 1917, possibly from Beaverbrook. This is the rough draft of a letter, and the final version only describes Jeapes as 'a first class producer of film'.
52. HLRO, BBK Papers E/2/5, 15 May 1917, Beaverbrook to Colonel Hutton Wilson.
53. HLRO, BBK Papers E/2/5, 22 May 1917, William Jeapes to William Jury; E/2/5, 30 May 1917, letter from Beaverbrook.

54. Part of the attraction of Topical to the WOCC must have been the descriptive name: it was both a topical budget and the *Topical Budget*. During its Official period the newsreel was usually referred to on paper as the *War Office Topical Budget*. See discussion about the various names employed by the newsreel later in the chapter.

55. These titles and footages (which exclude the length of the titles) are taken from the first of the issue sheets for the *War Office Official Topical Budget*.

56. HLRO, BBK Papers E/2/17, sales report 2 March 1918.

57. First issue 16 January 1917.

58. HLRO, BBK Papers E/2/8, 8 August 1917, Holt-White to Beaverbrook.

59. Ibid.

60. HLRO, BBK Papers E/2/8, 15 August 1917, Holt-White to Beaverbrook.

61. Issue number 324–1, release date 7 November 1917, length 66 feet.

62. Issue number 316–1, release date 12 September 1917, length 60 feet.

63. Issue number 324–1, release date 7 November 1917, length 77 feet.

64. For example, *Bioscope*, 27 September 1917, pp. 6 and 23 [quoted at head of chapter], *The Times*, 21 September 1917, p. 3.

65. HLRO, BBK Papers E/2/9, 3 October 1917, Holt-White to Beaverbrook.

66. By 19 November 1917 12,281 shares in the company were settled for. A further 1,000 were held by Topical director D. W. Player, then thought to be in Mesopotamia. There were 14,782 shares in all, eventually purchased at the average price of 15s 1d each, from a total of 15,000. The company directors also resigned on this date. HLRO, BBK Papers E/2/13, 19 November 1917; *The Times*, 23 September 1918, p. 5; BLMB, 1913–1947, pp. 66–8.

67. HLRO, BBK Papers E/1/14, 6 December 1917, Scott to Beaverbrook.

68. The first issue so named was either 328–2 (8 December 1917) or 329–1 (12 December 1917).

69. HLRO, BBK Papers E/2/13, 16 November 1917, Tewson to Beaverbrook.

70. HLRO, BBK Papers E/2/8, 27 April 1917, William Jeapes to WOCC.

71. *Bioscope*, 28 February 1918, p. 2.

72. HLRO, BBK Papers E/2/18, draft report [undated].

73. HLRO, BBK Papers E/2/14, sales reports 10 November 1917, 24 November 1917, 5 January 1918, 26 January 1918; BBK E/2/17, sales report 2 March 1918.

74. The twenty million attendance figure, a generally accepted number for the period, includes people going to the cinema more than once a week. The three million attendance figure means individual cinemagoers exposed to the newsreel at least once a week. See opening of next chapter for a more detailed discussion of audience figures.

75. John is quoted as saying, 'I would much like to help so excellent a purpose as the War Office Topical Budget, and will at once set about the problem of a Poster'. HLRO, BBK Papers E/2/14, 26 January 1918. Two further letters show Beaverbrook reminding him of his promise, and John saying that the design will be completed on Monday 27 May. BBK Papers E/3/34, 22 May 1918, Beaverbrook to John; BBK Papers E/3/34, 24 May 1918, John to Beaverbrook. The cartoon, which is held by the Canadian War Museum, is a design in charcoal, measuring 8 ×

5 feet (224.4 × 149.5 cm).

76. Issue number 339–2, release date 23 February 1918, length 318 feet. The whole issue consisted of this single item. The film was released in a number of versions during the war, and later the material was re-edited and re-released in various forms. Essentially there was the original newsreel version, 318 feet, and an extended version designed for worldwide release as an individual film, 720 feet. Details of these two main versions and the variations uncovered from surviving copies of the film are to be found in the catalogue to *Topical Budget* which accompanies this history.

77. 'It was a refreshing contrast to have T. E. L. about for a week . . . He went about happily in a second lieutenant's tunic and badges somewhere between a lieutenant and a captain, and no decoration and no belt. When he went to Jerusalem with Allenby he is reported to have borrowed from one person and another a regular staff outfit with proper badges and even decorations. I only hope he appears in the cinema pictures taken on that occasion, because, otherwise, an unknown aspect of him will be lost.' David G. Hogarth to his wife, letter quoted in John E. Mack, *A Prince of our Disorder. The Life of T. E. Lawrence* (London: Weidenfeld and Nicolson, 1976), p. 158.

78. BLMB, 1913–1947, pp. 71–72.

79. *Kinematograph and Lantern Weekly*, 26 September 1918, p. 70. Sir Graham Greene joined the WOCC in April 1917, representing the Navy, but it was only a token appointment.

80. This exasperating character returned from the Western Front in March 1917 to write up his experiences, but was turned down in November 1917 when he was suggested for home front coverage with the *War Office Official Topical Budget*, William Jeapes declaring that he was unable to get on with him. He subsequently joined the CWRO as a cameraman on the Western Front. His unreliable memoirs were published, after much official displeasure, as *How I Filmed the War* (London: Herbert Jenkins, 1920).

81. 'Only men of a category lower than "A" will be considered eligible for employment as proposed.' HLRO, BBK Papers E/2/2, 21 June 1917.

82. HLRO, BBK Papers E/2/8, 9 September 1917. Davies eventually filmed for the MOI and the newsreel in 1918, but only in Britain, and possibly only after being wounded in action.

83. HLRO, BBK Papers E/2/8, 9 September 1917, Faunthorpe to Beaverbrook.

84. Badsey, *British Official Film*, pp. 38–40. McDowell took over from Harry Bartholomew, who had taken over from Major Andrew Holt in November 1917.

85. In THE BATTLE SOUTH OF ARRAS, issue number 366–2, release date 2 September 1918, length 111 feet.

86. HLRO, BBK Papers E/2/2, Bovill papers.

87. Issue number 364–1, release date 15 August 1918, length 140 feet.

88. Issue number 365–2, release date 19 August 1918, length 207 feet. The last two intertitles, but not the action they describe, are missing from the surviving copy.

89. Reeves, *Official British Film*, pp. 169–74.

90. For example, *Against the Grain*, on the need to feed poultry with sunflower seeds; *What's the Use of Grumblin'?*, criticising those complaining about war conditions; and the notorious *The Leopard's Spots*, about the need to be wary of German businessmen after the war.

91. Issue number 374–2, release date 20 October 1918, length of first item 89 feet, length of second item 50 feet. Main edition.

92. *Kinematograph and Lantern Weekly*, 31 October 1918, p. 58.

93. PRO FO 395/233/241273, 12 September 1918, Frazer to Northam. The first foreign edition given on the issue sheets is 369–1 (release date 19 September 1918).

94. Issue number 374–2, release date 28 October 1918, length of items unknown. Foreign edition. Titles taken from issue sheets.

95. HLRO, BBK Papers E/2/9, 5 October 1917? memorandum from Beaverbrook?

96. PRO FO 395/233/68245, 17 April 1918, Northam to Gaselee.

97. PRO FO 395/233, various reports and accounts between 17 April 1918 and 12 September 1918.

98. PRO FO 395/233/113861, 27 June 1918; FO 395/233/121197, 25 June 1918.

99. *Report of the Work of the British War Information Committee for China During 1918*, 31 March 1919, pp. 13–18, PRO FO 395/269/003893.

100. HLRO, BBK Papers E/2/17, 20 January 1918?

101. Information about the *British War Office Official News Film* and *British Government Official News* comes from surviving copies catalogued by the Library of Congress, Motion Picture, Broadcasting and Recorded Sound Division, detailed in Imperial War Museum Department of Film (Topical Film Company file) 26 July 1989, letter from Duncan to Smither. It is quite likely, with different parties handling the newsreel in the USA, that it was released under other names as well.

102. HLRO, BBK Papers E/1/29, 30 March 1918, report by Lord Beaverbrook on the work of the Canadian War Records Office.

103. BLMB, 1913–1947, pp. 78–81.

104. Harold Jeapes was the only Official cameraman; recent evidence has made it clear that there was a second cameraman, possibly American, filming from a high vantage point at the side of the hall to Jeapes' left.

105. Issue number 410–1, release date 3 July 1919, length 323 feet. Length of special release version 944 feet.

106. *Kinematograph and Lantern Weekly*, 10 July 1919, p. 108.

The Nineteen Twenties

1. There are no precise figures for cinema audiences in Britain until the 1930s and any such estimate is necessarily very vague. Rachel Low, in *The History of the British Film 1914–1918* (London: George Allen & Unwin, 1950), p. 23, reports an approximate figure of 20,000,000 attendances a week for 1917, and in *The History of the British Film 1918–1929* (London: George Allen & Unwin, 1971), p. 47, refers to a figure for 1927 of 14,000,000 people, or 20,000,000 attendances a week.

2. The audience survey conducted by exhibitor Sidney Bernstein in 1927 reported that 33.5 per cent of those interviewed went once a week,

47.5 per cent twice a week, 14.75 per cent three times, and 4.5 per cent four times. Bernstein's figures actually add up to 100.25 per cent. *Bioscope*, 4 August 1927, p. 20. In 1929 he reported a figure of 60 per cent going twice a week. *Bioscope*, 3 April 1929, p. 21.

3. *Kinematograph and Lantern Weekly*, 15 March 1917, p. 96.
4. *Kinematograph and Lantern Weekly*, 21 February 1918, p. 1.
5. F. A. Enders, 'Minutes of the Convention Held at Film Booking Offices (1919) Ltd on Saturday, August 30th [1924]', pp. 8–10. Papers of Mr John Enders.
6. Figures for February 1925, BLMB, 1924–1937, 1937–1944, p. 54.
7. *Bioscope*, 4 August 1927, p. 20.
8. *Kinematograph Weekly*, 19 March 1931, p. 38.
9. Issue number 486–1, release date 16 December 1920, length 71 feet.
10. Issue number 582–2, release date 23 October 1922, length 177 feet.
11. Hulton's titles in 1919 included the *Daily Sketch, Daily Dispatch, Evening Standard, Illustrated Sunday Herald, Evening Chronicle, Sunday Chronicle, Ideas, Sporting Chronicle* and *Athletic News.*
12. Ken Gordon, 'Forty Years with a Newsreel Camera', *The Cine-Technician*, Mar–Apr 1951, pp. 44–50.
13. Film Booking Offices are sometimes confused with the American company Film Booking Offices of America, also known as FBO. Although they both handled the same kind of fiction films there was no connection between them. The British FBO predated the American by four years, having been founded in 1917. The American FBO became part of the merger in 1928 that resulted in RKO Pictures.
14. The Clozenburg brothers shortly afterwards changed their surname to Clavering.
15. For the period 10 February 1919 to 2 August 1919, Topical made a loss of £3,301 14s 7d. In May 1922 they were able to show a profit for the previous financial year of £13,769. BLMB, 1913–1947, pp. 99, 107.
16. These dates are provisional and based on examination of prints. However, the latter date seems to be related to Sir Edward Hulton's retiring to the south of France in 1923 and selling his papers to Beaverbrook. Beaverbrook sold them again to Lord Rothmere, keeping the *Evening Standard.* In 1924 Rothmere (who owned the *Daily Mirror*) sold the Hulton press to the Berry group, keeping the *Daily Sketch*, which he then sold to the Berry group in 1925. Taylor, *Beaverbrook*, p. 214.
17. 'There is reason to believe that cinema attendances in any area are the resultant of two principal conditions: first, the weather; and second, the attractiveness of the principal picture.' Simon Rowson, *A Statistical Survey of the Cinema Industry in Great Britain in 1934* (London: Royal Statistical Society, 1936), p. 115.
18. Leslie Wood, in *The Miracle of the Movies* (London: Burke Publishing, 1947), p. 193, suggests that the most common introduction for the silent newsreels was 'Blaze Away'.
19. Topical used a number of slogans over the years, on both the opening titles and their advertising:

    News of the World in Animation (1912–15)
    All British News-Film (1916)

The British Animated News-Film (1917)
The Reuter of the Screen (at least 1920 to 1927)
The Great British News Film (1920? to at least 1928)
The Only British News Film (1922)

20. D. R. P., 'Cinema Music', *The Cinema*, 9 August 1917, p. 20d.
21. Issue number 648–2, release date 28 January 1924.
22. Issue number 851–1, release date 15 December 1927.
23. Issue number 645–1, release date 3 January 1924.
24. Issue number 699–1, release date 15 January 1925.
25. For example, THE DUBLIN REBELLION, issue number 245–2, release date 6 May 1916, length 284 feet.
26. Issue number 758–1, release date 4 March 1926, length 57 feet.
27. Issue number 823–1, release date 1 June 1927, length 345 feet. The structure referred to is the new grandstand.
28. Issue number 549–1, release date 2 March 1922, length 518 feet. Newsreel cameras were not allowed inside the Abbey and a photograph was used for the scene inside.
29. Examples taken from issue numbers 502–1, 505–2, 534–2, 544–2, 555–1, 589–2, 591–2, 608–2, 619–2, 635–1, 676–1, 713–2, 721–2, 731–1 and 738–2.
30. Issue number 645–1, release date 3 January 1924. The figures all refer to 35mm footage. There are 65 feet of titles.
31. Issue number 233–2, release date 12 February 1916, length 67 feet.
32. Issue number 601–2, release date 5 March 1923, length 89 feet.
33. Issue number 627–2, release date 3 September 1923, length 49 feet.
34. Issue number 490–1, release date 13 January 1921, length 115 feet.
35. Topical's fashion items, such as the 'My Lady's Boudoir' series in 1926, only exist in negative form, so it is not known if they would have been coloured, and to what degree.
36. A detailed breakdown of the issue numbers and dates covered by these books is given in the list of sources.
37. In 1927 a series of short films, under the title *Fortune of Faces*, was released by FBO, featuring 'character studies' of famous people from various walks of life. Taken from the *Topical Budget* library, the project appears to have been connected with phrenology (there is a separate section in the portraits contained in the subject index cards thus entitled), and to have been a pet idea of F. A. Enders. See *Bioscope*, 17 February 1927, p. 72.
38. The foreign distribution of the Official newsreel had largely come to an end by December 1918, but copies appear to have been shown for a short while thereafter in France and America. Curiously, in July 1919, long after the company had been sold by the WOCC, they were still producing a 'Colonial Budget', which showed a gross profit of £75 0s 3d a week. BLMB, 1913–1947, p. 97. Presumably an opportune hangover from the Official period, and no more than the standard edition issued abroad, there is one further reference to it in 1920. Accounts of Topical Film Company, 1 January 1921. Papers of Mr John Enders.
39. There were no camerawomen in the regular British newsreel business. General's daughter Jessica Borthwick took film of the 1913 Balkan War

which she subsequently showed on lecture tours, and it is alleged (by Ken Gordon) that Will Barker made use of women operators before the First World War at 15 shillings a week, half a cameraman's wage. If this is so, it is likely to have been for topical events requiring a larger numbers of operators than usual.

40. A detailed analysis of the background and experience of newsreel cameramen in the silent era is given in James Ballantyne (ed.), *Researcher's Guide to British Newsreels Volume II* (London: BUFVC, 1988), in the section 'British Newsreel Staff 1910–1920', pp. 28–31, by Nicholas Hiley.

41. All seventy-six are given in an index to the catalogue of *Topical Budget* issues which accompanies this history. This contains detailed biographical summaries of the careers of the main cameramen, as well as other major figures connected with the newsreel.

42. Philip Norman, 'The Newsreel Boys', *Sunday Times Magazine*, 10 January 1971, p. 10.

43. *Kinematograph Weekly*, 20 November 1919, suppl. p. xix.

44. BLMB, 1924–1937, 1937–1944, pp. 78–9.

45. MEN WHO FILM THE WORLD FOR YOU, issue number 576–1, release date 7 September 1922, length 31 feet; MOUNT ARARAT OF STEEL, issue number 727–2, release date 3 August 1925, length 94 feet.

46. Issue number 644–1, release date 27 December 1923, length 358 feet. Topical issued reviews of the year for 1923 and 1924 only.

47. Article in *The Cine-Technician*, Sep–Oct 1941, pp. 112–17.

48. *The Times*, 5 September 1916, p. 6.

49. *Kinematograph and Lantern Weekly*, 27 February 1919, p. 62.

50. *Kinematograph and Lantern Weekly*, 8 May 1919, p. 78.

51. Paul Wyand, *Useless If Delayed* (London: George G. Harrap, 1959), pp. 23, 30, 39, 40.

52. Low, *British Film 1918–1929*, p. 275.

53. Herbert Tracey (ed.), *The British Press. A Survey, a Newspaper Directory, and a Who's Who in Journalism* (London: Europa Publications, 1929), p. 44.

54. *Kinematograph and Lantern Weekly*, 20 March 1919, p. 63.

55. *The Cine-Technician*, Oct–Dec 1940, p. 94.

56. BLMB, 1924–1937, 1937–1944, p. 26.

57. Accounts for Topical Film Company, 31 December 1921. Papers of Mr John Enders.

58. BLMB, 1924–1937, 1937–1944, pp. 90–1.

59. Wyand, *Useless If Delayed*, pp. 27–8.

60. Gordon, 'Forty Years', p. 46.

61. John 'Bunny' Hutchins, 'All in a Day's Work', *The Cine-Technician*, Aug–Sep 1937, p. 114.

62. Barnes, *The Rise of the Cinema*, p. 189. The film of the 1895 Derby taken by Birt Acres was not shown publicly until several months after the event, thus denying its status as 'news'. Barnes, *Beginnings of the Cinema*, pp. 31–2.

63. Barnes, *Pioneers*, p. 157.

64. *Gaumont Graphic* secured a much closer shot, which subsequently became famous, but their long-held claim that the shot was exclusive

is false.

65. Hutchins, 'All in a Day's Work', p. 114.
66. Gordon, 'Forty Years', p. 49.
67. Issue number 504–2, release date 25 April 1921, length 505 feet.
68. Issue number 557–2, release date 1 May 1922, length 482 feet.
69. *Bioscope*, 4 May 1922, p. 42.
70. Bernard Grant, *To the Four Corners. The Memoirs of a News Photographer* (London: Hutchinson, 1933), pp. 189–90.
71. Jock Gemmell, 'Newsreels – Ancient and Modern', *The Cine-Technician*, Jan–Feb 1952, p. 3.
72. Fred Wilson recalled: 'Once on a job of this kind I got into the Cup Final disguised as a parson, with a girl companion who carried my automatic cine-camera in her bag.' 'Searching the World for News', *Newcastle Sunday Sun*, 10 February 1935, p. 16.
73. Wyand, *Useless If Delayed*, p. 63.
74. The dead chicken was a regular feature. On one occasion Pathé stole the chicken from its flag-pole, cooked it in 'the most nauseating oil', carefully packed it, and sent it by special messenger to the editor of *Topical Budget* with the message, 'Pathé have cooked your Goose!' Gordon, 'Forty Years', p. 49.
75. Jim Wilde, 'Just the Winkers, Old Boy!', *Eyepiece* vol. 7 no. 5, Sep/Oct 1986, pp. 197–203. This is an article on the life of cameraman Ernie Palmer, who was grader in the *Topical Budget* labs between 1921 and 1925. Palmer recalled working on a Cup Final (probably 1922) from Saturday evening to 2.00 pm on the Monday, turning out 480 prints.
76. Advertisement in the *Bioscope*, 26 April 1923, p. 38.
77. Issue number 609–2, release date 30 April 1923, length 349 feet.
78. Charlie Chaplin, *My Wonderful Visit* (London: Hurst and Blackett, 1922). Originally published in the USA as *My Trip Abroad* (New York: Harper and Bros, 1922).
79. Ibid., p. 38.
80. Ibid., pp. 45–6.
81. Ibid., pp. 50–2.
82. Ibid., pp. 57–8.
83. Ibid., p. 72.
84. Ibid., p. 78.
85. Issue number 524–2, release date 12 September 1921, length 372 feet. The main title features a cartoon of Chaplin. 'Charlie on the Ocean' was also an alternative title for Chaplin's film *Shanghaied*.
86. This is a reference to Chaplin's own description of himself at the time, which he repeats in *My Wonderful Visit*, p. 56: 'When they see me minus my hat, cane, and shoes, it is like taking the whiskers off Santa Claus.'
87. Issue number 461–1, release date 24 June 1920.
88. John Hutchins, 'A Paper Read to the Hornsey Branch, British Legion, on Sunday, February 21st, 1937', pp. 13–14. Reprinted, with some alterations, as 'All in a Day's Work' in *The Cine-Technician*, Aug–Sep 1937, pp. 112–16.
89. Rudi Blesh, *Keaton* (London: Secker & Warburg, 1967), p. 218.
90. *Kinematograph and Lantern Weekly*, 15 May 1919, p. 67. In the regular

column, 'What the Kine Would Like to Know', it says, 'H. G. Wells doesn't go to the pictures because of snobbery in the topicals. But illustrated papers are just the same.'

91. Wyand, *Useless If Delayed*, p. 34.
92. Issue numbers 743–2, release date 23 November 1925, length 138 feet; 744–1, release date 26 November 1925, length 112 feet; and 744–2, release date 30 November 1925, length 216 feet.
93. *The Times*, 27 February 1922, p. 8.
94. *Bioscope*, 2 March 1922, p. 5. *Gaumont Graphic* had ten cameramen, with a back-up staff of one hundred, and Topical had fifteen, 'including such "stars" as J. B. McDowell.'
95. Issue number 609–2, release date 30 April 1923, length 687 feet.
96. A. Cochrane, in *The Dictionary of National Biography 1922–1930*.
97. *Bioscope*, 23 October 1924, p. 47.
98. *Kinematograph and Lantern Weekly*, 25 June 1908, p. 127. See also Rachel Low, *The History of the British Film 1906–1914* (London: George Allen & Unwin, 1949), p. 151.
99. Cecil Hepworth, 'The Secret History of the Cabinet Film', in *Kinematograph Year Book Diary and Directory 1917*, pp. 43–6. Reprinted with further comment and different memories of the events in Hepworth's *Came the Dawn. Memories of a Film Pioneer* (London: Phoenix House, 1951), pp. 99–104. Hepworth's original film 'interviews' were subsequently released in September 1916 as three one-reelers, featuring extracts from the politicians' speeches in the intertitles. *Bioscope*, 31 August 1916, p. 791.
100. THE NEW GOVERNMENT, issue number 584–1, release date 2 November 1922, length 160 feet.
101. *The Times*, 4 November 1922, p. 12.
102. In 1918 Elvey directed a feature film, *The Life Story of David Lloyd George*, for the Ideal Film Company. The film was withdrawn before release.
103. Low, *British Film 1918–1929*, p. 44.
104. 'The Newspaper "Boss" – and the Kinema', *Kinematograph Weekly*, 4 March 1920, p. 79.
105. Newspaper circulation figures supplied by Dr Nicholas Hiley.
106. MODERN 'HUNS' LEAVE THEIR MARK, issue number 162–2, release date 3 October 1914, length 54 feet.
107. Issue number 361–1, release date 25 July 1918. The titles are taken from the issue sheets.
108. Issue number 310–1, release date 1 August 1917, length 46 feet.
109. Issue number 423–2 complete, 6 October 1919. Descriptions taken from *Kinematograph and Lantern Weekly*, 9 October 1919, p. 98. Lengths unknown.
110. Issue number 502–1, release date 7 April 1921, length 81 feet. The titles may not be in the correct order.
111. Examples from 14 April 1921 to 30 June 1921.
112. Issue number 767–1, release date 6 May 1926, length 192 feet. This is a description of the surviving copy of film, which is 160 feet long with the shots of Ramsay MacDonald and J. H. Thomas missing. It would appear to be otherwise complete. 192 feet is the length given in

Topical's own issue books.

113. Issue number 523–2, release date 5 September 1921, length 123 feet.
114. Issue number 414–2, release date 4 August 1919, length unknown. Titles given in *Kinematograph and Lantern Weekly*, 7 August 1919, p. 100.
115. Issue number 245–2, release date 6 May 1916, length 284 feet.
116. Examples taken from 11 July 1921 to 11 December 1922. Titles in parentheses taken from issue books only.
117. Issue number 515–2, release date 11 July 1921, length 39 feet.
118. An interesting half-exception is DO YOU KNOW THIS HANDWRITING?, issue number 540–2, release date 2 January 1922, length 28 feet, which shows a telegram sent to a murder victim, the titles inviting the audience to identify the handwriting.
119. Issue number 564–1, release date 15 June 1922, length 107 feet.
120. Issue number 566–2, release date 3 July 1922, length 152 feet.
121. Issue number 586–1, release date 16 November 1922, length 134 feet.
122. Forsyth Hardy (ed.), *Grierson on Documentary* (London: Collins, 1946), p. 134.
123. BLMB, 1924–1937, 1937–1944, p. 88.
124. HLRO, BBK Papers C/180A, 25 February 1925, Beaverbrook to Hulton; C/180A, 28 February 1925, Hulton to Beaverbrook.
125. HLRO, BBK Papers E/1/29, 30 March 1918, report by Lord Beaverbrook on the work of the Canadian War Records Office.

APPENDIX 1
Chronological List of Newsreel Events

Note: This covers major events in *Topical Budget*'s history and the silent newsreels in general. Significant historical events and newsreel subjects are also included.

	1895	Birt Acres films the Boat Race (March), the Derby (May) and the opening of the Kiel Canal (June)
Feb	1896	Lumière programme at Regent Polytechnic, London
Mar	1896	Paul begins film shows at the Alhambra
Jun	1896	Paul films the Derby and screens it the following night
	1897	William Jeapes enters film industry as showman
Jun	1897	Queen Victoria's Diamond Jubilee
	1898	Charles Urban turns Maguire & Baucus into the Warwick Trading Company
Oct	1899	Start of Boer war
	1900	Will Barker's Autoscope Company founded at 50 Gray's Inn Road
Feb	1901	Funeral of Queen Victoria
	1902	*Jeapes' Animated Graphic* founded
May	1902	End of Boer war
Aug	1902	Coronation of King Edward VII
Dec	1902	Delhi Durbar
Dec	1903	Wright brothers' flight
Feb	1904	Russo-Japanese war
Sep	1905	Peace between Russia and Japan
Jan	1906	Autoscope Company merges with Warwick Trading Company under Will Barker
Feb	1906	Liberal Party returned to power
Apr	1906	San Francisco earthquake
May	1906	Daily Bioscope opens
Jul	1906	Barker's *London Day By Day* issued
	1908	*Pathé Fait-Divers* (later *Pathé Journal*) first issued in France
Apr	1908	Asquith becomes Prime Minister
Mar	1909	Edward Hulton founds *Daily Sketch* in Manchester
Apr	1909	Peary reaches the North Pole
Jul	1909	Blériot flies the Channel
Aug	1909	Barker forms own company (Barker Motion Photography)
May	1910	Funeral of King Edward VII
Jun	1910	*Pathe's Animated Gazette* first issued in Britain

Jul	1910	*Warwick Bioscope Chronicle* founded by William Jeapes
Jul	1910	Johnson-Jeffries boxing match
Oct	1910	*Gaumont Graphic* founded
Jan	1911	Siege of Sidney Street
Jun	1911	Coronation of King George V
Jul	1911	Investiture of Prince of Wales at Caernarvon
Aug	1911	Railway strike
Sep	1911	First *Topical Budget* issue released
Dec	1911	Amundsen reaches the South Pole
Dec	1911	Delhi Durbar
Apr	1912	Sinking of the *Titanic*
Sep	1912	First Balkan war
Mar	1913	*Eclair Journal* founded
May	1913	End of first Balkan war
May	1913	*Williamson's Animated News* founded
Jun	1913	Emily Davison killed following Derby
Jul	1913	Second Balkan war
Sep	1913	Topical Film Company Ltd registered
Aug	1913	End of second Balkan war
	1914	*Daily Sketch* moves to London
Apr	1914	Topical's offices move to 76–78 Wardour Street
Jul	1914	Assassination at Sarajevo
Aug	1914	World War begins
Aug	1914	Cherry Kearton founds *The Whirlpool Of War*
May	1915	Sinking of the *Lusitania*
Oct	1915	Agreement between War Office and Cinematograph Trade Topical Committee
Nov	1915	First Official cameramen sent out to the Western Front
Dec	1915	Retreat at Gallipoli
Dec	1915	*Britain Prepared* released
Jan	1916	Beaverbrook creates the Canadian War Records Office
Jan	1916	First films of the British Topical Committee for War Films shown
Apr	1916	Dublin rebellion
Jul	1916	Battle of the Somme
Aug	1916	*Battle Of The Somme* film released
Oct	1916	War Office Cinematograph Committee formed
Dec	1916	Lloyd George becomes Prime Minister
Apr	1917	USA enters war
May	1917	Formation of *War Office Official Topical Budget*
Nov	1917	WOCC purchases the Topical Film Company
Nov	1917	Russian revolution
Dec	1917	Allenby enters Jerusalem
Feb	1918	Beaverbrook becomes head of new Ministry of Information
Feb	1918	Official newsreel becomes *Pictorial News (Official)*. Release of GENERAL ALLENBY'S ENTRY INTO JERUSALEM in the first issue
May	1918	Pattern of issue changed from Wednesdays and Saturdays to Mondays and Thursdays in line with other newsreels
Sep	1918	Separate foreign edition introduced
Nov	1918	German surrender. Temporary offices at 80–82 Wardour

		Street during enlargements at 76–78 Wardour Street
Dec	1918	Women over thirty vote for first time
Feb	1919	War Office sells its interest in Topical Film Company. Bought up by Edward Hulton
Feb	1919	Topical moves to offices at 47 Shoe Lane (home of *Daily Sketch*)
May	1919	Agreement between Topical Film Company and Film Booking Offices (FBO)
May	1919	Newsreel becomes *Topical Budget* once more
Jun	1919	Versailles treaty, filmed by Harold Jeapes
Jun	1919	Ken Gordon filming for *Topical Budget* in North Russia
Sep	1919	Company returns to 76–78 Wardour Street
Oct	1919	FBO reincorporated as Film Booking Offices (1919) Ltd
Oct	1919	Transport workers' strike
Oct	1919	*Daily Cinema News* founded (closed January 1920)
Jan	1920	League of Nations formed
Apr	1920	*Fox News* first issued in Britain
Apr	1920	French army occupies the Ruhr
Apr	1921	Miners' strike
Jul	1921	Dempsey beats Carpentier
Sep	1921	*Topical Budget*'s tenth anniversary issue
Sep	1921	Charlie Chaplin's visit to England
Dec	1921	Formation of Irish Free State
Mar	1922	Princess Mary marries Viscount Lascelles
Jun	1922	First regional issue
Aug	1922	Michael Collins assassinated
Oct	1922	Mussolini marches on Rome
Oct	1922	Lloyd George coalition government falls
Oct	1922	Margaret Leahy competition
Nov	1922	Discovery of Tutankhamen's tomb
Nov	1922	General Election
Feb	1923	Full 'territorial scheme' begun for regional issues
Apr	1923	Wedding of Duke of York and Elizabeth Bowes-Lyon; the 'White Horse' Cup Final at Wembley
Dec	1923	General Election
Jan	1924	First Labour government formed
Apr	1924	Opening of British Empire Exhibition at Wembley
Sep	1924	Topical's offices now at 22 Soho Square, labs and editorial department at 76–78 Wardour Street
Oct	1924	Fire at 76–78 Wardour Street
Nov	1924	General Election
Jan	1925	Pathé introduce longer newsreel, *Pathé Super Gazette*
May	1925	Topical start up again their own printing at 76–78 Wardour Street
May	1925	William Jeapes resigns from *Topical Budget*
May	1925	Death of Sir Edward Hulton
Oct	1925	Locarno Conference
Nov	1925	Death of Queen Alexandra
Nov	1925	Company bought up by F. A. Enders, who takes majority shareholding

Jan	1926	Baird demonstrates television
Mar	1926	William Jeapes founds *Empire News Bulletin*
May	1926	General Strike
May	1927	Lindbergh flies the Atlantic solo
Jul	1928	*British Screen News* founded
Aug	1928	Enders' majority shareholding in company taken over by FBO
Aug	1928	Signing of Kellogg-Briand peace pact
May	1929	Labour government formed
Jun	1929	*British Movietone News*, the first British sound newsreel begins
Oct	1929	Wall Street crash
Nov	1929	King George V falls seriously ill
Dec	1929	Topical's Wardour Street lease runs out
	1930	Brent Laboratories opens
Jun	1930	First sound version of *Pathé Gazette*
Jul	1930	*Universal Talking News* founded
Oct	1930	Crash of R101 airship
Mar	1931	*British Paramount News* founded
Mar	1931	Last *Topical Budget* issue
Mar	1937	Company reincorporated and renamed Brent Laboratories Ltd.
Oct	1937	Topical Film Company incorporated once again (run jointly with Brent Laboratories at Cricklewood)
May	1986	Brent Labs in liquidation

APPENDIX 2
Cameraman Fred Wilson's Assignments 1920–1923

Cameraman: Frederick Ling Wilson
Period: May 1920–March 1923
Note: This does not cover Wilson's time for the Topical Film Company in 1918 as an Official cameraman, but otherwise represents all the surviving information about his time with *Topical Budget*. Where figures are given in brackets these relate to all cameramen used on that story, individual records not having been kept. 'Notes' refers to other cameramen employed on the story and the use made of the material if it did not go directly into the newsreel. The occasional additional footage shot for overseas sales has been omitted. All details are from the *Topical Budget* issue books.

Date	No.	Subject	Notes	Length	Used	Expenses
Year: 1920						
May 17	455–2	German fleet at Rosyth			100	£9 12 9
May 20	456–1	Order of the Bath	1 other	60	?	2 0
May 24	456–2	King and Queen at Aldershot		600	40	£8 08 9
May 27	457–1	King and Queen at Aldershot			131	£8 08 4
May 31	457–2	No story				
Jun 3	458–1	The Derby	5 others	(470)	(233)	£8 00 6
Jun 7	458–2	The Oaks	2 others	(254)	(70)	£4 00 0
Jun 10	459–1	No story				
Jun 14	459–2	Ascot frocks		250	73	£1 00 9
Jun 17	460–1	Isle of Man/Motor cycling	1 other/Not used	(520)		£24 10 4
Jun 21	460–2	Wimbledon		200	37	£1 00 3
Jun 24	461–1	Mary Pickford/ Douglas Fairbanks	4 others	(900)	(241)	£26 17 0
Jun 24	461–1	Lloyd George and Foch at Folkestone		150	38	£6 14 1
Jun 28	461–2	Unveiling memorial to Viscount Wolseley		100	45	3 0
Jul 1	462–1	Anglo-Catholic congress	1 other	(210)	(31)	18 2

Date	No.	Subject	Notes	Length	Used	Expenses
Jul 1	462–1	Stoke Poges/Golf		150	56	£1 12 0
Jul 1	462–1	Opening scenes at Henley		60	27	£1 1 11
Jul 5	462–2	No story				
Jul 8	463–1	King in Edinburgh		400	60	£8 03 0
Jul 8	463–1	Edinburgh investiture	Not used	100		£3 19 6
Jul 12	463–2	King and Princess Mary in Edinburgh		400	40	£1 15 0
Jul 12	463–2	King and Queen at Rothsay	Not used?	150		£2 05 6
Jul 15	464–1	King in Edinburgh		770	146	£20 07 1
Jul 19	464–2	No story				
Jul 22	465–1	No story				
Jul 26	465–2	Aerial derby	2 others	(230)	(68)	£1 19 8
Jul 26	465–2	Lady Channel swimmer	½ used in 466–1	200		£5 14 5
Jul 26	465–2	March foal show	Used in 466–2	100		£1 18 8
Jul 29	466–1	Holiday tax/Folkestone	1 other	(105)	(39)	£2 17 2
Jul 29	466–1	Chief scout/Richmond		180	40	£1 03 8
Aug 2	466–2	March foal show	Used from 465–2		33	
Aug 5	467–1	No story				
Aug 9	467–2	Ranjitsinhji		25	19	12 9
Aug 12	468–1	Dr Mannix/Liverpool/London	3 others	(360)	(66)	£21 09 1
Aug 12	468–1	Devon & Somerset stag hounds		120	38	£6 11 9
Aug 16	468–2	Grouse shooting		183	108	£10 04 6
Aug 19	469–1	HMS Vindictive	Special	330	75	£19 19 0
Aug 19	469–1	Fête at Sydenham	Local	?	?	£1 04 5
Aug 23	469–2	Shorncliffe sports	Held	200		£2 10 7
Aug 26	470–1	No story				
Aug 30	470–2	Coal story/Wales	2 others	41	?	9 6
Aug 30	470–2	Opening of football season	2 others	50	?	6 6
Aug 30	470–2	Police sports/Richmond	No picture			8 7
Sep 2	471–1	Woman Channel swim	See 465–2?	?	?	£5 14 5
Sep 2	471–1	Miners' executive	No picture			?
Sep 6	471–2	No story				
Sep 9	472–1	Deauville		165	30	£20 03 6
Sep 9	472–1	Fire at Woolwich		140	29	£1 08 3
Sep 9	472–1	St Leger	1 other	142	(83)	£4 06 9

Date	No.	Subject	Notes	Length	Used	Expenses
Sep 13	472–2	Ryde children regatta		140	43	£2 14 8
Sep 16	473–1	Mystery ships/ Shoreham		200	43	£4 03 9
Sep 20	473–2	Stoke Poges/Golf		130	70	£1 11 3
Sep 20	473–2	Prince Henry in camp		45	26	£2 19 6
Sep 23	474–1	English team for Australia	Not used	56		£1 01 0
Sep 27	474–2	Fashions in suburbia	1 other	(350)	(70)	£2 11 0
Sep 27	474–2	South (?)	Not used	56		£5 15 4
Sep 27	474–2	Yarmouth	No picture			" "
Sep 30	475–1	Autumn hats	Used from 474–2	14		
Sep 30	475–1	*Sketch* office Sunday	No picture			£1 00 0
Oct 4	475–2	St John's Wood Barracks/Hussars		158	47	11 6
Oct 4	475–2	Wedding of the Hon. (?) Jenkins	Not used	71		£6 04 5
Oct 7	476–1	No story				
Oct 11	476–2	No story				
Oct 14	477–1	Prince of Wales' arrival in England	9 others	(844)	(258)	5 6
Oct 14	477–1	Cesarewitch	2 others	158	?	£3 05 0
Oct 14	477–1	Fire resisting demonstration	Held			9 6
Oct 14	477–1	Our Day (?)	Held			4 6
Oct 18	477–2	Fire resisting demonstration	Used from 477–1		31	
Oct 18	477–2	Cruiser/Chatham		?	36	£1 13 10
Oct 18	477–2	Our Day	Used from 477–1		36	
Oct 18	477–2	*Daily Sketch*		?	?	£1 00 0
Oct 21	478–1	Coal		377	81	£9 11 4
Oct 25	478–2	Coal		176	103	£7 15 6
Oct 28	479–1	Terence MacSwiney/Brixton	3 others	20?	?	16 0
Oct 28	479–1	City Specials	1 other	103	32	10 0
Oct 28	479–1	Unemployed/ Trafalgar Square	No picture			3 9
Nov 1	479–2	Departure of Duke of Connaught		?	24	15 6
Nov 1	479–2	Crystal Palace/ Civil Service exam		122	52	17 3
Nov 4	480–1	Greenwood trial	1 other	?	(66)	£11 18 8
Nov 8	480–2	Lloyd George/ RSC (?)		136	40	3 0

Date	No.	Subject	Notes	Length	Used	Expenses
Nov 8	480–2	End of coal strike	Old material used		13	
Nov 8	480–2	Queen at Wandsworth	Not used?	118		16 6
Nov 11	481–1	Sir Charles Townsend/ by-election		252	55	£4 07 0
Nov 11	481–1	Homecoming unknown warrior	2 others	?	(170)	£3 03 0
Nov 11	481–1	Duke of York at York	Not used	103		£4 3 11
Nov 15	481–2	Burial of unknown warrior in W. Abbey	8 others	180	(467)	16 6
Nov 18	482–1	Cheltenham races	2 others	63	(81)	£5 0 10
Nov 22	482–2	Norwich cattle show		186	41	£3 15 1
Nov 25	483–1	No story				
Nov 29	483–2	Sinn Fein gunmen victim's funeral	5 others	110	(223)	3 6
Nov 29	483–2	Ditto/Holyhead	No picture			£6 09 0
Dec 2	484–1	Lingfield	1 other	158	(51)	£1 08 2
Dec 2	484–1	Wedding	1 other	120	(37)	14 0
Dec 2	484–1	Liverpool Sinn Fein outrages/ London	1 other	141	16	3 0
Dec 6	484–2	Stars at Variety Ball	All-night duty	151	61	£3 00 6
Dec 6	484–2	Rugger at Richmond	No picture			17 9
Dec 9	485–1	Stage v Press		100	51	13 6
Dec 9	485–1	Prince in the city	2 others	41	(69)	6 0
Dec 9	485–1	Asquith/Albert Hall	Not used	10		11 6
Dec 13	485–2	Fatty Arbuckle	1 other	88	40	18 6
Dec 13	485–2	Distinguished scientist's burial		97	55	£5 07 3
Dec 16	486–1	Our wonderful climate/Torquay	1 other	(79)	(62)	£9 05 1
Dec 20	486–2	Jumper competition		97	87	3 0
Dec 20	486–2	Xmas leave Portsmouth	No picture			£1 16 2
Dec 20	486–2	Mr Scott's dogs	No picture			£1 07 7
Dec 20	486–2	Passport Kaiserin (?)	No picture?			£1 01 4
Dec 23	487–1	Father Xmas at hospital	1 other/Held	(189)		£1 07 6
Dec 23	487–1	*Daily Sketch*	Held?	?	?	£1 12 6

Date	No.	Subject	Notes	Length	Used	Expenses
Dec 27	487–2	Hospital Xmas	Used from 487–1		(69)	
Dec 30	488–1	Football/Chelsea	1 other/ Xmas day duty	(205)	(44)	£2 10 0
Dec 30	488–1	Circus/Olympia		454	45	£1 04 6
Year: 1921						
Jan 3	488–2	No story				
Jan 6	489–1	Children at hospital		200	38	9 6
Jan 6	489–1	Lloyd George at Chequers	Held	21		£1 13 1
Jan 6	489–1	(Expenses re continental trip)				4 4
Jan 10	489–2	RA flag	Held	35		?
Jan 13	490–1	Downing St in Buckinghamshire/ Chequers		174	85	?
Jan 17	490–2	Lambing season		135	62	£1 15 0
Jan 20	491–1	No story				
Jan 24	491–2	No story				
Jan 27	492–1	St Moritz			46	£73 01 7
Jan 31	492–2	Alfred Lester/ Switzerland			48	(total)
Feb 3	493–1	St Moritz			57	
Feb 3	493–1	Nice			104	
Feb 7	493–2	St Moritz			72	
Feb 7	493–2	Riviera season			51	
Feb 10	494–1	Ashbourne street football		258	85	£4 12 10
Feb 10	494–1	(Dover for Riviera film)	Customs etc			£7 14 2
Feb 10	494–1	Football Horley (?)	Special	?	?	£1 03 3
Feb 14	494–2	Monte Carlo			69	See above
Feb 17	495–1	Parliament reassembles	4 others	117	(115)	17 0
Feb 21	495–2	Highest golf club			47	See above
Feb 24	496–1	Oban cattle show		179	42	£10 03 3
Feb 24	496–1	Students' rag	No picture			5 0
Feb 28	496–2	Wedding of Elinor Glyn's daughter		61	37	12 0
Feb 28	496–2	Princess Mary Horse Guards	1 other/Held	70		10 0
Mar 3	497–1	Princess Mary presenting colours	Used from 496–2		(35)	
Mar 3	497–1	Chequers		117	69	£2 18 10
Mar 7	497–2	No story				

Date	No.	Subject	Notes	Length	Used	Expenses
Mar 10	498–1	Carnival/Paris		?	66	?
Mar 10	498–1	Baptism/Monte Carlo	Held	?		£20 08 4
Mar 14	498–2	British troops in Germany		?	97	£53 12 4
Mar 17	499–1	Lincoln Handicap	2 others	30	?	£6 10 2
Mar 21	499–2	Grand National	3 others?	?	(180)	£7 13 4
Mar 24	500–1	FA Cup semi-finals/Wolves v Cardiff	1 other	?	81	£2 15 2
Mar 24	500–1	Pulham aerodrome	1 other/Held?	?		£2 06 0
Mar 28	500–2	Oxford & Cambridge practice	3 others	?	(118)	£1 00 0
Mar 31	501–1	Oxford & Cambridge boat race	6 others	?	81	£2 15 6
Apr 4	501–2	Warriors' Day/Unemployment	1 other	40	(41)	£1 09 0
Apr 4	501–2	Prince at Hawthorn Hill	4 others	(93)	(81)	?
Apr 7	502–1	Coal strike	2 others	?	?	?
Apr 11	502–2	Coal	2 others	?	56	£23 17 7
Apr 11	502–2	Sunday duty/Cardiff	Not used?	?		£1 00 0
Apr 14	503–1	No story				
Apr 14	503–2	No story				
Apr 21	504–1	Public's struggle for coal		?	47	7 6
Apr 21	504–1	Funeral of ex-Kaiserin/Germany		?	77	£111 10 1
Apr 25	504–2	FA Cup Final	8 others	?	(514)	£1 11 6
Apr 25	504–2	Rifle inspection	Not used?			6 0
Apr 28	505–1	Ladies' football	Held			14 0
Apr 28	505–1	Prince of Wales & lifeboat	Held			8 0
May 2	505–2	Prince boards the lifeboat	2 others/From 505–2	49		
May 2	505–2	Tea-cup final	Used from 505–1	73		
May 2	505–2	Horse-racing/Newmarket	2 others		(111)	£1 16 6
May 5	506–1	No story				
May 9	506–2	France's homage to Napoleon			60	From above?
May 12	507–1	Joan of Arc/Verdun			120	From above?
May 16	507–2	No story				

Date	No.	Subject	Notes	Length	Used	Expenses
May 19	508–1	Prince's visit to West Country		?	?	?
May 23	508–2	Prince in Devon		?	?	?
May 26	509–1	Prince's tour in the West		?	?	?
May 30	509–2	Prince of Wales concludes tour		?	?	?
Jun 2	510–1	The Derby?				

[510–2/6 June 1921 to 574–2/28 August 1922: camera credits missing]

Year: 1922

Date	No.	Subject	Notes	Length	Used	Expenses
Aug 31	575–1	Collins' funeral	1 other	370	49	£12 00 0
Aug 31	575–1	Open air cinema	Held	89		£1 03 6
Sep 4	575–2	Ebor Handicap	2 others	15	7	£3 15 0
Sep 4	575–2	Leyton carnival	Local	360		15 6
Sep 7	576–1	Princess Nina's wedding	1 other	71	8	16 0
Sep 7	576–1	Partridge shooting		185	29	£3 00 0
Sep 11	576–2	Boys' golf championship		202	41	£2 14 0
Sep 14	577–1	Air race	3 others	315	43?	£3 00 0
Sep 14	577–1	Arsenal in training	1 other/Held	(160)		£1 5 11
Sep 18	577–2	RAF leave for the East	1 other	145	21	£3 00 0
Sep 18	577–2	St Leger	2 others	185	45	£4 10 0
Sep 21	578–1	Locomotive smash	2 visits/ Not used	231		£2 10 0
Sep 21	578–1	Trotting at Greenford	1 other/Held	109		£1 00 0
Sep 21	578–1	Cabinet meeting/ Downing St	Not used	44		10 0
Sep 25	578–2	Labour Party/ Downing St		30	27	3 0
Sep 25	578–2	Mounted police sports		316	31	£1 05 0
Sep 28	579–1	Bloodhound trials	Not used	111		£2 16 5
Oct 2	579–2	No story				
Oct 5	580–1	Golf academy		338	55	£3 05 0
Oct 9	580–2	Turkish ambassador	Not used	44		5 6
Oct 9	580–2	Indoor football	Not used	240		£1 10 0
Oct 12	581–1	Prince at Alexandra Park	5 others	160	(88)	£5 00 0
Oct 12	581–1	King at Edinburgh		183	30	£5 00 0
Oct 16	581–2	Landship at Hull	Not used	191		£10 00 0
Oct 19	582–1	*Daily Sketch* beauties/ Bournemouth		66	10	£1 10 0

Date	No.	Subject	Notes	Length	Used	Expenses
Oct 19	582–1	Child beauties/ Bournemouth		183	183?	£2 00 0
Oct 19	582–1	*Daily Sketch* beauties/ Soho Square	1 other/ Not used	21		
Oct 19	582–1	*Daily Sketch* beauties/ Southampton	Held	165		£3 00 0
Oct 19	582–1	*Daily Sketch* beauties/ Shaftesbury Av	Held	106		4 0
Oct 19	582–1	Dairy show	Not used	180		10 0
Oct 19	582–1	PLA building	Not used	49		7 0
Oct 23	582–2	Prince/Guildhall	4 others	72	(51)	£1 15 0
Oct 26	583–1	Lloyd George at Leeds		176	73	£6 00 0
Oct 26	583–1	Bonar Law at Cecil	3 others/ No picture/ None used			7 0
Oct 30	583–2	Cambridgeshire	3 others	103	(73)	£2 08 0
Oct 30	583–2	Dissolution of parliament	1 other	111	(60)	£1 12 0
Oct 30	583–2	Asquith at Peterborough	Not used	25		£2 00 0
Oct 30	583–2	Floods at Skegness	No picture			£3 12 0
Nov 2	584–1	Prince at Stamford Bridge	1 other	185	(56)	8 3
Nov 6	584–2	Prince at drag hunt near Windsor	3 others	119	18	£3 00 8
Nov 6	584–2	Bonar Law at Drury Lane	3 others	159	(85)	£2 10 0
Nov 9	585–1	Prince/Mill Hill	1 other	112	12	£1 0 10
Nov 9	585–1	Lloyd George at Opera House	2 others	80	(22)	17 0
Nov 9	585–1	Victory Ball/ London	4 others	125	(88)	£2 10 0
Nov 12	585–2	Lord Mayor's Show	4 others	76	(67)	£1 00 6
Nov 12	585–2	Remembrance Day	6 others	126	(135)	3 6
Nov 12	585–2	Battalion at Tooting	Not used	45		14 6
Nov 16	586–1	Limbless walk	Held	87		£1 10 0
Nov 20	586–2	Election/ Chamberlain/ Birmingham		101	15	£3 10 0
Nov 20	586–2	Election/Baldwin		121	15	£4 00 0
Nov 20	586–2	Election/ Saklatvala/Battersea	Not used	33		18 6

Date	No.	Subject	Notes	Length	Used	Expenses
Nov 23	587–1	Unemployed	7 others/Not used	100		15 0
Nov 23	587–1	Grimsdell wedding	No picture			£1 00 2
Nov 27	587–2	Opening of parliament	8 others	35	(176)	5 6
Nov 27	587–2	Mrs Swynnerton (?)/Artist	Not used	64		12 0
Nov 30	588–1	Spurs' Captain's wedding		36	12	£1 05 0
Nov 30	588–1	Racing/Lingfield	2 others	46	(50)	£2 10 0
Dec 4	588–2	Redhill cattle show		129	21	£1 05 0
Dec 7	589–1	Xmas leave for Navy		78	35	£2 05 0
Dec 7	589–1	Plunkett wedding	1 other	131	80?	£1 05 0
Dec 7	589–1	Miners' leaders at No. 10	Held	104		5 6
Dec 11	589–2	Shoot in Yorkshire	No picture			£8 18 3
Dec 14	590–1	Whippet racing	Held?	?		5 6
Dec 18	590–2	Oxford & Cambridge/Crystal Palace	Not used	59		15 0
Dec 18	590–2	Submarine memorial	Held?	85		4 0
Dec 21	591–1	No story				
Dec 25	591–2	No story				
Dec 28	592–1	No story				

Year: 1923

Date	No.	Subject	Notes	Length	Used	Expenses
Jan 1	592–2	Varsity hockey		271	80	£20 00 0
Jan 1	592–2	Winter sports	Held	283		" "
Jan 4	593–1	Dogs' home/Battersea		108	20	17 0
Jan 8	593–2	Uncle Oojah visits hospital		164	37	£1 05 0
Jan 11	594–1	Tame fox		151	27	£2 15 0
Jan 15	594–2	Football/Corinthians v Brighton	1 other	213	30	£2 02 0
Jan 18	595–1	Oxford crew		142	45	£2 05 0
Jan 18	595–1	Ship on fire/Millwall	No picture			£1 01 0
Jan 22	595–2	Lambing/Pangbourne		163	44	£2 05 0
Jan 22	595–2	Corinthians v Brighton replay	1 other	66	28	7 6
Jan 25	596–1	No story				
Jan 29	596–2	Cadets/HMS Thunderer		255	65	£9 00 0

Date	No.	Subject	Notes	Length	Used	Expenses
Jan 29	596–2	Kempton Park	3 others/ None used			£1 00 0
Feb 1	597–1	Grigg-Poynder wedding	2 others	92	15	
Feb 1	597–1	Madame Melba	No picture			£1 10 0
Feb 5	597–2	Horne (?) wedding	2 others/ None used	40		£1 00 0
Feb 8	598–1	Lloyd George's return		84	22	£5 03 3
Feb 12	598–2	No story				
Feb 15	599–1	Cross-country run	1 other/Held	93		12 0
Feb 15	599–1	Opening of parliament	10 others/ Not used	28		5 6
Feb 19	599–2	Cambridge Lent races	1 other	89	30	£1 12 0
Feb 22	600–1	Horse show	No picture			4 9
Feb 22	600–1	Master Lascelles	1 other/No picture			5 0
Feb 26	600–2	Wedding/Honora Ward		191	60	£5 10 0
Mar 1	601–1	Football/Charlton v West Brom		132	38	15 0
Mar 5	601–2	No story				
Mar 8	602–1	Gatwick races	3 others	34	10	£1 10 0
Mar 12	602–2	Prince at Hawthorn Hill	6 others/ Not used	54		£2 00 0

SOURCES

Little has been written about the British newsreel, particularly for the silent period. Steer and Talbot have useful accounts of the early newsreel industry, and the full article in *Cassell's Saturday Journal* is an invaluable description of newsreel work. Ken Gordon's article 'Forty Years With A Newsreel Camera' is informative and entertaining and has much on newsreel filming in *Topical Budget*'s time. Raymond Fielding's history of American newsreels also has information on British newsreels and serves as a general guide. The memoirs of Paul Wyand and Ronnie Noble are excellent accounts of the life of a newsreel cameraman, though mostly covering the sound era. James Ballantyne's guides contain abstracts from a wide range of publications and much essential information culled from newsreel research. But the greatest sources of information are the contemporary trade papers, notably the *Bioscope* and the *Kinematograph Weekly*. The later journal *The Cine-Technician* is also useful.

Official filming during the First World War has, on the other hand, been well covered in the past few years, and this book owes a great deal to such researches. The main history behind the British filming of the war, of which *Topical Budget* formed but a part, has been covered by three writers in particular. Steve Badsey's introductory history contains all the essential information, relating it to the surviving footage in the Imperial War Museum (IWM). Nicholas Hiley's thesis comprehensively covers the progress of the news media in the first two years of the war, with a detailed account of newsreel production as well as the first efforts of the Official film-makers. His account of newsfilming before 1910 is also very useful. Nicholas Reeves' history, published in association with the IWM, is a thorough account of the range and kinds of Official films, although it contains some errors in the sections on the *War Office Official Topical Budget*. Also, Kevin Brownlow's book includes a wide-ranging account of filming during the war and is essential reading, although it makes no mention of newsreels.

The records of the Topical Film Company came into the possession of the National Film Archive after Brent Laboratories Ltd went into liquidation in 1986.

Topical Film Company records

Held by the Imperial War Museum
i) Loose issue sheets for the *War Office Official Topical Budget* and the *Pictorial News (Official)* from 301–1 (29 May 1917) to 376–2 (11 November 1918), including issue number, release date, footages of

individual items (less opening titles), main titles and descriptive titles (these do not always correspond with the actual words used on release). The two issues for the week are sometimes given without any indication of a division between the two. From issue 369–1 (19 September 1918) there are separate sheets for the foreign edition, although they are not always named as such. Copies of the sheets are also held by the National Film Archive.

ii) Various papers relating to Official film-making held by the IWM Film Department, and MOI (Film) papers held by the Department of Photographs. The Film Department also holds some other papers and correspondence, including that between William Jeapes and Frederick Wile for 1915–16.

Held by the National Film Archive

i) 'Records And Details Of Budget Subjects.' Editorial records of *Topical Budget* from 393–1 (6 March 1919) to 638–1 (15 November 1923). These include the issue number, date, a descriptive title of all assignments, which were used, held over or not used, name of cameraman or other source, length taken, length used and operator's expenses. The records are not divided into separate issues until 455–1 (13 May 1920).

ii) 'Budget Book 1922–23 [sic].' Issue book covering 541–1 (2 January 1922) to 579–2 (2 October 1922). Gives newsreel as released, with issue number, date, descriptive title, lengths of individual items and total length with titles. Also records of when items were handed in for printing from 567–2 (10 July 1922). Following issue books include the same information.

iii) 'Budget Book 580–1 to 636–1.' Issue book covering 580–1 (5 October 1922) to 636–1 (1 November 1923). Includes details of additional items for regional issues. Following issue books also contain the same information.

iv) 'Budget Book 636–2 to 686–2.' Issue book covering 636–2 (5 November 1923) to 686–2 (20 October 1924).

v) 'Budget Book 687–1 to 744–1.' Issue book covering 687–1 (23 October 1924) to 744–1 (26 November 1925).

vi) 'Budget Book 744–2 to 800–1.' Issue book covering 744–2 (30 November 1925) to 800–1 (23 December 1926). No further printing details after 769–1 (20 May 1926).

vii) 'Budget Book 800–2 to 855–2.' Issue book covering 800–2 (27 December 1926) to 855–2 (16 January 1928).

viii) 'Budget Book 911 – 966–1.' Issue book covering 911–1 (7 February 1929) to 966–1 (27 February 1930).

ix) 'Budget Book 966 – .' Issue book covering 966–2 (3 March 1930) to 1000–2 (27 October 1930).

x) 'Budget Book from 979–1–2 to .' Issue book covering 979–1 (29 May 1930) to 1019–2 (9 March 1931).

xi) Subject index cards. From 'Abbeys' to 'Zoo', covering issues 500–1 (24 March 1921) to 1017–2 (23 February 1931), with separate sections for 'locals and specials', 'portraits' and 'portraits (phrenology)'.

xii) 'Brent Laboratories Minute Book 1913–1947.' Minute book covering period from incorporation of the Topical Film Company in October 1913 to June 1947. Includes Topical's operations up to 1917, the WOCC and then the MOI take-over, and the purchase of the company by Edward Hulton. Continues after the newsreel had closed and the company turned to laboratory work, becoming Brent Laboratories Ltd in 1937.

xiii) 'Brent Laboratories Ltd Minute Book 1924–1937, 1937–1944.' Includes detailed records of weekly meetings 1924–1925, covering the fire, William Jeapes' departure and Sir Edward Hulton's death. Detailed accounts at this time of the weekly progress of the newsreel and comparisons with the output of *Gaumont Graphic* and *Pathé Gazette*.

Further records held include share registers, Memorandum and Articles of Association for 1913 and 1937 (when the Topical Film Company was reincorporated), share certificates, a further minute book covering Brent Laboratories Ltd 1945–1964, records of the reuse of negatives in the library, of material sent by *MGM International News*, and incidental papers and records relating to the newsreel and to the subsequent activities of the company.

Held by Mr John Enders

i)   General Minute Book for Film Booking Offices, 14 February 1917 to 14 October 1919.
ii) Accounts for Topical Film Company, 1 January 1921.
iii) Accounts for Topical Film Company, 31 December 1921.
iv) Minute Book for meetings of directors of Film Booking Offices (1919) Ltd, 16 February 1922 to 21 February 1924.
v)   Auditors' report for the Topical Film Company for year ending December 1923 with balance sheet.
vi) Minutes of the convention held at Film Booking Offices (1919) Ltd, 30 August 1924.
vii) Register of meetings of the board of directors of Film Booking Offices (1919) Ltd, 11 September 1924 to 13 August 1925.

Also further papers and records relating to the Topical Film Company, FBO and its related company H & W Ltd. John Enders is the son of F. A. Enders.

Published Sources

Books and Pamphlets

Ballantyne, James (ed.), *Researcher's Guide to British Newsreels*, London, BUFVC, 1983.
Ballantyne, James (ed.), *Researcher's Guide to British Newsreels Volume II*, London, BUFVC, 1988.
Balshofer, Fred J. and Arthur C. Miller, *One Reel a Week*, Berkeley & Los Angeles, University of California Press, 1967.
Barnes, John, *The Beginnings of the Cinema in Great Britain*, Newton Abbott, David & Charles, 1976.
Barnes, John, *The Rise of the Cinema in Great Britain*, London, Bishopsgate

Press, 1983.

Barnes, John, *Pioneers of the British Film*, London, Bishopsgate Press, 1983.

Beaverbrook, Lord, *Men and Power 1917–1918*, London, Hutchinson, 1956.

Bennett, Colin N., *The Handbook of Kinematography*, London, Kinematography Weekly, 1913.

Bennett, Colin N., *The Guide to Kinematography*, London, E. T. Heron, 1917.

Blakeston, Oswell, *Through a Yellow Glass*, London, Pool, 1928.

Blesh, Rudi, *Keaton*, London, Secker & Warburg, 1967.

Boughey, Davidson, *The Film Industry*, London, Sir Isaac Pitman & Sons, 1921.

Brownlow, Kevin, *The War, the West and the Wilderness*, London, Secker & Warburg, 1979.

Brunel, Adrian, *Nice Work*, London, Forbes Robertson, 1949.

Butler, Ivan, *Silent Magic; Rediscovering the Silent Film Era*, London, Columbus Books, 1987.

Chaplin, Charlie, *My Wonderful Visit*, London, Hurst and Blackett, 1922.

Chesmore, Stuart, *Behind The Cinema Screen* (Discovery Books no. 5), London, Thomas Nelson & Sons, 1934.

Coe, Brian, *The History of Movie Photography*, London, Ash & Grant, 1981.

Commission on Educational and Cultural Films, *The Film in National Life*, London, George Allen & Unwin, 1932.

Dench, Ernest A., *Making the Movies*, New York, The MacMillan Company, 1915.

Fielding, Raymond, *The American Newsreel 1911–1967*, Norman, University of Oklahoma Press, 1972.

George, W. Tyacke, *Playing to Pictures*, London, E. T. Heron, 1914.

Gifford, Denis, *The British Film Catalogue 1895–1985*, London, David & Charles, 1986.

Grant, Bernard, *To the Four Corners; the Memoirs of a News Photographer*, London, Hutchinson, 1933.

Hardy, Forsyth (ed.), *Grierson on Documentary*, London, Collins, 1946.

Hepworth, Cecil, *Came the Dawn. Memories of a Film Pioneer*, London, Phoenix House, 1951.

Holt-White, W., *The Super-Spy*, London, Andrew Melrose, 1916.

Hugon, P. D., *Hints to Newsfilm Cameramen*, Jersey City, Pathé News, 1915.

Hulton, Edward, *When I Was a Child*, London, Cresset Press, 1952.

Humfrey, Robert, *Careers in the Films*, London, Pitman, 1938.

Huret, Marcel, *Ciné Actualités. Histoire de la Presse Filmée*, Paris, Henri Veyrier, 1984.

Judd, Denis, *The Life and Times of George V*, London, Weidenfeld and Nicolson, 1973.

Low, Rachel and Manvell, Roger, *The History of the British Film 1896–1906*, London, George Allen & Unwin, 1948.

Low, Rachel, *The History of the British Film 1906–1914*, London, George Allen & Unwin, 1949.

Low, Rachel, *The History of the British Film 1914–1918*, London, George Allen & Unwin, 1950.

Low, Rachel, *The History of the British Film 1918–1929*, London, George Allen & Unwin, 1971.

Low, Rachel, *Films of Comment and Persuasion of the 1930s*, London, George Allen & Unwin, 1979.

McBain, Janet, *Pictures Past*, Edinburgh, Moorfoot Publishing, 1985.

MacBean, L. C., *Kinematograph Studio Technique*, London, Pitman, 1922.

Mack, John E., *A Prince of Our Disorder. The Life of T. E. Lawrence*, London, Weidenfeld and Nicolson, 1976.

Malins, Geoffrey H., (Low Warren, ed.), *How I Filmed the War. A Record of the Extraordinary Experiences of the Man Who Filmed the Great Somme Battles etc.*, London, Herbert Jenkins, 1920.

Miller, Maud M. (ed.), *Winchester's Screen Encyclopedia*, London, Winchester Publications, 1948.

Mould, David H., *American Newsfilm 1914–1919. The Underexposed War*, New York, Garland, 1983.

National Film Archive, *Catalogue. Part 1. Silent News Films 1895–1933*, London, BFI, 1965.

Noble, Ronnie, *Shoot First! Assignments of a Newsreel Cameraman*, London, George G. Harrap, 1955.

Pearson, George, *Flashback. The Autobiography of a British Film-maker*, London, George Allen & Unwin, 1957.

Proceedings of the British Kinematograph Society no. 38, 'Before 1910, Kinematograph Experiences', February 3 1936.

Ramsaye, Terry, *A Million and One Nights*, New York, Simon and Schuster, 1926.

Reeves, Nicholas, *Official British Film Propaganda During the First World War*, London, Croom Helm, 1986.

Rowson, Simon, *A Statistical Survey of the Cinema Industry in Great Britain in 1934*, London, Royal Statistical Society, 1936.

Simonis, H., *The Street of Ink. An Intimate History of Journalism*, London, Cassell & Co., 1917.

Smith, Paul (ed.), *The Historian and Film*, Cambridge, Cambridge University Press, 1976.

Steer, Valentia, *The Romance of the Cinema*, London, Arthur Pearson, 1913.

Steer, Valentia, *The Secrets of the Cinema; Your Favourite Amusement From Within*, London, Arthur Pearson, 1920.

Talbot, Frederick A., *Moving Pictures. How They Are Made and Worked*, London, William Heinemann, 1912.

Taylor, A. J. P., *Beaverbrook*, London, Hamish Hamilton, 1972.

Tracey, Herbert (ed.), *The British Press. A Survey, a Newspaper Directory, and a Who's Who in Journalism* (Parchment Guides), London, Europa Publications, 1929.

Warren, Low, *The Film Game*, London, T. Werner Laurie, 1937.

White, Henry E., (ed.), *The Pageant of the Century*, London, Odhams Press, 1933.

Winchester, Clarence (ed.), *The World Film Encyclopedia. A Universal Screen Guide*, London, The Amalgamated Press, 1933.

Wood, Leslie, *The Miracle of the Movies*, London, Burke Publishing, 1947.

Wyand, Paul, *Useless If Delayed*, London, George G. Harrap, 1959.

Microfiche
Slade Film History Register, *British Newsreel Issue Sheets 1913–1970*,
London, Graphic Data Publishing in association with British Univer-
sities Film & Video Council, 1984. (These do not include *Topical
Budget*.)

Trade papers consulted
Bioscope
British Kinematography
The Cinema
Eyepiece
Film Renter
Journal of the Association of Cine-Technicians (1935–37)
    Became *The Cine-Technician* (1937–1957)
    Then *Film and TV Technician* (1957–)
Kinematograph and Lantern Weekly
    Became *Kinematograph Weekly* in November 1919.

The annual *Kinematograph Year Book, Diary and Directory* (1914–19), later
the *Kinematograph Year Book*, from 1921 to 1938 includes biographical
details of newsreel cameramen and is an excellent first source of information.

Articles
Anon., 'The Newspaper "Boss" – and the Kinema', *Kinematograph Weekly*,
    4 March 1920, p. 79.
Anon., 'Running The Topical Films', *Cassell's Saturday Journal*, 29 May
    1915, p. 2.
Cotter, Jack and Scales, Tommy, 'My Life of . . . Reel Thrills', *Newcastle
    Sunday Sun*, 20 January 1935, p. 8.
Gemmell, Jock, 'Newsreels – Ancient And Modern', *The Cine-Technician*,
    Jan-Feb 1952, pp. 2–5.
Gordon, Ken, 'The Early Days of the News-reels', *British Kinematography*,
    August 1950, pp. 47–50.
Gordon, Ken, 'Forty Years With A Newsreel Camera', *The Cine-Techni-
    cian*, Mar-Apr 1951, pp. 44–50.
Hutchins, John, 'The Trials and Troubles of the Topical Taker', *Bioscope*,
    12 December 1912, pp. 800–1.
Hutchins, John, 'All in a Day's Work', *The Cine-Technician*, Aug-Sep 1936,
    pp. 112–16.
Jeapes, Harold, 'How News-films Were Taken in Pre-war Days', *Newcastle
    Sunday Sun*, 17 February 1935, p. 16.
Norman, Philip, 'The Newsreel Boys', *Sunday Times Magazine*, 10 January
    1971, pp. 8–15.
Wilson, Fred, 'Searching the World for News', *Newcastle Sunday Sun*, 10
    February 1935, p. 16.

Newspapers and Journals Consulted
Cassell's Saturday Journal
Daily Mirror

Daily Sketch
Newcastle Sunday Sun
·The Picturegoer
The Star
The Times

Unpublished Sources

Badsey, S. D., *British Official Film in the First World War*, 1981. Typescript held by the Imperial War Museum Film Department.

Brownlow, Kevin, transcript of interview with Bertram Brooks-Carrington, 1972. Held by Brownlow, with extracts published in *The War, the West, and the Wilderness*.

Hiley, Nicholas, *Making War. The British News Media and Government Control, 1914–16*, 1985. Open University PhD thesis held in the Library of the Open University.

Hutchins, John, *A Paper Read to the Hornsey Branch, British Legion, on Sunday, February 21st, 1937*, 1937. Held by Mr David Hutchins. Reprinted with some alterations as 'All in a Day's Work', in *The Cine-Technician*, Aug-Sep 1936, pp. 112–16.

Pontecorvo, Lisa, *Newsreel in Europe*, 1977. Typescript held by the author.

Other sources

i)   Papers of Lord Beaverbrook. Held by the House of Lords Record Office. These include a great deal of information about the workings of the War Office Cinematograph Committee and its control of *Topical Budget* in 1917–18. Papers consulted: C/180, C/180A, E/1/1–9, 14–17, 29, 39, E/2/1–19 complete, and E/3/34.

ii) Public Record Office. Nicholas Reeves' book contains in its list of sources a detailed breakdown of PRO papers relating to Official film-making. Foreign Office papers from file FO 395/233 contain much information on the handling of the Official newsreel overseas.

iii) Papers, newspaper cuttings and autobiographical notes relating to William Jeapes. Held by Mr Clifford Jeapes.

iv) Papers relating to cameraman Fred Wilson. Held by the National Film Archive.

The surviving films of the *Topical Budget* newsreel, with only a handful of exceptions, are held by the Imperial War Museum Department of Film and the National Film Archive.

INDEX